THE ZOOM

▓▓ TMI ▓▓ TECHNIQUES of the MOVING IMAGE

Volumes in the Techniques of the Moving Image series explore the relationship between what we see on-screen and the technical achievements undertaken in filmmaking to make this possible. The books explore some defined aspect of cinema—work from a particular era, work in a particular genre, work by a particular filmmaker or team, work from a particular studio, or work on a particular theme—in light of some technique and/or technical achievement, such as cinematography, direction, acting, lighting, costuming, set design, legal arrangements, agenting, scripting, sound design and recording, and sound or picture editing. Historical and social backgrounds contextualize the subject of each volume.

Murray Pomerance
Series Editor

THE ZOOM

Drama at the Touch of a Lever

NICK HALL

RUTGERS UNIVERSITY PRESS

New Brunswick, Camden, and Newark, New Jersey, and London

2017002128

Cataloging-in-publication data is available for this book at the Library of Congress.

A British Cataloging-in-Publication record for this book is available from the British Library.

∞ The paper used in this publication meets the requirements of the American National Standard for Information Sciences—Permanence of Paper for Printed Library Materials, ANSI Z39.48-1992.

www.rutgersuniversitypress.org

Manufactured in the United States of America

For Demelza and Milly

CONTENTS

THE ZOOM

1 · INTRODUCTION

Zoom is an unmistakably twentieth-century word. It is an onomato-
poeia of the late industrial age, brought into language by the steam train, the
motorcar, and the jet engine. In one of its original meanings, it described
the rapid upward flight of an aircraft—a sudden, noisy, bracing surge into the
heavens. No wonder, then, that when an invention made it possible for cinematographers to quickly magnify their images without moving the camera, it should
be called a zoom lens. On-screen, or through a viewfinder, the zoom shot creates
an impression of being transported forward or backward at high speed. Not only
is the zoom lens the creator of a special effect, but it is also a labor-saving device.
An early advertisement promised that it offered "drama at the touch of a lever."[1]
This bald overstatement is typical of one of the strangest, most interesting, and
most divisive of film techniques. Both a technology and a technique, the zoom
was available before the birth of cinema and developed alongside the industry.
Breakthroughs in zoom technology have exerted a significant influence on film
and television style and production logistics, yet the zoom has never been an
industry changer. It is not irresistible, as sound and color have proved to be. Nor
has it been abandoned or marginalized, like 3-D, CinemaScope, or Smell-O-
Vision. Instead, since the 1930s, the zoom has been a constant and controversial
presence in the notional kitbags of directors and cinematographers. For some,
the zoom is a vulgar time saver, inherited from television and beloved of hacks
and corner cutters. For others, it is the tool that most strongly distinguishes
Robert Altman, Roberto Rossellini, and Alfred Hitchcock from their contemporaries. There are few cinematic techniques so immediately recognizable by audiences and fewer still that can elicit such violent and visceral objections.

This book presents a historical account of the zoom lens and zoom shot as
it has developed and appeared in American film and television. It explores the
zoom's precedents in precinematic entertainment and first appearances in late
silent and early sound features. It traces the complex web of inventions that

led to the breakthrough zoom lenses of the twentieth century: in television, the Zoomar lens of the mid-1940s, and in film, the Angénieux 10:1 zoom lens, which followed in the 1960s. Alongside this account of technological history, the book discusses and analyzes the stylistic consequences of these inventions and improvements. This is not achieved exclusively through analysis of film images and sequences; the book discusses the ways in which filmmakers—especially directors and cinematographers—have accepted or rejected zoom lenses through negotiation and experimentation. The stylish, self-conscious use of the zoom by New Wave and TV Generation filmmakers in the 1960s presented a powerful challenge to the established "self-effacing" mode of filmmaking preferred by Hollywood cinematographers. But the story does not end with the dramatic and much-lampooned shock zooms of the 1970s. Afterward, zoom technology brought more subtle changes, playing a part in the "intensified" style of post-1980s cinema and enabling a refreshment of television style. Zoom lenses have become more commonplace in recent years, while zoom shots have been woven more successfully into film style and accepted more readily by the production culture. This book brings the story of the zoom lens and zoom shot as close as possible to the present moment.

Three broad periods can be discerned in the history of the zoom lens. Almost a century of development in zoom technology is made up of numerous individual case studies of new technologies, each of which follows its own path. Broadly, however, it represents a familiar pattern of invention, innovation, and diffusion.[2] Until the late 1940s, zoom shots only rarely appeared in Hollywood features, and their use was no more widespread in newsreel or documentary film. This was largely because the zoom lenses that did exist were made in small batches and could not offer the optical clarity or brightness of equivalent prime (fixed focal-length) lenses. Despite the rarity of the zoom, the device was used in interesting and highly creative ways. When zooms do appear in late silent and early sound features, directors and cinematographers generally limit their use to one or two shots. But it is not reasonable to describe such shots as mere "trick shots" or "special effects": they were carefully woven into broader stylistic and narrative choices. As the case studies in this book's second chapter show, the use of the zoom to save effort in craning or dollying the camera, to emphasize the subjective psychological reactions of characters, and to emphasize moments of high drama or lavish production design were all rehearsed on a limited scale in the late 1920s and early 1930s.

In the 1940s and 1950s, zoom lenses were manufactured in greater numbers than before. It is possible that in the 1930s, little more than a handful of Varo zoom lenses were manufactured by Taylor and Hobson. By contrast, after the Second World War, hundreds of Zoomar lenses were manufactured. Most of them were initially destined for electronic television cameras, but the successful film camera zooms manufactured by SOM-Berthiot and Angénieux—which arrived a little later—were similarly mass-produced and mass-marketed. In the broad history of the zoom, this is the point at which the technology was innovated—the moment when it was successfully introduced to the market as a stable, lasting product. That period laid the groundwork for the third, and current, phase in the history of the zoom lens: commercial production, diffusion, and ultimately ubiquity. If hundreds of Zoomar and Pan Cinor lenses were manufactured, then thousands of Angénieux 10:1 lenses were produced; since then, consumers and professionals alike have witnessed a rapid proliferation of zoom lenses, attached to and integrated within everything from professional motion picture cameras, costing hundreds of thousands of dollars, to cheap camcorders.

Because the nature and application of these inventions as well as the industrial response to them changed across the decades, the nature of the evidence differs during each period. As my discussion of the zoom lens in the late 1920s and early 1930s demonstrates, the early history of the zoom lens is rather mysterious. Many of the earliest efforts to develop zooms have left little trace in the archives. For example, we know a little about the lenses developed at Paramount and by Joseph Walker. However, it is possible that other studios developed their own zoom lenses but never shared these trade secrets beyond studio walls and used their zooms (which they may have called by another name) only in films that have since been lost. In this case, such technology would be entirely invisible to the historian. The earliest history of the zoom lens, therefore, is an incomplete history reliant on what was written down, patented, or recalled years later. Almost completely absent from this part of the history is the "industrial debate" around the use of the zoom lens. It is safe to assume that the appropriate use of the zoom was a topic hotly debated by cinematographers. However, little to none of this debate was recorded in trade periodicals. The cinematographers of the day have died and cannot be interviewed. We can, therefore, only imagine discussions among the producers, directors, and cinematographers involved in the production of the 1920s and 1930s films highlighted by this book.

By the end of the book's historical range, the problem is reversed. In the 1990s, the zoom—often rebranded as a "variable prime"—was more prevalent than ever. In twenty-first-century film, television, and digital media, there are so many zoom shots that describing them comprehensively would be an impossible and unrewarding feat. If the final chapter—which looks at the uses of the zoom since 1980—seems compressed, it is because a great deal of the "debate" around the zoom is no debate at all; rather, it is the continual restatement of attitudes, preferences, and received wisdom first developed in the 1970s. However, the conclusion of this book traces two gradual shifts: one toward the use of "variable primes," the other toward the settling of the zoom into a number of specific referential categories. With some decades of history behind it, the zoom now evokes moods, eras, and genres in a way that was not possible when the technology was new and had a scant history of usage on which to draw. Recent ways of using the zoom make readily apparent what has always been true: the zoom is a device that, for much of its history, has been intermedial in its design and usage. Therefore, though it would be easier and tidier to look at film in isolation, as if there were not a porous border between film and television production, this book considers film and television together. It also looks out toward amateur filmmaking and video recording to consider the effect of the zoom across the broad field of the popular American moving image.

Across the chapters that follow, this book draws on three types of evidence. First, where possible, it delves into primary evidence of the research and development of new inventions, referring to original documents including patents, court papers, and studio scripts in order to trace the early development of zoom technologies. Second, the book examines discussions of the use of the zoom lens in the trade press in order to trace the ways in which directors, cinematographers, and other Hollywood film and television craftspeople have responded to the availability of the zoom lens at various points since the late 1920s. Third, alongside traditional trawls through paper copies of these periodicals, this book has benefited considerably from a wide range of technical journals now available via the Media History Digital Library and David Gleason's American Radio History website, among other electronic sources.[3] Finally, because it is unwise to take craft descriptions of creative practice at face value, this book analyzes films and television programs themselves so as to examine the impact of the zoom lens on the audience in the cinema or the viewer at home. Not all of the films and television shows significant to the early development of the zoom are available to the researcher—the gaps are especially problematic in early cinema and early postwar television—and so, like all histories, this book is to some degree an account of what has survived and been remembered. I have no doubt that there are "forgotten" zooms in early American film and early postwar American television; I hope that, where they survive, this book may help draw them to the surface. Equally, later chapters of the book aim to offer a detailed overview of developments in technology and style rather than an exhaustive account. While this book introduces new evidence and discusses the zoom from a range of new perspectives, the territory is not entirely untouched. In addition to the range of critical essays discussed in the introduction, several important works of film history have broadly mapped the history of the zoom. Most textbooks that discuss the zoom trace their evidence to some combination of Barry Salt's perennially useful *Film Style and Technology* and John Belton's important *Film Comment* essay on the subject. This book is no different: it builds on, extends, and in some cases questions these foundational accounts.[4]

More recently, Patrick Keating's collection *Cinematography* has been an indispensable historical reference to the complex history of the art and craft of cinematography. Keating and his coauthors rightly shift the focus of attention from the director to the cinematographer, but such a focus comes with its own risks. It would be no more useful to suggest that the decision to use a zoom shot falls exclusively to the cinematographer than to cling to the idea that the director must be responsible. As Chris Cagle points out, since the beginning of the 1930s, the role of the Hollywood cinematographer has been primarily managerial; directors of photography tend not to "run the camera," leaving this job to assistants.[5] As a result, assistant camera operators or focus pullers are far more likely than directors of photography to physically operate the zoom. This was particularly the case for early zooms, because before motors or electronic controls, the simplest zoom shot required the coordinated effort of a team. Today, unless a camera operator shoots "documentary style," twisting the zoom ring manually while operating the camera, the same teamwork is required. However, to the frustration of academic film historians, the minuscule details of who made what decision when and why are rarely recorded for posterity. The efforts and ideas of the assistants and grips instead accrue to their team leader, the director of photography; as a result, some cinematographic auteurs have emerged, their elevation encouraged by the very trade that is so essential to this history.[6]

In any event, the decision to use a zoom lens is not always made on a film or television set. Decisions made far away from a soundstage or location shoot can have significant bearing on whether a zoom shot ends up in a finished film. A film may feature lots of zoom shots because of a creative decision made by producers at the time of its commission. If a producer today wants "vérité," a "documentary effect," or a "cheesy 1970s aesthetic," then the chances are he or she has the zoom at least partly in mind. Production accountants and other budget setters play a passive role too: when a tighter budget means fewer setups, there may be less time to adjust prime lenses and cover action from multiple angles. In these circumstances, a zoom may be the most expedient way to get the required footage in the can. When zooms were newer and more expensive, the reverse was sometimes true: newer, high-quality zoom lenses were reserved for higher-budget productions. If the cinematographer did not have his or her own zoom lens and the production would not fund the hire of one, then zooms were unlikely to appear in the film. Not that the lack of a zoom lens precludes a zoom: in postproduction, zooms might be added or subtracted from a film's final edit. An optical zoom, effected during printing, can focus on a particular part of the frame in a way never envisaged by the director or cinematographer. This approach may be applied years after production: "panned and scanned" home video releases, which adapted widescreen movies for squarer television screens, sometimes added zooms to films in which they never originally appeared. Inversely, with a slice of the razor, an editor can excise any trace of a zoom shot, however meticulously constructed and carefully executed it may have been; such decisions are easier than ever thanks to nonlinear editing and CGI special effects. Therefore, to the extent that any zoom appears in a film by "choice," that choice is informed as much by myriad technological and economic considerations as by aesthetic and stylistic concerns. As a result, the history of the zoom lens and zoom shot is diffuse, complex, and often highly contested.

"USE AND ABUSE"

The zoom shot divides opinion. Many people—professional filmmakers and casual film fans alike—simply hate it. Sometimes this is for artistic preference: the jolt of a rapid zoom is thought to remind the audience that they are watching a film or (worse) that the film was made under the supervision of a director and cinematographer. The zoom is further tied to a series of artistically negative cultural associations, especially television and amateur cinematography, both of which are discussed in the chapters that follow. This book does not advocate for the zoom lens; it is not a call for the rehabilitation of the technique. Nevertheless, it does call for a cautious assessment of strong arguments against the zoom, especially when trying to understand the history of the technique. This is particularly the case when such arguments link mass or amateur media to the zoom. For example, television was a key incubator of the zoom lens. Television has often been considered artless and vulgar. But as the following chapters make clear, the cultural status of television means little or nothing to the place of the zoom in cinema. Of equal importance—though this book does not extensively discuss the zoom in non-Hollywood cinema—is the significance of the zoom in cinema industries across the world. Both Indian and Nigerian ("Bollywood" and "Nollywood") cinemas make lavish use of zoom shots. In these contexts, the zoom has its own technological imperatives and stylistic implications. Yet by embracing too uncritically the notion that the zoom is amateurish, vulgar, "televisual," and self-conscious, we might easily end up sneering at unfamiliar cultural products and failing to assess them on their own terms.

Aside from debates about the zoom in film and television scholarship, an entirely different debate can be observed within historical industrial discourse. Filmmaking professionals—principally directors and cinematographers—have debated the merits of the technique in trade journals such as *American Cinematographer*. Yet these sources must be investigated with caution. A single issue may display both the enthusiasm of a zoom lens manufacturer and the entrenched caution of a cinematographic grandee but never quite reflect actual industrial practice. In light of this complexity and confusion, the following pages establish the precise technological, stylistic, and conceptual meanings of the zoom alongside a critical account of existing industrial and academic responses. Out of these debates emerge a series of key issues that shape the history of the zoom lens. Often these have broader implications for the way in which we consider the historical handling of new and controversial technologies and how academic history and criticism interacts with industrial discourse. Despite the contradictions and lacunae in these accounts, the zoom has inspired passionate and wide-ranging debate that touches key issues in the very meaning of film and television. It is precisely the controversy of the zoom that makes it a valuable target for attention.

Few documents better illustrate the confusion surrounding the development and use of the zoom than an article published in *Daily Variety* in March 1990. Written by the film historian Joseph McBride, it recounts a disagreement between the Academy of Motion Picture Arts and Sciences and the daughter of cinematographer Joseph Walker. The academy had announced its intention to give an award to the French lens designer Pierre Angénieux for designing "the first practical zoom lens." Marjorie Walker, on learning of the citation's wording, protested that "her father's much earlier work on the zoom was being slighted." As a result, just prior to the broadcast of the ceremony, the academy deleted the word *first* from Isabelle Huppert's announcement of the award. However, they stood by their original claim on the basis that earlier lenses had been "impractical." McBride's article attempted to unpick the mess. Who had invented the first zoom lens depended on which historian or industry veteran he consulted. Perhaps a practical zoom lens had been invented before Walker's; perhaps, as Marjorie Walker argued, her father's was the first; or perhaps zoom lenses were of little use until other technologies, such as reflex viewfinders, had been perfected. (This suggestion was made by Ed DiGiulio, who made his fortune retrofitting reflex viewfinders to cameras.) And what about medium? Should television innovations be considered on the same level as cinema innovations? If *practicality* was the operative word in the academy's award citation, how should that concept be defined?[7]

These issues of novelty, practicality, medium specificity, industrial recognition, practice, and preference are negotiated throughout this book. However, before addressing these questions, it is necessary to provide a basic technical definition of the zoom lens and discuss some of the challenges posed when distinguishing between zoom lens technology and the zoom-shot technique. In purely technological terms, a zoom lens is deceptively easy to define; as a technique, the zoom shot is far more complicated. A zoom lens is any lens with a continuously variable focal length. The shot it creates is an apparent movement forward or backward effected by a change in the focal length of the lens. The zoom shot may be fast or slow. It may exhibit a very large change in focal length or hardly any change at all. However, the movement is different to that created by physically moving the camera. When a camera moves, the position of objects in the images it captures change relative to one another. From these movements, viewers can infer the size, shape, and depth of the space in front of the camera. The zoom, by contrast, simply magnifies the image in front of the camera, and no change occurs to the relative position of the objects in front of it. It is possible, of course, to move a camera and zoom in or out at the same time, and in some circumstances, as in the creation of a "dolly zoom" of the sort made famous by *Vertigo* (Alfred Hitchcock, 1958), a zoom shot may be made while the camera moves in the opposite direction. The flexibility of the term *zoom* has made it ideal for use as a metaphor or to describe movements having nothing to do with a photographic zoom lens. It is no surprise that critical discussions of the zoom have been varied and often contradictory.

For several decades after the introduction of the zoom shot to Hollywood filmmaking, the only writing about the subject came not from film historians or critics but from directors, cinematographers, equipment manufacturers, and distributors. Save for the occasional iconoclast, their views were firmly practical. They urged restraint and self-effacement in all aspects of cinematography. The general aim was to prevent the work of the camera crew from becoming obvious to the audience and thereby outshining the strength of a film's narrative.[8] Because the zoom was new and more noticeable for its novelty, the approach to the zoom shot voiced through the pages of trade periodicals during the 1950s and 1960s was entirely in line with this "classical" thinking. In 1957, Joseph V. Mascelli made one of *American Cinematographer*'s first significant interventions into the debate over the use of zoom lenses. Under the heading "Use and Abuse of the Zoom Lens," he counseled "restraint" and urged readers not to "show-off" but to use the zoom "intelligently." For Mascelli, restraint meant making the zoom look as much as possible like a "good dolly shot"—one that "starts up slowly, moves smoothly and steadily, and then decelerates to a stop." Though the zoom was relatively new, camera operators were urged to think about it in terms of its similarity to familiar techniques. When faced with a zoom lens, Mascelli advised cinematographers to "visualize how the shot would appear if it were being filmed from a dolly and imitate the action with the zoom lens." This left little room for the unique creative potential of the zoom and far less tolerance for the experimental or stylish use of the technology. In the pages of trade periodicals, the zoom was an inherently dangerous tool, prone to exposing the show-off tendencies of inexperienced camera operators. By the 1960s, cinematographers were reflexively defensive of their choices to use the zoom. When Philip Lathrop used a zoom in *Experiment in Terror* (Blake Edwards, 1962), *American Cinematographer* maintained that it was "so expertly devised and executed that few persons are aware that it is anything but straightforward photography."[9] Gerald Hirschfeld's zooms in *Fail Safe* (Sidney Lumet, 1964) were necessitated, it was claimed, by "the size of the set and the physical distances covered within split seconds."[10] James Wong Howe made lavish use of the zoom when filming *The Outrage* (Martin Ritt, 1964) only months after he had used the photography of *Hud* (Martin Ritt, 1962) to express his dislike for the technique. *American Cinematographer* duly explained that the zoom had been used only "in combination with dolly and pan movement to create certain desired visual effects."[11] In these ways, the zoom was sanctioned only when used "appropriately"—that is, where no alternative existed—and ideally hidden from the audience. Only under these circumstances could the zoom be said to have been "used"; anything else was, by implication, an "abuse."[12]

Why linger over yellowing magazine articles? It may be tempting to dismiss trade discourse as ephemera, but in this case, as in many others, ephemera echoes across decades of scholarship. Consider, for example, David A. Cook's discussions of the zoom in the context of 1970s Hollywood cinema. As a critic and historian rather than a working cinematographer, Cook's interests and priorities are different to those reflected in *American Cinematographer*. Nevertheless, his assessment, like others, is explicitly framed by the concept of "use and abuse" and conceptualizes the zoom as an alternative to other, more primary, techniques. Cook asserts, "The use (and abuse) of the zoom lens is an unmistakable hallmark of late 1960s' and early 1970s' film style in the United States and Europe. Most historians attribute this to the influence of television, whose cameras had been equipped with permanently mounted zoom lenses since the 1940s. During the 1950s and 1960s, as more and more films came to be shot on location, television production techniques were adapted to feature filmmaking for their flexibility and economy."[13] Cook then compares television-influenced American directors unfavorably with their European colleagues: "The European new-wave cinemas employed the lens expressively to create pictorial abstraction . . . or to structure scenic space by hovering and focusing selectively within it . . . but when American directors embraced the zoom in the late 1960s they initially used it to isolate detail within the frame, following the practice of television. In fact, many of them were veterans of television . . . and some indulged in orgies of self-conscious zooming in otherwise worthy films."[14]

"Use and abuse" is a problematic frame of reference in which to discuss the zoom, which relies in part on judgments of artistic quality or value, implicitly limiting discussion to texts in which artistry is the more important factor. This approach also holds the zoom shot to a standard not generally applied to other techniques of representation and narration: it is far rarer to see more commonplace camera movements—such as panning, tilting, and tracking—discussed in terms of *use* and *abuse* and more common for a spectrum of skill, quality, or inspiration to be invoked. The result is that the critical approach to the zoom shot has been technologically deterministic: a certain critical frame of reference has been applied only because a certain technology has been used to produce the text.

In an essay offering a "historical overview" of cinema and technology, Peter Wollen sheds some light on the critical thought processes behind the use/abuse concept. Wollen criticizes avant-garde cinema for its "mis-use of existing technology," identifying among other examples "the hyperbolic use of the zoom lens (as in *Wavelength*)" and concluding that "in all these areas . . . there is an ambivalence between contravening legitimate codes and practices (a negative act) and exploring possibilities deliberately overlooked within the industry, or tightly contextualised (in contrast, a positive act)."[15] This perspective is representative of the priorities that lie beneath much writing on the zoom. Seeded by trade discourses that urged restraint, rhetorical strategies such as Wollen's appear many times in relation to the zoom lens. The zoom is frequently considered along with other, supposedly cognate, devices. Bernard F. Dick considers "zooms and freezes" together on the basis that the freeze-frame is the "opposite" of the zoom. Dick adopts the metaphor of a balance sheet. On the credit side, "there are occasions when a zoom is useful: to single someone out in a crowd. . . . On the debit side, zooming flattens the image and creates an unreal sense of depth. . . . The zoom and the freeze are similar in that they can call attention to details more dramatically than other devices. Because of their strong underscoring power, they are as easily misused as italics are by inexperienced writers."[16] The use/abuse framework reveals not only a certain critical arrogance but also a sense that critics feel personally offended by the effect that the zooming technique has on them. Negative attitudes toward the zoom have often taken the form of an objection against the way in which the device seems to enable filmmakers to do what is contrary to the desires of the audience.

Describing camera movements, Robert Edmonds argues that "changes in camera position can be comfortable or uncomfortable. If the change is from a position far from the subject to one that is closer, we must also move to a different angle as well. If this did not happen, if we were to see one shot of a person followed by another shot of the same person, seen from the same axis but much closer, we would feel that someone had grasped us by the back of the neck and pushed us into the person." Edmonds singles out the zoom as a technology that, because of its "usual speed," particularly lends itself to such unwelcome manipulations of the viewer's attention. He then goes one step further to suggest that cinema can diminish viewers' agency, somehow reducing their ability to consent to filmic experience.[17] The zoom, at a certain speed, is seen as insisting on creating a relationship between audience and film that seems more "physical" than other techniques. Consequently, because much early (and some contemporary) critical writing on the cinema describes a personal relationship between the filmmaker/director and the individual audience member, the abuse of the zoom lens manifests itself as a breach of social convention. It moves in a few rhetorical steps from being a technique that falls foul of an individual critic's personal preference and becomes a social error rather like an invasion of personal space. Thus the zoom inhabits a privileged position in the sort of critical language that ascribes physical reactions and sensations to psychological perception. Zooms can be "jarring" or—according to a 1964 advertisement—"neck-snapping."[18] The zoom's link to synesthesia, described later in this chapter, is also part of this equation.

In the early 1970s, anxieties about the zoom inevitably found their way into the new academic discipline of film criticism. In an influential *Sight & Sound* article, Paul Joannides expressed key characteristics of the zoom lens taken as axiomatic by many early critics: the zoom is unique among camera "movements," it denies perspective, and it "flattens" the photographed object. In doing so, he conflated the effects of the zoom and telephoto lens, characterizing them as the "mobile and static halves of the same problem," with "aesthetic problems" that "merge naturally into each other." Nevertheless, for Joannides, the zoom was different because it "has an emphatic quality, demonstrating points in a context rather than combining those points in a new whole; it is less often used to create a new composition, that being more easily achieved by a cut to a different set-up." Here, the zoom is best defined by its difference from other technologies and techniques: unlike other camera movements, it takes place inside the camera rather than outside. In Joannides's estimation, it "can never, or almost never, be mistaken for a track." Joannides sees the zoom as a "dangerous tool" that "jars the audience and unless it is very necessary, as in a long distance shot, it usually looks out of place in a filmed context." Giving the example of a fast zoom designed to frighten horror audiences, Joannides argued that the zoom is "essentially false because the eye cannot zoom, whereas a cut to a different angle or a fast track . . . can approximate more truthfully to the frightened person's perception." In addition to its "falseness," Joannides also claims that the zoom shot is an intrinsically self-conscious device, conspicuously different to "normal" vision. Nevertheless, Joannides sees some potential for the zoom, along with the telephoto lens, to open new possibilities in filmmaking in which "the camera will play a more passive role dramatically, but a more potent one visually." However, this applied only to certain sorts of film—such as "symbolic montage *á la* Eisenstein"— and not to the formally conservative narrative applications to which the zoom had been applied. For Joannides, the zoom's potential was limited to intellectual implications of the art film, and then only within certain circumstances and modes of use.[19] While the essay offers a useful introduction to the aesthetic properties of the zoom and the telephoto lens, its key drawback is its dismissal of the powerful forces of formal convention that encouraged the use of the zoom as a substitution device. While the zoom indeed went on to play a more potent visual role within film and television style, it did not break out from stylistic norms but continued to operate within them. As the final chapters of this book demonstrate, though the zoom did not herald a new way of seeing in film and television, it did gradually develop new properties specific to its visual characteristics. By the dawn of the twenty-first century, the zoom was playing a role in enhancing the "intensified" style of Hollywood features, while in television, it became one of the clearest markers of the self-conscious, reflexive mockumentary sitcom.

Joannides's critique has been cited in numerous subsequent discussions of the zoom. In one of the first such responses, Stuart M. Kaminsky developed a somewhat more nuanced critical approach to the zoom. He imagined an alternative history of cinema in which tracking was impossible and the zoom shot was the only way to "move" the camera. Under such circumstances, Kaminsky argued, "cinematic grammar would then accept the zoom as the proper medium for tracking," while physical movement of the camera, if invented later, "would clearly be opposed on the grounds that the track was being used as an elaborate substitute for the more simple and natural device of the zoom." Upon the foundation of this counterfactual thought experiment, Kaminsky draws a parallel between the use of the zoom and the use of informal words and phrases in English speech and writing, arguing that "the repeated use of the zoom to 'track' will become aesthetically acceptable if it continues to be used—just as new words, phrases, and grammatical constructions become accepted through usage though they are initially considered vulgar."[20] Like Joannides, Kaminsky's preoccupation is the overuse of the zoom. Like a profane word whose impact is rooted in the shock of its occasional use, Kaminsky presses for the limited use of the zoom. This analogy, however, creates confusion. Kaminsky maintains that the zoom is little used and disapproved of merely because of its unfamiliarity, yet when placing it within the established grammar of filmmaking, he chooses to compare it with profanity, which would suggest entirely different reasons behind its unpopularity. Kaminsky pledges support for directors whose films stand as exceptions to general rules but disapproves of the essential creative impulse that would allow such independence to flourish. He maintains that the zoom is popular because "it allows the camera operator to insert his personality on that which he is shooting. Personality is probably too affirmative a word; 'presence' is more in keeping with the impetus." Kaminsky's ultimate solution to the problem of the zoom is to contain its use within certain categories—"to duplicate an atmosphere of verite," for example, or "to express a psychological reaction through the eyes of a character"—its appropriateness deriving in part from what is familiar: "The way in which the zoom is used in the non-fiction film, primarily in news photography and cinema verite."[21] Here, Kaminsky's argument is in broad accord with the trade discourse of the day, which was battling with the zoom as an increasingly attractive—but dangerously self-conscious—technology.

During the burgeoning of technology-focused and formalist film history in the 1970s and 1980s, a more detailed and somewhat more complete history of the zoom lens began to develop. Writing in *Cineaste* in late 1980, John Belton contributed a detailed history of the zoom that considered both the philosophical and the industrial aspects of its development and aesthetics. Drawing on debates published in *American Cinematographer* as well as Joannides's and Kaminsky's interventions of a decade earlier, Belton was the first historian to offer a comprehensive history of the zoom lens, accounting for its use in 1920s and 1930s feature films, its development in television during the 1940s and 1950s, and its subsequent popularity in Hollywood feature films after the 1960s.[22] Barry Salt was similarly diligent in *Film Style and Technology*, published in 1983. Yet despite their unprecedented level of detail, these accounts were missing an important component: while the development of the zoom in feature film production was carefully charted, scarcely any attention was paid to the technology's applications in television. Belton's assessment of the stylistic impact of the television zoom lenses of the 1940s and 1950s is limited to relatively brief remarks on their particular use in live television and sporting coverage. In later years, similar underestimations of the zoom's use in television can be found in some of David Bordwell's work. In *On the History of Film Style*, he characterizes this complex, intermedial interaction as follows: "In the 1940s the lens was improved for television and used for covering sports events. As filmmakers began to shoot on location more frequently during the 1950s and 1960s, the zoom proved very handy. . . . That cliché of television news—the telephoto shot of citizens on the street, jammed together and stalking to and from the camera—has its source in early 1960s films aiming at greater naturalism."[23] In fact, as the following chapters demonstrate, the zoom lens was used by television far more widely than just for "sports events." Television had a more complex interaction with zoom technology, and a more nuanced influence on film style, than accounts that foreground "use and abuse" (while passing quickly over television history) imply. If 1950s television technologies and techniques influenced subsequent film style, then it is useful to have a detailed account of the nature of the influence and a fuller assessment of how smooth and straightforward an influence it was. It is for this reason that this book closely examines early uses of the zoom in postwar television and newsreel.

Television, however, is not the only aspect of the zoom lens insufficiently served by historians of film style and technology. Many of the limitations of existing scholarship seem to stem, in one way or another, from the reductive "use and abuse" framework established so long ago by advertisements for zoom lenses, in manuals explaining how to use them, and in the pages of *American Cinematographer*. In the absence of a substantial body of stand-alone scholarship on the zoom, strangely skewed accounts of the technology and descriptions of its properties permeate general film histories. One problem is the tendency to emphasize films in which it appears at its most stylistically extreme. In multiple editions of their influential textbook *Film Art*, David Bordwell and Kristen Thompson limit their discussion of zooms in specific films to *The Conversation* (Francis Ford Coppola, 1974), *Barravento* (Glauber Rocha, 1962), *Serene Velocity* (Ernie Gehr, 1970), and—especially—*Wavelength* (Michael Snow, 1967). These examples are linked by their artistically motivated, and often extreme, uses of the zoom. The opening of *The Conversation*, for example, may be a powerful classroom example of a dramatic zoom shot; it is not, however, representative of American mainstream cinema's approach to the zoom. Connected to this problem is the challenge posed by the frequent conflation of the zoom shot and the telephoto shot. Joannides adopted this strategy when considering the zoom, and a more puzzling example is to be found in Bordwell's work when, in *On the History of Film Style*, three examples of striking zoom shots are given in the midst of a reflection on the formal implications of the telephoto lens.[24] There is no doubt that Bordwell knows the difference between zoom and telephoto, but there is a question as to whether all of his readers do, and the conflation of the two devices, strongly implied here, means that neither are given the critical consideration they deserve.

In addition, this approach tends to magnify the role of the director in the creative production of film texts. Much of what has been written on the zoom lens derives from auteurist critical accounts written by those who have noticed that certain directors seem to have a special preference for the zoom. But this approach has also inhibited some accounts of the zoom. Geoffrey Nowell-Smith's account of New Wave and avant-garde world cinemas (2008), which finds the subject of the zoom "worthy of brief mention," emphasizes Roberto Rossellini's early adoption of the zoom: "Now a staple of television and of home video, the first truly viable zoom lens for professional film-making was introduced by the Angénieux company in 1963, just too late for the early new waves.... Most film-makers at the time chose to ignore the new technology entirely and it was not until the 1970s that its use became widespread. Two film-makers, however, took it up with enthusiasm, though for very different purposes.... Rossellini in fact jumped the gun, using an early Pancinor zoom lens in *Viva l'Italia!* in 1960 and *Vanina Vanini* in 1961."[25] This passage concisely exemplifies some of the crucial problems with existing history and criticism on the zoom lens. Nowell-Smith's approach to the zoom is easy to understand but tough to defend. A number of these key facts are in the wrong order and seem twisted to fit a preexisting narrative that treats art cinema as its telos. The history of the Zoomar lens, discussed in chapter 3, demonstrates that the zoom shot was a "staple of television and of home video" before it became commonplace in feature filmmaking.[26]

The idea that Rossellini "jumped the gun" with regard to using the zoom lens is a particularly unproductive way of historicizing such a stylistic development. There was no starting gun—Rossellini was simply an early adopter of a technology that had been relatively unexploited by the industrial context in which he operated. Nor was he an early adopter of the Pan Cinor when he used it in the early 1960s: Pan Cinor lenses were introduced in the early 1950s. If this is recognized, then Nowell-Smith's claim that the Angénieux 10:1 lens was "the first truly viable zoom lens for professional film-making" is unsupportable. Insofar as they were developed and used, zoom lenses were viable in professional filmmaking as early as the late 1920s—and possibly much earlier. The Pan Cinor lens was also "viable" not only in Hollywood but also in Europe: as Nowell-Smith himself states, Rossellini used it. In truth, the history of the zoom lens is uneven and untidy. It begins decades before the New Wave experiments of the 1960s and encompasses popular television drama and amateur cinematography. Though a potent symbol of a particular era in American film, the zoom cannot be so neatly packaged as a product of any one historical moment.

WAVELENGTH AND BEYOND

Somewhat more recently, scholars approaching film studies from more purely philosophical and phenomenological directions have attempted to explain the significance and meaning of the zoom shot. These accounts almost always focus on exceptionally "showy" or artistic uses of the zoom. In place of direct formal analysis, inflected with technological and authorial determinism, such accounts speculate more adventurously on what the zoom shot may *mean* to audiences and how its use can be linked to other forms of cinematic address. At the same time, the term *zoom* has been adopted by scholars in other disciplines and by journalists in the wider media landscape as a flexible metaphor for concepts including magnification, bending, and the focusing of attention on a subset within a whole. In film and visual studies, such metaphorical uses of the term can be seen looping back on themselves, and it is clear that those who have substantially addressed the zoom have chosen to do so with reference to visual techniques that are "zooms" in only the metaphorical sense. In this phase of analysis, the zoom has become much more than an optical technique.

William C. Wees offers one of the earliest critical attempts to understand *how* zooms make meaning. Taking *Wavelength*—a film without camera movement except for a long, slow zoom in throughout its length—as his central text, Wees lays out his central questions: "What, then, *is* the visual event created by the zoom in *Wavelength*? How does it come about? How is it perceived? What, in a word, *happens* during a viewing of that forty-five minute zoom? And what does it mean?"[27] In attempting to answer these questions, Wees pays particularly close attention to the manner in which the zoom simultaneously is and is not "movement." He argues,

> The first thing to remember is that, unlike a tracking shot, a zoom shot is not based on "forward movement." In fact, it is a commonplace of technical manuals, as well as more general texts on film techniques, to point out that a zoom shot, which creates its effects through the optics of the zoom lens, should not be confused with a tracking shot, which depends for its effects on actual movement of the camera forward (or backward) in space. . . . The fact that so many people refer to "movement" in describing their perception of *Wavelength* suggests that, despite what I have just been saying, the zoom does provide visual cues for movement. If I actually walk toward a photograph pinned on a wall, I find that the photograph does, indeed, get larger in my visual field, and that things around it slip out of view at the peripheries of my vision. The zoom produces equivalent effects, hence the tendency to describe it as "moving forward." But I am really imitating a tracking shot, not a zoom. . . . I think it is safe to say that no perceptual experience in the every-day world can prepare us for the kind of vision produced by the zoom.[28]

Wees theorizes that the mental processes of the viewer cause him or her to make a "best guess" about what the optical alteration brought about by the zoom equates to. In the context of *Wavelength*, therefore, the zoom is seen by the viewer as a "functional equivalent" of camera movement, even if in production and in a variety of optical characteristics, it differs significantly.[29]

While Joannides and Kaminsky explored the uses and implications of the zoom shot from a critical perspective, Donald Skoller took a more experimental approach to the same question. He carried out an experiment in which a film camera fitted with a zoom lens was used to film a bowl of soup. The footage began with a close-up of the soup, then slowly zoomed out to show the soup bubbling within the pan, then zoomed farther out to show a man stirring the soup—in other words, from an extreme close-up, to a close-up, to a medium shot. Skoller showed the footage to a test audience and observed their reaction. He recognized a change in the audience's understanding as the zoom movement progressed, transforming an unrecognizably abstract swirl of red liquid into a recognizable, quotidian domestic scene. Among viewers, Skoller remarked, "there is usually chuckling and 'the shock of recognition' more along the lines of the viewer having experienced a quick cut that has juxtaposed two disparate images that set each other off in some unique way. But there hasn't been a cut at all and the viewer knows this and it tones his response." In contrast to this quotidian example, Skoller uses *Wavelength* to unpick the workings of the zoom.[30]

He finds that "as the zoom lens increases its focal length and compresses and flattens the field as viewed on the screen . . . a 'dramatically' different realm is entered. It is filled with ironies accessible only through *visceral discernment*. As the zoom slowly progresses, it reduces the degree of illusionistic depth of field presented to the viewer. . . . There is a liberation of illusioned energy, a release from willing suspension of perceptual disbelief occurring to the viewer's consciousness as depth-illusion itself is reduced."[31] Skoller finds two clearly distinct uses for zooms: to play with an audience's expectation for a short-term narrative advantage and to effect a more fundamental and long-lasting change in their artistic interpretation. Like Joannides and Kaminsky, Skoller argues that the zoom has interesting effects at either end of this spectrum.

At times, though the language is more complex, the message conveyed is not hugely developed beyond some of the arguments advanced during the 1970s. Vivian Sobchack, advancing a "phenomenology of cinematic vision," is a case in point: "As we all know (whether consciously or pre-consciously), there is a radical difference between the movement of a 'zoom-in' on an object and a 'forward track' toward it. In the former, the film's 'viewing view' is *compelled by* the object; in the latter, the film's material 'body' and its 'viewing view' literally *move toward* the object. The one is an intrasubjective visual gesture, experienced only introceptively as *im-pressive*. The other, while also experienced intrasubjectively and introceptively, is intersubjectively available as visible gesture, as *ex-pressive*."[32] This is worth comparing with Joannides and Kaminsky, both of whom outline arguments about the "psychological" properties of the zoom lens and maintain that there is a difference, of some sort, between the zoom and the track-in. Sobchack continues, "In optical movement, it is the film's 'viewing view,' not its material 'body,' that changes its address and situation in the world; that viewing view traverses worldly space without materially inhabiting the distance between itself and the object which compels its attention. That is, from its initiation, the 'zooming' gaze locates itself in its object, and literally *transcends* the space between the film's situation as an embodied viewing subject and the situation of the viewed object."[33] Here again, Sobchack describes in great detail a phenomenon more concisely noted by numerous critics and practitioners since the earliest days of the zoom: zooming in or out does not result in a change in the relative positions of various items ranged in depth in the mise-en-scène. Despite Sobchack's apparent restatement of earlier arguments, these interventions are worth considering because although they are reiterations of much earlier observations, they form a key reference point for scholars who make philosophical and phenomenological approaches to the zoom shot.

Sobchack's influence is particularly evident in discussions of the "cosmic zoom," which is, as Jennifer Barker describes its appearance in *Moulin Rouge!* (Baz Luhrman, 2001), "a digitally effected camera movement that races over

[Paris] rooftops at dizzying speed towards the legendary nightclub." In *Sweeney Todd* (Tim Burton, 2007), the effect "hurls us into the city ahead of [Todd], with speed and agility that only a digital effect can produce."[34] Barker adapts the term *cosmic zoom* from Garrett Stewart, who describes "a technique of digital rhetoric capable of drastic shifts in scale—as when plummeting from a satellite-range scan to a facial close-up, or lifting back out again—that also appears lately, in muted variants, for such radical shifts (in temporal rather than spatial orientation) as a precipitous tunnelling from present into biographical past."[35] The definition of the cosmic zoom is, on this basis, confused. For Stewart, it is a downward plunge or a sudden upward flight covering an effective focal length many times greater than any "real" zoom lens. For Barker, the cosmic zoom's trajectory is primarily horizontal: it produces the effect of a spectator surging through the mise-en-scène, which surrounds the viewer from start to finish. All that Barker and Stewart agree on is that the movement must be "digitally effected." Barker does not conceal such difficulties of definition: "The cosmic zoom," she writes, "is ontologically puzzling: neither a 'zoom' nor a 'travelling' or 'tracking' shot in the conventional senses of those terms, it exists somewhere in between the two."[36] After brief recourse to Sobchack, Barker attempts to solve the puzzle:

> As the cosmic zoom plummets, swerves, tunnels, and swoops through space and time, it clearly does not "travel" the same way a tracking shot travels, but it *does travel*, as the conventional zoom does not. Its digital aspects allow it to exceed the laws of physics by tunnelling through solid objects and moving at speeds no tracking camera could achieve. However, the part(s) of a cosmic zoom that involve an actual camera moving through sets or models are kinetic in a way the optical zoom can ever [*sic*] be; hence the cosmic zoom's ability to swerve around corners as the zoom cannot. . . . Faced with a well-executed cosmic zoom, the viewer is hard-pressed to tell the difference between physical movement and optical movement; the difference is rendered obsolete.[37]

Such confusion only reestablishes the flexibility of the term *zoom* in both etymological and conceptual terms. It is evident that the "cosmic zoom" as defined by Stewart and Barker is a *form* of zoom shot: it involves an apparent onrush of the camera, quickly closing in on an aspect of the frame. However, this approach shares the same limitation found in a number of other critical accounts. Discussions of visually exceptional techniques such as the cosmic zoom, Snow's creeping zoom-in in *Wavelength*, and the zoom-in/track-out combination described as the "*Vertigo* zoom" can be useful.[38] They also highlight the fact that close formal attention has not been paid to the more commonplace types of zoom shot used in American film and television from the mid-1940s onward.

It is not difficult to understand why such films have repeatedly caught the attention of critics and scholars. The unfamiliar can be easier to write about than the everyday and can fit more easily with existing norms and approaches in film criticism. *Wavelength* is an avant-garde film meant to provoke discussion and appreciation: it submits itself for aesthetic analysis. The *Vertigo* zoom, finally, is so strange in appearance that it is nearly always used to describe some specific and visceral psychological or physiological condition, such as the condition of vertigo. Addressing the famous queasy zoom-in/pull-back in *Vertigo*, Sobchack writes, "The difference between optical movement as a movement of the film's attention which transcends space and camera movement as a movement of the film's material 'body' through space is nowhere so marked as in Alfred Hitchcock's *Vertigo*. Indeed, Hitchcock constitutes vertigo as the dizziness which emerges when the *attention of consciousness* and the *intention of the body* are at odds with each other . . . Hitchcock makes Scotty's illness visible and intelligible through the simultaneous combination of optical movement (a forward zoom) and camera movement (a track out)—each opposed to the other in their immediate project."[39]

This raises a further important question: Is there a psychological basis for treating the zoom differently than other forms of editing or camera movement? There has been little direct investigation of this matter, but there have been limited comparative studies of the effect of zoom shots on video viewers. Colleen Birchett showed two groups of college students "videotaped paintings." One group saw a "slide treatment" of the paintings, in which the camera cut directly from one image to the next, while the other group saw images in which "the videotape camera zoomed into details."[40] Sun-Kyung Hong examined the cognitive styles of viewers of different categories of television programming, including a class of programming that was thought to contain "longer zooms and more moderate levels of action."[41] Both studies concluded that there was some suggestion of difference in the responses of test groups shown footage featuring zoom shots when compared with those shown footage without (or with fewer) zooms, though both studies also noted numerous confounding factors and called for further research. Whatever effects the zoom may have on a viewer's brain remain to be speculated by critics of the visual arts and are not yet confirmed by empirical study.

The history and theory of the zoom are sparse and unsatisfying. Decades of critical and academic interest in film and television history give the researcher a sheaf of journal articles and index entries from which to construct a history of the technology. They offer an encouraging diversity of views and perspectives: Joannides draws attention to the zoom's relationship with the telephoto and closeup shot, while Kaminsky's catalog of uses for the zoom provides a useful paradigm for formal analysis, and Belton and Salt represent an early mapping of the historical territory. But these approaches are, in themselves, of limited value. Historical accounts have not, so far, contributed a detailed account of the ways in which the zoom was used before the Second World War, and they have ignored television and amateur technology almost completely. Critical accounts, meanwhile, have leaned too heavily on a "use and abuse" dichotomy that emerges from trade discourse and does not fully represent the diversity of approaches to the zoom as it appears in film and on television. This study provides a more detailed account of some of the historical developments described by Belton and Salt—especially the Zoomar lens, the history and significance of which has not been fully accounted for. Formalist accounts such as Bordwell's indicate some further significant gaps in knowledge. They too gesture toward a necessary but untold history of zoom technology in the television context. In addition, their focus on artistically motivated New Wave and European examples—and their frequent insistence on the zoom as either a "special effect" or a "cheap alternative"—suggest a neglected corpus of mainstream American films requiring further investigation. In short, while the films of Robert Altman and Stanley Kubrick have rightly been lavished with affirmative critical attention for their uses of the zoom, more popular fare—films like *Planet of the Apes* and *The Thomas Crown Affair*—have not been considered in such detail. While the influence of storied TV Generation directors has been glancingly considered, close attention has not been paid to how they really used the zoom, and no examination has revealed the approach taken by camera operators sent to cover baseball games, parades, and political conventions—the mundane coverage watched by millions. Equally as important is the question of what happened after the zoom lost its novelty and unfamiliarity, for zooms did not disappear from film and television but were an essential aspect of the quickening pace of moving-image media at the dawn of the video age and into the twenty-first century. All of these issues are discussed in the chapters that follow.

CHAPTER PREVIEWS

Chapter 2 begins with an examination of the earliest origins of the zoom shot. To do so, it reaches back to precinema optical toys, lantern shows, and telescopes in order to demonstrate that zoom technology and zoom effects were familiar to audiences and showmen long before the invention of cinema. This chapter explores the etymology of the word *zoom* to elucidate the conceptual link between the word's original meaning—the flight of an aircraft upward at great speed—and its application to variable focal length lenses for motion picture cameras. The chapter explores the earliest zoom lenses for which records exists.

It analyzes in detail the zoom's earliest applications, from the adventurous and painstakingly rehearsed establishing shots in Paramount films, to the more complex and motivated zoom shots trialed by MGM directors. The chapter discusses the best known zoom lens of the period, the Varo, and also considers the significance of ostensibly "failed" and largely forgotten zoom technologies such as the Durholz lens.

Chapter 3 considers how zoom technology was improved and augmented in order to provide a tool that could be used on a day-to-day basis in television. It was during the late 1940s and early 1950s that American audiences first became familiar with the zoom lens, and during this period, the key innovative impulse came from television. This chapter shows how the inventor Frank Back converted wartime innovations into the Zoomar lens, which, after proving its worth on newsreel cameras, became ubiquitous in television. The chapter demonstrates that far from being only occasionally used for sports and news programming, the Zoomar lens made a substantial impact on the look and feel of a wide range of American television, both on location and in the studio. This chapter analyzes newsreel footage of baseball and football games televised with the aid of Zoomar lenses, demonstrating how the technology made possible screen-filling images of players and spectators and helped establish the style and grammar of sports coverage on television. The chapter also examines the critical contribution Zoomar lenses made to television networks' breakthrough coverage of the political conventions of 1952, which helped establish the role of American television as a purveyor of news reporting as well as entertainment.

The fourth chapter covers the initial intervention of European zoom lenses into both the amateur and the professional markets. This chapter explores the legal and technological implications of the introduction of Pan Cinor lenses and highlights some of the most innovative uses of the technique in mid-to-late 1950s television and late 1950s feature films. The first half of this chapter examines the battle between the two manufacturers and shows how legal arguments over the patentability of the Zoomar lens affected the long-term availability of European zoom lenses to American cinematographers. The chapter then examines the benefits of the newly available Pan Cinor lenses to the makers of television shows and the directors of feature films. The lens became available at a time when the production of American television comedy and drama serials was shifting from New York to Hollywood and from live video to film. This chapter focuses on several detailed case studies of television serials, which were particularly affected by the new availability of zoom lenses. In addition, the chapter reviews the television work of some of the directors who were to become known as the "TV Generation"—including John Frankenheimer, Robert Mulligan, Blake Edwards, and Sydney Pollack. This chapter analyzes the ways in which these directors used the zoom lens during their television careers and questions the assumption that their later uses of the zoom in features were straightforward stylistic importations from television.

Chapter 5 discusses one of the better-known developments in the history of the zoom lens, the introduction of the Angénieux 10:1 lens in 1963. This chapter argues that the Angénieux lens was an incremental development rather than a radical one and that the "zoom boom" that followed in American film was as much a product of earlier zooms as of the technological superiority of the new technology. While most accounts begin their analyses of the 1960s zoom boom during that decade, this chapter pays attention to late 1950s features that made significant use of the zoom shot. The chapter then analyzes the increasingly vigorous debate in trade periodicals around the appropriate usage of the zoom lens and examines how directors and cinematographers negotiated innovation and stylistic norms when using the zoom shot during the 1960s and early 1970s. Finally, it considers case studies of two directors—John Frankenheimer and Sydney Pollack—whose transition from television to film helped break new ground in the use of the zoom in Hollywood features.

Chapter 6 examines how, following the "zoom boom" of the early 1960s, new technologies broadened the appeal of the zoom lens for both amateur and professional cinematographers. Amateur filmmakers benefited from smaller, lighter, and more convenient zoom lenses on 8mm cameras. Meanwhile, a wide range of new technologies—including advances in smooth, predictable zoom motors and higher-quality glass technologies—led to improvements in professional-grade lenses. Against this backdrop, many feature cinematographers became increasingly resistant to the attractions of the zoom lens, as the enthusiastic uptake of the zoom in the 1960s began to look like overuse. Television, however, saw some of the most adventurous and comprehensive adoptions of the zoom, and this chapter looks closely at early 1970s television drama in order to demonstrate the influence of the zoom lens on small-screen production logistics and style.

The book's final chapter looks at zoom technologies and the zoom shot since 1980. It considers how new technologies that have enabled easier, swifter, and more economical camera movement have reduced the usefulness of the zoom lens. Thanks to portable cranes, lightweight jibs, and the Steadicam, moving action can be captured with greater ease and speed. The rise of digital nonlinear editing and acquisition means that it has become more efficient to film from multiple angles and save decisions for postproduction than to cover a scene from a single angle using a zoom lens. Overt zooms, meanwhile, have become unfashionable; from the 1980s onward, cinematographers increasingly used zooms as a substitute for a set of prime lenses. Lens manufacturers responded by producing faster, but often less flexible, zooms marketed explicitly as variable primes.

However, since 1980, the zoom shot has been highly important in other areas of moving image entertainment. The development of lightweight portable video cameras broadened the scope and ambition of live television news while camcorders with miniaturized zoom lenses created a generation of videographers. This chapter demonstrates the centrality of the zoom in making possible news coverage from a distance, whether on the ground, as in the case of camcorder footage of the beating of Rodney King in Los Angeles in 1992, or from the air, as in the case of helicopter news coverage of the police pursuit of O. J. Simpson. Finally, this chapter addresses how television's approach to the zoom changed. Though news and soap operas continued to make extensive use of the production economies of the zoom lens, high-budget television eschewed the zoom in favor of the Steadicam or the "cinematic" look of carefully lit, single-camera shooting. Meanwhile, television drama's move away from the zoom created new stylistic opportunities: unstable, jolting zooms became a signifier of nervous energy or smartphone-age vérité, and the zoom itself became a knowing and self-referential stylistic marker of the documentary-style sitcom.

2 · DRAMA AT THE TOUCH OF A LEVER

Before the zoom lens was invented, zooming was invented, and it had nothing to do with cinematography. When American army and navy personnel returned from the European battlegrounds of the First World War, they brought with them a panoply of new slang, including fresh vocabulary to describe flying. Among these new words was *zoom*, meaning "to climb speedily after level flight."[1] The word had for some time been used to describe fast movement or "a continuous humming, buzzing, or droning sound": earliest attestations describe the flight of bees and the bass notes of orchestral string instruments.[2] But after the war, associated with the new technology of flight, *zoom* meant something altogether new and exciting. To zoom was to do just about the most exhilarating thing a pilot could do with an aircraft: open the throttle, point the nose toward the sky, and surge away from the ground. From the end of the 1910s and throughout the 1920s, newspapers, magazines, newsreels, and feature films filled with firsthand accounts of derring-do by aviators and "aerobats." Zooming became all the rage.

Perhaps the epidemic of zooming can be dated to the antics of army air force pilots Fred Kelly and L. F. Pritchard. On December 4, 1918, Kelly and Pritchard took off from New York's Mitchel Field and flew toward the USS *George Washington*. The ship had just set sail for France, carrying President Woodrow Wilson to peace talks. The aviators' flight plan had been cleared by the Army Air Service, but what they did when they reached the *George Washington* had not been approved. A few hundred feet above the president and first lady, and watched by thousands of spectators from the shore, Kelly and Pritchard launched a breathtaking aerobatic display. Reporters sent to cover the Wilsons' departure watched in astonishment as the planes "looped the loop, made nose dives, and performed other feats that made the thousands on shore and on ships gasp at the audacity of the pilots."³ Newspapers in California, where Kelly had been a star college athlete, took particular note of the stunt. Recounting the story to reporters a few days later, Pritchard claimed that Kelly's display had so terrified Edith Wilson that she retreated belowdecks. He was particularly keen to boast about the zooming, which, he told reporters, "means to strain the plane beyond its tested endurance and get away with it." The getaway, however, was not perfect. Though the planes landed safely, Kelly was punished with two weeks of menial tasks back at the base.⁴

Kelly's aerobatics—probably not quickly forgotten by anyone who witnessed them—heralded the first age of the zoom. Newspapers filled with stories of powered flight, and zooming was often prominent. In August 1919, the *Los Angeles Herald* reported that the first supply flight was due to "zoom off" to Catalina Island "on the first aerial overseas merchandise delivery ever made in the history of this high-flying cosmos."⁵ Another aerobatic pilot, explaining to readers the attractions of stunt flying, described adventures between "fleecy clouds that turn the whole world into a fairyland": "Just as you come to the great cloud you suddenly pull back the old joy stick and zoom down the other side, perhaps into a lake—that is, it looks like a lake. Then you come to a succession of hills or mountains and you go zooming up and then down like a big roller coaster."⁶ Decades would pass before flying would become so familiar to wealthy Americans as to be unremarkable. Nevertheless, newspapers already imagined their readers fretting about airsickness, which would surely be exacerbated if the pilot were to try a little "zooming" on a passenger flight. Such a stunt, warned Dr. Leonard Keene Hirshberg in the *Herald*, "is bad for delicate constitutions." In a zoom, he explained, "the nose of the airplane is headed straight toward the sky. Then the control is shoved forward, the tail of the ship flips up until the nose points straight earthward. After a short downward course it is again headed towards the heavens, the operation being repeated as long as its effects can be enjoyed, which for the novice isn't very long."⁷

In the early 1920s, it was the "zoom" of an aircraft—whether its sound or the action of hurtling toward the sky—that was most evocative of flight. The act and sound of zooming took on a metonymic quality. Thus one newspaper enlivened a dull report on California state aircraft licensing laws with a declaration that "birdmen cannot in [the] future zoom down over the shrinking heads of city crowds," while the lead paragraph in a report on Armistice Day ceremonies in California in 1921 highlighted that "the 'zoom' of a German Gnome engine will be heard again by thousands of veterans."⁸ It was not long before earthbound Californians were encouraged to zoom in their motorcars. "Borrow the skyman's slang," suggested one car advertisement. "No earthly word fits as well. You 'zoom' up a hill in an HCS. Short of flight itself, no greater pleasure than this."⁹ "Man alive, what a difference," declared a newspaper advertisement for General

Gasoline, "when you zoom up hills in high that have always called for a gear-shift before . . . then you'll know what we mean by a 'different' gasoline."[10]

The film industry, then, did not coin the term *zoom*. Instead, it was adopted from aeronautics, along with a powerful set of cultural and technological associations. This etymology tells us something important about the expectations of engineers and opticians who developed the earliest zoom lenses. Long before articles in the pages of *American Cinematographer* urged cinematographers to use the zoom with restraint and self-effacement, this borrowing of aeronautical jargon implied that the lens should be used with power and energy to create an impact on audiences as shocking and visceral as aerobatic flight. As we shall see, this is exactly how the earliest commercially marketed zoom lens—the Varo—was promoted. It would be decades before either technology or film style would allow for such visually arresting zooms, but the seeds of these later developments were planted in the 1920s and 1930s, and the zoom's heritage stretches back even further. Before the Varo could be introduced, a series of optical experiments and experimental lenses were tried. These laid the earliest groundwork for a technology that would eventually revolutionize motion picture cameras by extending the reach and flexibility of their vision.

THE ZOOM BEFORE CINEMA

A form of zoom shot predates cinema by at least a century. In the late eighteenth century, an itinerant lanternist named Étienne-Gaspard Robert—better known by his stage name, Robertson—traveled Europe displaying *Phantasmagoria*, a show of glass slides and shadow play. Robertson was an innovator who combined multiple lenses and mechanisms to create novel effects. His projector was mounted on rails so that it could be moved forward and backward, and "to enable the lens to be always in focus, a rackwork mechanism was added, so that the image could be kept sharply defined throughout the advancing and retreating process of the machine."[11] In a memoir, Robertson described the zoom-like special effect this mechanism created: "At a great distance a point of light appeared; a figure could be made out, at first very small, but then approaching with slow steps, and at each step seeming to grow; soon, now of immense size, the phantom advanced under the eyes of the spectator and, at the moment when the latter let out a cry, disappeared with unimaginable suddenness."[12]

This surprisingly early record of a zoom shot reminds us that even though motion picture zoom lenses would not be developed until the 1920s, the fundamental optical and mechanical principles required for their design were established centuries earlier. In Italy, artisans had manipulated glass to create lenses for spectacles since the thirteenth century.[13] The historian Vincent Ilardi argues that the optical theory of the day would have been of little use to glassworkers but suggests that there is strong evidence to indicate that they carried out experiments to devise other forms of optical devices comprising multiple lenses. After experimenting with the different capabilities of spectacles, Ilardi argues, "other inquisitive artisans would have been equally tempted to place combinations of two convex lenses or convex and concave lenses in alignment and move one back and forth in front of one eye for focusing to achieve modest magnification for distance viewing. In other words, the construction of spectacles and tubeless telescopes by trial and error would not have presented enormous difficulties for talented individuals."[14] On this basis, it seems likely that the "zooming" property exhibited when multiple lenses were combined was known early on. A medieval glassworker would have only to hold two lenses before him, one in front of the other, and move one lens forward and back to see a primitive zoom effect. Because such experiments were carried out by artisans rather than scientists and predate the patent record, little evidence of any such experimentation survives. There is no trail of invention and experimentation to lead from putative medieval experiments to the devices such as the one evidently used by Robertson; all that we know is that in order to be effective, Robertson's device would have been a sophisticated and precise piece of engineering, the likely result of substantial experimentation with combinations of lenses and types of movements. It is possible that Robertson built this device alone and from first principles, but it is not unlikely that he was drawing on centuries of unrecorded expertise.

Experimentation of this type continued after Robertson, and more recent development work has left a more accessible trail of evidence. During the nineteenth century, efforts to develop variable focal length lenses were taken up by mathematicians and optical designers interested in creating improved astronomical telescopes. In 1848, the Italian photographer Ignazio Porro designed a zoom telescope in order to observe a solar eclipse.[15] Later, he adapted the lens for photographic purposes.[16] In the early 1890s, when the first motion picture cameras were under development, Thomas R. Dallmeyer was granted a patent for a telephoto lens that allowed the continuous variation of focal length. This, he promised, would "assist the user of the 'hand-camera' and smaller sizes of cameras . . . by enabling the operator to be at greater distance from the foreground of his subject and yet maintain a sufficiently large image, also to obtain by the addition of the enlarging system to his lens enlarged details in subjects of general interest."[17] As with later motion picture zoom lenses, this was achieved by manipulating sliding tubes of lenses so as to alter the focal length.

None of these devices was a zoom lens in the modern sense, and it is unlikely that any of them were used during the production of a motion picture. Nevertheless, the precinema history of the zoom effect and zoom-type lens is important. From the details of Robertson's *Phantasmagoria*, we understand that zoom effects were familiar to showmen and enjoyed by audiences; they also demonstrated the sophistication and innovation of lens systems used by lanternists. Sustained international efforts to develop variable focal length lens systems during the nineteenth century show that the convenience of these systems was appreciated by lens designers. The publication of designs in patents, journals, and other professional papers indicate an active research culture surrounding variable focal length optics.

Despite all this scientific research and innovative effort, for the first quarter of the twentieth century, the extent of the development and application of zoom lenses in motion picture production is largely unrecorded. The zoom shot itself cannot be traced further back than 1927. One account hints at the appearance of a zoom in *Second in Command* (William Bowman, 1915), but this is uncorroborated.[18] There is no confirmed zoom until *It* (Clarence G. Badger, 1927).[19] The lack of zoom shots before 1927 may be due to a lack of directly applicable innovation. While opticians experimented with zoom-like devices in the early years of the twentieth century, none developed a zoom lens, and none were working with motion picture photography in mind. Nonetheless, zoom-type lens designs were well researched by the turn of the twentieth century, while their various attractions—of economy and novel visual effect—would undoubtedly have piqued the interest of early filmmakers. As cinema underwent its earliest developments at the turn of the nineteenth century, this research and innovation continued. Efforts to design zoom-type lenses for optical toys continued into the early twentieth century: the earliest zoom lens patent of the cinema age, by Chicago-based inventor Clile C. Allen in 1901, makes no mention of moving pictures, intending its application instead for stereopticons and other optical toys.[20] In 1914, a patent was granted to Albert Konig, a lens designer working for the German firm Carl Zeiss, for a variable power telescope, which promised to offer two levels of magnification without the need to detach or decouple lenses while in use.[21] Such a variable focal length setup would have been useful in itself to motion picture camera operators, and as Richard Koszarski notes, the dominant design of early Mitchell film cameras, which featured a turret of multiple lenses, "prefigures one use for the modern zoom."[22] However, the complexity of zoom lenses, in addition to their typically poor performance when compared with contemporary fixed focal length lenses, would have rendered their use impractical in many situations. All these factors weighed against the use of a zoom before the late 1920s: the technology simply was not sufficiently advanced to be used in the production of commercial motion pictures. However, great caution is needed in relation to this conclusion. The patchy preservation of films and the lack of key technical trade publications from this era (the *Journal of the Society of Motion Picture Engineers* began in 1916, while *American Cinematographer* did not get started until 1920) means that the absence of an extant zoom shot prior to 1927 tells us little about the earliest inception of the technique. It is likely that zoom lenses were used—even if only experimentally—long before this date. However, hunting for the "first" zoom shot is most likely a futile activity.

THE EARLIEST ZOOMS

Whichever film truly contains the "first" zoom—*It* or some earlier lost or unnoticed film—it is evident that the potential advantages of zoom lenses were well known by the closing years of the silent era. During the 1920s, a special effects technician at Paramount named Rolla T. Flora developed a zoom lens, for which he filed a patent in 1927. Flora's invention consisted of a "movable lens system controllable by a single operation to have relatively short-focal, telephoto or any intermediate focal characteristics with respect to a given focal plane . . . accomplished generally by the provision of a pair of lenses movable with relation to each other to vary the resultant focal length."[23] Most significant in Flora's patent filing is his evocative description of how the lens might be used in practice. He anticipates both fundamental uses of a zoom lens—namely, as a substitute for fixed lenses of different focal lengths and as the progenitor of the dynamic zoom effect:

> Assume, for instance, that it be desired to take a relatively "long shot" of a landscape and then take a close-up of some detail thereof. The usual method of accomplishing this would involve either two camera settings . . . or else the mounting of the camera on a car. . . . Both of these operations call for laborious preparations and are necessarily costly. In contradistinction to this, the same situation may be handled by my device but with a single setting of the camera. The camera is set up to take the long shot and while the film is being exposed the lenses are moved as described above to cause the gradual magnification or increase of linear dimensions of the image on the film, thus giving the effect of a gradual change from a long shot to a close-up.[24]

At the same time, cinematographer Joseph Walker became one of the first independent innovators to develop a zoom lens for motion picture use and later documented the process in his autobiography. Walker recalls the notion of a zoom shot having "tantalized" him for some years before he began work on his zoom lens during the early 1920s. Like all other zoom lens developers, Walker faced significant optical challenges. One of the gravest of these was the elimination of focusing problems caused by varying the position of the two lenses. Walker's solution was to change the way in which the lens's optical elements moved relative to one another. He abandoned a linear movement and designed a cam that would provide for an irregular relationship between one group of lenses and another: "I resorted to making the cam from a flat piece of phosphor bronze, cutting the edge to the required shape. It worked well; the lens stayed in focus while it moved from wide angle to telephoto. The image appeared to travel through space, therefore I called it the 'Traveling Telephoto' lens. In February, 1929, I applied for a patent."[25] Walker was by this point an established cinematographer who had worked for a range of studios and would go on to forge a creative alliance with Frank Capra, in whose films some early examples of zoom shots would appear. Walker's patent, written with the detail and passion of an expert, described twin inconveniences that might be avoided by his new lens. With the help of a zoom, studio technicians would no longer be required to adjust their "carefully arranged" lights and screens when the camera was moved to facilitate a closer shot. Nor would two cameras, shooting simultaneously, be required to capture the two shots on a sound production.[26] Unlike Flora, who worked within Paramount and filed his patent on behalf of his employer, Walker worked more or less independently, personally machining components for his prototypes and solving problems through trial and error. The combined efforts of corporate research and development and independent inventing, always the dual drivers of innovation in the motion picture industries, would continue to typify the zoom lens industry for decades.

The inventive efforts of Flora, and later of Walker, were immediately evident in films released from 1927 onward, though zoom-ins and zoom-outs remained infrequent.[27] The earliest of these films tend to feature only one or two zoom shots, always combined with a very high or low camera angle. This is most famously the case in *It*, which opens with a single establishing shot featuring two zooms. This earliest known example of a zoom shot transforms a series of ordinary establishing shots into a tour de force of narrative efficiency. The film's opening image, a frame-filling low-angle view of a sign that reads "Waltham's / Worlds Largest / Store," gives way, via a zoom-out, to a pan down the façade of a twelve-story building. The camera rests for a few moments on a high-angle view of the building's lower stories, which dwarf the motorcars on the street. The camera then zooms toward the store's main entrance, excluding the cars from the frame and drawing attention to shoppers walking along the sidewalk and in and out of the department store. A lap dissolve transports the viewer inside the store, where shoppers, store assistants, and products for sale can more clearly be seen. The opening shot thus shifts the audience from the starkly functional rooftop advertisement to individual shoppers inside—from the bland, self-promoting architecture of the commercial enterprise (the film's broad setting) to personal relations on the human scale (the material of the film's narrative). The zoom maintains the spatial continuity of the shot and in doing so emphasizes the contrast between the vastness of the store building and the relative smallness of the mass of consumers and employees who populate its inner spaces. Remarkably, these shots have been mistaken for tracking or dollying.[28] The distinction is important: that such a visual impact is achievable from a single camera position, for the sake of the few moments of footage that establish the film's setting, testifies to the significant attraction of the zoom shot. *It*'s opening shot is narratively complex, visually appealing, and unusual but required fewer camera setups and less effort in editing than an equivalent sequence achieved through montage.

A more adventurous zoom shot is to be found in *The Four Feathers* (Merian C. Cooper, 1929), which uses a zoom to focus attention on two soldiers keeping watch from the lookout tower of a besieged citadel. The shot appears unremarkable to modern eyes—a slow zoom-in combined with a slight upward tilt of the camera. However, it must have required significant effort in planning and coordination because the zoom-in occurs as one of the soldiers climbs a ladder to the roof of the tower to join his comrade. The zoom begins precisely as the soldier's head appears over a parapet on a lower level of the building and finishes on a long shot of the two soldiers beneath the British flag. The film then cuts to a closer view of the two soldiers, who discuss—in an intertitle—their besiegement and apparent abandonment by the British. This shot shares the same fundamental style as the opening scene in *It*: in both establishing shots, the zoom contrasts

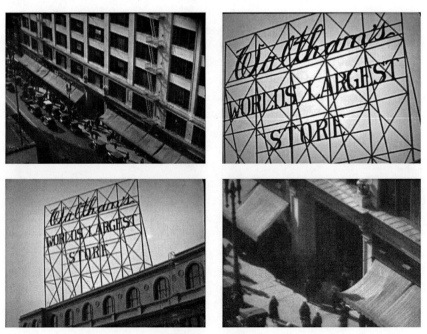

FIGURE 2.1. Zooms in the opening shot of *It* (Clarence G. Badger, 1927)

a massive building with the comparatively tiny human figures within it. However, *The Four Feathers* zoom is considerably more adventurous than the earlier example because it focuses on the directed action of specific actors and ends in a match-on-action cut to the next shot. This scene would not have worked without careful orchestration and rehearsal of actors and camera crew and is unlikely to have been captured by chance in a moment of whimsical experimentation by a cinematographer. Instead, it suggests that by 1929, Paramount camera crews had acquired a significant degree of confidence and practice in using the zoom lens. Indeed, zooming into a match-on-action cut was an approach repeated in *The Silent Enemy* (H. P. Carver, 1930), which features a zoom shot toward a shaman and two other characters on top of a rocky outcrop, followed by a well-matched lap dissolve to a slightly closer view of the same setup. Both of these scenes lay bare the photographic limitations of the zoom lens in the late 1930s: images taken with the zoom lens are far darker and less well defined than the equivalent footage shot with standard primes. While the apparent camera movement is visually appealing, the tactic of moving from a zooming establishing shot to a well-matched fixed focal length shot creates a juxtaposition that was not flattering to the skill of the cinematographer. Nor was the technique flattering to the editor: in both of these examples, the imperfectly matched zoom and prime shots create a jarring jump cut that is poorly concealed by the lap-dissolve transition.

This may be why Paramount's zooming establishing shots were the exception rather than the rule. The opening sequence of *Only the Brave* (Frank Tuttle, 1930) features a series of zooms onto a map of the United States of America, a *New York Times* front page, and the muzzle of a cannon. The sequence concludes with a fast and remarkably precise zoom toward a galloping horse, executed while the camera pans from left to right—a bravura shot that may reflect the confidence and practice of the Paramount crew in the use of the zoom. But it is not matched by the rest of the film, which, though it displays a great deal of fluidity and experiment in camera movement, does not repeat its use of the zoom shot.

More elaborate experiments with early zoom lenses are to be found in MGM's late silent pictures. These include zooms that animate establishing shots, as in *Tide of Empire* (Allan Dwan, 1929), which features three zoom shots. Each of these slowly pulls back from a wide view of the gold-prospecting town in which the film is set. The first of these shots is the most impressive. Starting on a telephoto long shot of a horse-drawn wagon, the camera zooms back to reveal the scale of the exterior set constructed for the film. The zoom transports the viewer from the tented outskirts of the town to the older wooden buildings at its heart. At its widest angle, the zoom also takes in a multitude of people bustling through the town and working on the hillside far in the distance. The same zooming movement from the same angle and position is then repeated twice more during the film, during the arrival of the Wells Fargo stagecoach and when the town is attacked by a band of outlaws. These latter zooms make less of an impact because they are murky night shots in which only lights and indistinct outlines of people and horses can be made out.

The tactic of zooming out to reveal a lavish set, as rehearsed in *Tide of Empire*, is exploited to far greater and more self-conscious effect in the frenetic romantic drama *Our Modern Maidens* (Jack Conway, 1929). As Lucy Fischer observes, the film's focus on "beautiful single women of the Jazz Age . . . allowed MGM to flaunt its gorgeous Art Deco set designs and costumes."[29] One scene, which depicts a Fourth of July party inside a cavernous mansion, is particularly enhanced by the cinematographer's adventurous and skillful use of the zoom lens. The studio set for the scene is huge: an exaggerated cathedral of a space, with (at least) quadruple-height ceilings, the room looks more like a grand ballroom than any private home. The set for this scene is, as Fischer puts it, "replete with such Art Deco design and architectural touches as geometric wall sconces, accordion-pleated molding, abstractly decorated door panels, *moderne* pedestals topped by sleek statuary."[30]

The set is an object of visual pleasure in itself, and the cinematography flatters it to the greatest possible extent. The scene is preceded by an energetic montage sequence superimposing a series of musical instruments and dancers, all treated with a bewildering array of optical effects, including zooms. In the shots that follow, Kentucky Strafford (Anita Page) and Gil Jordan (Douglas Fairbanks Jr.) join the orchestra. While Jordan plays the piano, Strafford sits on it, playing a ukulele. These shots do not disclose the scale of the set; they simply frame the players in medium close-ups, with hints of architectural styling in the background. In the next shot, however, the set is shown in its full glory. Starting from a long shot of the band, the camera languidly zooms out. As it does so, the set's various decorations are gradually revealed. The "accordion-pleated molding," glimpsed in the background of an earlier shot, appears at the right of the frame, and as the zoom draws farther back, it is revealed that this molding forms the edge of an archway that spans the room. Drawing back still farther, we see that the party is taking place in two connected spaces. In addition, there is a third space—largely off screen, to the right of the frame. As the zoom reaches its widest angle, a couple appears from the right of the screen and sweeps onto the dancefloor. Their appearance confirms the substance of the set: despite the symmetry of the archways, there are no mirrors or other special effects making possible the vast scale of the scene. At the left of the frame, a spiral staircase winds up an internal column.

This gradual zoom shot, which takes about ten seconds to fully unfold, is a masterpiece of showmanship. The slow rate of the zoom-out has two effects. It withholds the full grandeur of the set, gradually disclosing more of the scenery as the angle becomes wider. The zoom, longer in duration than the shots that precede it, also represents a brief pause in the film's headlong narrative. The shot offers a breathing space in which there is nothing for the audience to do but enjoy the scale and detail of the set. It testifies to the reality and wholeness of the stage—proof that the scene is not composed of a series of shots assembled so as to deceive. The story does not advance for these eleven seconds; the opulent set is all that is revealed. This scene is therefore as much a demonstration of the wealth of MGM as it is an exposition of the opulence of the film's characters. The zoom provides an excuse to stop and take in the view without halting the film's frantic pace.

Directly after this spectacular shot, *Our Modern Maidens* does something entirely different—but equally novel—with the zoom. Billie Brown (Joan Crawford) climbs the spiral staircase seen at the edge of the frame in the earlier zoom-out and pauses at a high balcony, where she cavorts in an attempt to draw Gil Jordan's attention. A zoom-in moves past Brown to center Jordan in the frame as he climbs onto the piano; this is followed by a cut to his perspective of Brown on the balcony. The camera again zooms in and remains on a shot of

FIGURE 2.2. Zooms animate the flirtatious gaze of Billie Brown (Joan Crawford) and Gil Jordan (Douglas Fairbanks Jr.) in *Our Modern Maidens* (Jack Conway, 1929).

Brown until she dances off the screen and up the staircase. When Brown subsequently reappears at the top of the staircase wearing a new outfit, the zoom is used once more. On this final occasion, however, the zoom is combined with an exaggerated theatrical lighting transition that fully emphasizes Brown's sensual display. As she reappears at the balcony, most of the lights dim, leaving her picked out as if by spotlight. The zoom then advances toward Brown, roughly approximating Jordan's point of view, as she strikes a provocative pose. After a brief view of Jordan applauding her display, we see a closer shot of Brown exposing her midriff and bikini.

Another example of the shot/reverse shot zoom strategy can be found in *Where East Is East* (Tod Browning, 1929), another MGM feature released just a few months prior to *Our Modern Maidens*. The subject and setting of the film—tiger trapping in Laos—is equally as exotic as the East Coast luxury of *Our Modern Maidens*. The film gave an early starring role to Lupe Vélez, and it is to the glamorous image of Vélez—and her costar, Lloyd Hughes—that the zoom lens is applied. Like *Our Modern Maidens*, *Where East Is East* uses the zoom shot subjectively to demonstrate the gaze of two characters and illustrate their romantic attachment. These shots occur during a sequence in which the film's protagonists—Bobby Bailey (Hughes) and Toyo Haynes (Vélez)—are separated by Bailey's departure for a hunting expedition. As Bailey's steamer makes ready for departure, Toyo's father finds the couple passionately embracing behind piles of cargo on the quayside and resorts to physically manhandling his daughter's suitor onto the boat. They embrace again on the gangplank, and Toyo attempts to board the vessel in order to travel with her lover. Once the couple is finally separated, a pair of zoom shots simulates the boat's departure. A slow zoom-out, from Bailey to Haynes, is intercut with the corresponding shot of Haynes waving from the quay. The zoom's role in the scene's spatial relations is rather more complex than the simple high-angle zoom shots seen in earlier films. At first, the zoom slowly pulls back from Bailey on a level angle before he motions that he will move to the upper deck of the boat. From there, zooms from a high and low angle emphasize the physical separation of the lovers as the boat departs. The zoom thus operates on several levels. It creates a sense of attachment to the points of view of the two lovers, it reinforces the spatial relationship between the departing boat and quayside, and it emphasizes, not only spatially but emotionally, the gradual and reluctant separation of Haynes and Bailey.

Where East Is East and *Our Modern Maidens* were significant films with high-profile leading players. They were produced with substantial budgets and had high production values. Before their release, they were heavily promoted in fan magazines, and they performed well at the box office. Nothing—not least the cinematography, and certainly not the use of a relatively novel technology such as the zoom lens—would have been left to chance in productions such as these.

FIGURE 2.3. A boat departs, and the zoom emphasizes the new distance between lovers Toyo Haynes (Lupe Vélez) and Bobby Bailey (Lloyd Hughes) in *Where East Is East* (Tod Browning, 1929).

As Patrick Keating has noted, by the end of the silent period, cinematography had become a highly "aestheticized" craft, as "cinematographers grew to think of themselves as artists, self-consciously drawing on the related arts of photography, theater and painting for inspiration."[31] By 1929, whether, how, and when to use a zoom shot would have been a deliberate decision motivated at least partly by the artistic priorities of the cinematographer and director. In light of this, it is worth considering how *Our Modern Maidens* does *not* use the zoom. In one scene, a character is seen looking out of a window, her attention drawn to a building in the distance. The camera adopts her perspective, and a circular wipe picks out the building on which she focuses. Later, during a wedding scene toward the end of the film, the camera adopts the visual perspective of the bride as she walks down the aisle toward the officiant. This movement is handled through a physical forward tracking movement of the camera, and not—as may have been possible—through a zoom shot. There was no question of using the zoom as a substitute dolly; it was reserved for its special effect, and its impact was protected by limited use.

It is important, therefore, to use examples such as these to correct the notions that the earliest uses of the zoom were for frivolous "trick" purposes or that the lenses were of such poor quality that they could not be used in the general run of a film's narrative. The conclusion that must be drawn from the zoom shots that appear in late silent Paramount films and MGM features is that the use of the zoom lens was strategically limited to specific moments in a film's production. *It*, *The Four Feathers*, and *The Silent Enemy* indicate that Paramount may have preferred to limit the zoom to tone-setting establishing shots. MGM's more adventurous zooms, integrated into and motivated by narrative, might suggest that the studio reserved its zoom shots for showing off its leading players in scenes that most strongly emphasized their glamour or its sets when they were particularly lavish or expensive. These, however, must be tentative conclusions because there are far too few surviving examples from this period to suggest any sort of "house style" with regard to the zoom.

"PACKED WITH DRAMA": THE VARO

If an advertisement placed in *International Photographer* in 1932 was to be believed, then a new zoom lens called the Varo was all that was necessary to create breathtaking cinematography. The Varo was the first zoom lens manufactured by an independent equipment firm and marketed under license by an equipment distributor; earlier lenses had been developed without fanfare for use internally by studios. As a result, it benefited from advertising that sought to excite directors and cinematographers about the creative potential of the product. One early advertisement informed cinematographers that "this totally different lens opens up a wide range of new possibilities and spectacular effects. It makes it possible to 'swoop' or 'zoom' down on a subject and to recede from it *without moving camera or scene*. 'Close-ups' can be taken in sound photography work without danger of extraneous noise. 'Zooming' scenes from far back to a close-up can be taken of actors on a cliff or other inaccessible locations. The new effects that skilful camera men will work out with it are many."[32] The Varo was marketed as a labor-saving device, but it promised a perfect compromise between technological convenience and artistic ambition—a shortcut that would not bypass the craft of photography and leave the cinematographer obsolete.

The Varo was developed through a partnership of the British optical lens firm Taylor and Hobson and the American camera company Bell & Howell. The principal inventor of the lens was Arthur Warmisham, Taylor and Hobson's director of research.[33] The Varo was not, however, a British invention imported to the United States under license. Instead, it appears to have been developed while Warmisham was working at Bell & Howell's headquarters in Chicago; both the British and the American patents for the lens give Warmisham's address as Evanston, Illinois.[34] At a meeting of the Society of Motion Picture Engineers (SMPE) in spring 1932, Warmisham—alongside R. F. Mitchell of Bell & Howell—explained the principal objectives in developing the Varo. Previous zoom lenses, Warmisham and Mitchell complained, had suffered from three main limitations: (1) small apertures, rating no better than $f/8$; (2) poor optical correction, meaning that zoom lenses would not hold their focus throughout the range of focal lengths; and (3) their heavy burden on camera crews, as zooms "required several pairs of hands working in unison to operate them." Warmisham attempted to improve the Varo's focus holding by making a zoom lens with three, rather than two, independently moving sets of lenses. This, he remarked, made "the mechanical problem more severe, but it [gave] much more command over the optical aberrations."[35] During their presentation, Warmisham and Mitchell also promised an accessory viewfinder for the Varo that would enable rehearsals of zoom shots. With some adaptation, the viewfinder could even be used to watch the zoom as the film ran, though this would require the operator to keep his or her eye pressed tightly to the viewfinder to prevent light leakage onto the film.[36]

The Varo was impressively engineered, with numerous complex levers and mechanisms designed to ensure that the lens always operated at the best aperture for its focal length. Moving three sets of lens independently but in harmony was a significant engineering challenge, yet footage of the lens in action suggests that the movement was easy and smooth. In other respects, however, the lens must have been tricky to work with and frustrating to maintain. The various moving parts displaced so much air that a permeable "breather" was included in the design. This in turn necessitated a "fine wire mesh . . . moistened with glycerine so as to act as a dust trap."[37] The mesh required periodic cleaning and remoistening, and it is easy to imagine how much of an encumbrance this would have been on a hot, dusty, or frozen location shoot.

One of the Varo's other key limitations—the requirement for auxiliary attachments to be added in order to change the point of focus—stemmed from an incorrect prediction as to how cinematographers would want to use the zoom lens. Warmisham and Mitchell assumed that camera operators would not want to move their cameras while zooming, and they gained "considerable mechanical simplifications" by fixing the focal point of the lens to infinity. "The only problem of operation," the makers claimed, "is that of following a moving object."[38] But this was not a trivial problem: cinematographers were already beginning to experiment with moving the camera while zooming, as the example of *Prestige* (discussed later on) demonstrates. The trade-off between adjustment of focus and adjustment of focal length may have been a significant mistake at a time when camera movement was becoming increasingly desirable.

Bell & Howell marketed the Varo through trade periodical advertisements throughout 1932 and until at least 1935. As the months wore on, Bell & Howell's advertisements for the Varo become increasingly laden with hype. The firm persuaded *American Cinematographer* to promise that the lens would eliminate "crane shots in professional movies."[39] In paid advertisements, the lens was described as "an object of wonder in the studios where it is used," providing the "magic 'zoom' which has distinguished so many of the better films."[40] Under the heading "DRAMA at the touch of a lever," another advertisement declared that the lens itself was "packed with drama, holding within its amazingly precise complexity a thousand possibilities for the kind of a scene that stirs the emotions of millions. An artist breathing life into a daring composition, the cameramen moves a crank and creates a masterpiece."[41] Bell & Howell's advertisements listed films in which "Varo shots" had appeared in an attempt to create the impression that there was no corner of the film industry not using the device.[42] Early marketing of the Varo also sought to give the lens the Army Air Corps' seal of approval. Marketing materials distributed to trade periodicals boasted that the new lens had been tested in the skies above Chicago, resulting in "tremendously interesting results from a military perspective." Rather optimistically, the same article claimed that by using the Varo, "a parachute jumper can be shot as a 'close-up' all the way down to a landing place."[43] A more detailed account of this test laid bare the army's real interest in the lens, observing that it might "readily obtain for minute military study large detail photographs of certain locations" from far higher altitudes than had been previously been required of surveillance flights.[44] The army's test of the lens was filmed by a Fox Movietone newsreel cameraman and was included in a newsreel released in early May 1932. Outtakes from the newsreel show Lieutenant George Goddard kneeling next to a camera with a mounted Varo and operating the lens's hand crank. A closeup shot of the lens in operation shows smooth, precisely machined movement of the lens's internal parts.[45]

Taylor and Hobson's marketing efforts also permeated the editorial content of *International Photographer*, as when newsreel columnist Ray Fernstrom exhorted his readers to buy a Varo and use it to enliven their news footage. The Varo, Fernstrom suggested,

> acts as if it were made to order for us newsreel men who have long wished we had something to save us from changing lenses in the middle of a swell shot. . . . Imagine a baseball or football game where you can shift from a close shot to a scene of the whole field while the action is also spreading out, then back to close-up of the guy who is in the center of action. Why, this one lens can change the whole method of newsreel coverage. Go to it and our hat is off to the first newsreel to use it, for that reel will pass a milestone in newsreel history.[46]

The absence of any Bell & Howell advertisement proudly proclaiming the appearance of a Varo shot in a newsreel would suggest that few news camera crews took up Fernstrom's challenge, and it was not until 1938 that a Gaumont crew working in Britain experimented with a Varo. Despite the six-year delay between the Varo's introduction and its apparent first use in Britain, Gaumont trumpeted their purchase of the "new thousand-guinea lens," which was used to film the Wimbledon campaign of the American tennis star Helen Wills Moody.[47]

A relative flood of zoom shots appeared in Hollywood features released in 1932 and 1933. Some of these zooms were, as Belton notes, "emphatic reaction shot[s]" made not with the new Varo but with older equipment designed by Joseph Walker—as in the "two-element zoom-in on an explorer's face frozen in ice" in *Dirigible* (Frank Capra, 1931). A similar reaction zoom is to be found in Capra's *American Madness* (1932) during the bank robbery scene.[48] *One Night of Love* (Victor Schertzinger, 1934) includes a particularly noticeable zoom-in that appears at the crescendo of Mary Barrett's (Grace Moore) operatic performance on an Italian balcony. Each of these films was photographed by Joseph Walker, but his lens also found its way into the hands of other cinematographers, such as Milton Krasner, who later recalled struggling to create a zoom shot with the unfamiliar equipment on the set of *Golden Harvest* (Ralph Murphy, 1933): "Zoom lenses weren't heard of in those days, but we had a primitive one—I think it was Joe Walker's that we used. I had to burn everybody up with about 2,000 footcandles and had to zoom up by hand. I was really confused, but I had a lot of help and we made a hell of a zoom shot."[49]

Perhaps as a result of the blaze of publicity surrounding the Varo, the zoom began to make an impact on the language of American film production. Scripts and other similar production materials from the late 1920s referred to zoom shots in a variety of ways. Final continuity scripts for *The Four Feathers* (Merian C. Cooper, 1929) and *The Island of Lost Souls* (Erle C. Kenton, 1932) use the phrases "the camera trucks up" and "the camera trucks toward" to describe zoom shots toward soldiers standing atop a watchtower and M'ling's ear, respectively.[50] A zoom shot in the opening sequence of *Love Me Tonight* (Rouben Mamoulian, 1932) is similarly described in the film's release dialogue script.[51] By the early 1930s, the word *zoom*—which had originally indicated merely a "fast tracking movement forward"—was becoming a more specific reference to an apparent movement made by optical means.[52] The first draft of the script for *Thunder Below* (Richard Wallace, 1932) contains several references to "camera zooms" during an early scene, while early scripts for *King of the Jungle* (H. Bruce Humberstone and Max Marcin, 1933) suggest a pair of shots to be taken "CLOSEUP—ZOOM LENS."[53] In 1932, the SMPE included *zoom* in a list of technical terms that were being used "without official recognition" and were therefore at risk of causing confusion.[54]

However, it is notable that despite technological progress in zoom lens design, few films produced during the 1930s match either *Where East Is East* or *Our Modern Maidens* for the creativity and psychological significance of their zoom shots. Across a range of genres, studios, directors, and cinematographers, the technique is used to create a momentary effect or for convenience rather than to bolster the narrative through an aesthetic approach. Hence while the zoom makes an appearance in *Island of Lost Souls* (Erle C. Kenton, 1932), it is used only once to focus on the shocking revelation of M'ling's doglike ear. *What Price Hollywood* (George Cukor, 1932) features a handful of special effects zoom shots: two, early in the film, animate establishing shots of a newspaper and a house in a landscape, and the zoom is also a part of a spectacular special effects montage sequence in which the protagonist, Mary Evans (Constance Bennett), dreams of stardom. *The Stranger's Return* (King Vidor, 1933) opens with a series of establishing shots of the farmhouse in which the entire film is set, concluding with a shot that zooms toward the house's front porch, as if inviting the audience into the home. But as with many other zoom shots of this period, it is very difficult to determine whether this zoom was made at the time of shooting or added as a special effect in the laboratory.

Night Flight (Clarence Brown, 1933) is slightly more interesting in its use of the zoom. Initially, the zoom is used simply to magnify the pilot's kneepad so that the audience can read the notes that he makes. Later in the film, as the aircraft begins to run low on fuel, the zoom is used in an entirely different way. A repeated zoom toward the aircraft's fuel gauge magnifies the film's final-reel drama. On its first appearance, the zoom emphasizes that the fuel is almost entirely depleted, and the aircraft's engine continues to run. The second zoom, by contrast, is longer in duration and leads to a more extreme close-up; it is also accompanied by a sharp string note that further enhances the dramatic tension and contributes to the subsequent contrast between the monotonous drone of the engine—the sonic backdrop to a significant portion of the film—and the unfueled plane's silent gliding once the gauge has reached zero. Though these zooms are similar in their optical properties to those seen in other films of this

FIGURE 2.4. The zoom reveals M'ling's doglike ear in *Island of Lost Souls* (Erle C. Kenton, 1932).

period, they are distinctive for the manner in which they are used repetitively and in conjunction with sound cues. Much as the zoom in *Our Modern Maidens* and *Where East Is East* flatters the set and stars of those films, in *Night Flight*, the zoom draws attention to the film's carefully constructed soundtrack.

A significant exception to the rather unadventurous use of zoom lenses in the early 1930s is to be found in the RKO sound picture *Prestige* (Tay Garnett, 1932). Here, zooms augment and enhance the film's astonishingly adventurous mobile camerawork. In the opening scene, the camera swoops over a miniature model of Parisian rooftops before cutting to a high-angle zoom-in on a court-martial taking place in a courtyard below. This is novel special effects work in itself, but it is far from the most innovative use of the zoom in the film. In a later scene, the zoom is the central component in a highly complex camera movement. As Therese Du Flos (Ann Harding) and Captain Verlaine (Melvyn Douglas) salute the flag, the camera zooms out and pans upward, revealing a soldier who has shimmied up the wooden pole so as to lower the flag. Without a cut, the camera zooms in to centrally frame the soldier, who descends the pole. As he reaches the ground, and while the camera is still panning downward, a zoom-out restores the original framing. This shot lasts about half a minute, and includes several distinct framings, without a cut. It reflects great confidence in the use of

FIGURE 2.5. A zoom reveals the critical shortage of fuel in *Night Flight* (Clarence Brown, 1933).

the zoom shot to structure a complicated action sequence and, as with many of the zooms found in Paramount and MGM silent features, suggests careful planning and rehearsal of shots involving zooms. This impression is only increased by the presence of one of the first examples of a snap zoom, which focuses on the impassive face of a soldier as his comrade is sentenced to death. In addition to this particular rapid change of focal length, the zoom is then more subtly operated in coordination with the moving camera to create a particularly complex and dynamic series of framings. This, again, could not have happened by happenstance but would have required careful planning and coordination on the part of the cinematographer and his camera-operating assistants. This sequence, and the technical work it implies, calls particular attention to the magnitude of the misjudgment made by Mitchell and Warmisham when they sacrificed the Varo's ability to follow focus on moving shots.

Despite optimistic promotion by Bell & Howell and the zoom shots noted in the films discussed previously, there is considerable doubt about the extent to which the Varo was used in routine film production. It was not mass-produced, and one source estimates that as few as six copies were manufactured.[55] As Barry Salt observes, it remained an impractical tool for most uses, with an aperture

FIGURE 2.6. In *Prestige* (Tay Garnett, 1932), one of the most complex zooms of the early 1930s transports the audience up and down a flagpole.

too small for use under normal studio lighting, and was significantly hindered by its inflexible focal point.[56] Salt suggests that because of these limitations, the Varo largely saw use in special effects work—especially in the creation of "optical zooms" created in postproduction. If the lens was of limited use in feature film production, it may have been more attractive to the industrial, documentary, and newsreel industries. Indeed, in contrast to Bell & Howell's evocative description of the zoom lens as an artistic tool, one of the first detailed accounts of its use in *American Cinematographer* was for the purpose of filming an "industrial talkie" for the benefit of the Independent Grocers Alliance of America. Here there was no promise of "drama at the touch of a lever"; rather, there was the pedestrian promise of "a tremendous saving in film footage."[57] A later article discussing the production of training films for the army describes the zoom's advantages in similarly prosaic terms: "Zoom shots from long views to close-ups and the opposite are effective in maintaining orientation and at the same time provide opportunities for examining minute details."[58] The Varo was not compatible with a wide range of cameras: the lens kept its place in the Bell & Howell catalog until World War II, but it was offered only as an option for the company's 2709 camera.[59] Bell & Howell's advertisements may have promised movie magic, but in practice, the Varo was a strictly practical tool, more likely to be found in the special effects lab than on the main soundstage. Bell & Howell continued to promote the Varo lens for conventional zoom shots well into the 1930s, but by 1934, filmmakers chafed at the limitations of existing zoom lenses. SMPE president A. N. Goldsmith complained in particular of the cluttered array of different lenses available to cinematographers: "Some workers are prepared to accept the theory that the optics of photographic lenses are not capable of basic improvement, but if some way to diminish the large number of lenses that are required in the studio for close-ups, medium, and long shots could be contrived, it would be a step forward. Zooming by more convenient and automatic means is desirable."[60]

The relative dearth of zoom shots after about 1935 has led some historians to conclude that zoom lens development did not continue after the Varo.[61] This is mistaken. Indeed, the Varo was not even the only zoom lens newly marketed in 1932. A few months after its introduction, cameraman Otto Durholz of Paterson, New Jersey, promoted a zoom lens of his own invention. A prominently placed full-page advertisement in *International Photographer* included an illustration of the "Durholz Lens" attached to a turret camera and promised that the device would enable "zooming shots when and where you want them."[62] Very little is known about this lens, or about Durholz, who was a news and location camera operator based in New Jersey. As Salt points out, the lens offered an aperture of only $f/8$, which was far slower than the $f/5.6$ Varo and thus "did not make much [of an] impression" on filmmakers.[63] In other respects, however,

Durholz's design appears superior. The Varo was encased within a vast oblong box that took up all the space on a camera turret, meaning that the lens could not be mounted at the same time as other lenses. Durholz's lens, by contrast, was slender and cylindrical and took up little more space on a turret than an ordinary lens. While the Varo's focal length was adjusted by means of a hand crank, Durholz's patent shows that he intended to provide the means for a semiautomated zoom movement by linking a cable from the camera's motor to the gears of the zoom lens.[64] This, in particular, was an ambition that would not be fully realized until the electromechanically and electronically controlled servo zooms of the 1960s.

Not enough is known about the Durholz lens to properly assess why it was unsuccessful. The Varo's superior aperture may, as Salt suggests, have been its key disadvantage. Other factors may have been more significant. We do not know how many—if any—Durholz lenses were manufactured and tested by studios and working camera operators. Otto Durholz claimed to have made at least one lens for himself, which he "carried about in [his] 'bag of tricks' on location and news assignments."[65] If Durholz lenses were manufactured, no evidence survives of the quality of their optics or general standard of workmanship. Most importantly, we do not know how Durholz would have overcome the advantage of Cooke's partnership with the powerful marketing force of Bell & Howell. However, even if the Durholz lens was a thoroughgoing commercial failure, it remains an important invention that has much to tell us about the state of the zoom lens in the early 1930s. First, the Durholz lens emanated from a new location. Rolla T. Flora and Joseph Walker were based in Hollywood, and the Cooke Varo had been developed in Chicago. Durholz's base in Patterson, New Jersey, suggests an active interest in zoom lens technology among camera operators on the East Coast of the United States. Second, the language of Durholz's ambitious *International Photographer* advertisement offers clear evidence that the word *zooming* was a widely understood term of art in cinematography by 1932—before the arrival of the Varo. In Durholz's marketing, there are no quotation marks around the term *zooming* to betray a newfangled word; "zooming shots" were simply assumed to be desirable.

Durholz also spells out, in greater detail than marketing materials surrounding the Varo, where he thought the zoom lens fit within the broader context of early 1930s motion picture production. In a short *International Photographer* article, he suggested that his new zoom lens might be a way around "difficulties" caused by the "requirements of the sound department—the cumbersome blimps and their uncertain devices for the change of focus which frequently require camera rehearsals."[66] This marketing may have been pure opportunism, but it points toward a key potential advantage of the zoom lens during Hollywood's transition from silent to sound shooting.

FIGURE 2.7. An advertisement placed in *International Photographer* in 1932 promises "camera wings" with the Durholz zoom lens, but few were ever produced.

Following the Varo's partial success and Durholz's inventive ambition, zoom lens innovation continued throughout the 1930s and 1940s. The patent record shows that a number of inventors and groups of inventors continued to carry out research into zoom lens technologies throughout the 1930s and during the war. Zoom lens development work continued at Paramount. In June 1936, Lewis Mellor and Arthur Zaugg filed a patent on behalf of the studio describing an invention that would "provide a variable equivalent focal length objective characterized by large relative aperture, as substantially $f/2.7$, throughout a range of magnification substantially as great as 1 to 3½, and which is corrected to an extent requisite for motion picture purposes throughout each range of use."[67] The most salient aspect of this patent, in view of the limitations of the Varo and its precedents, was the lens's large aperture, which would have enabled its use under normal studio lighting conditions as well as on location. Zoom lens research also took place in New York, where in September 1934, Lodewyk Holst, William Mayer, and Harry Menefee of the C-Lens Corporation filed a patent for a lens system that they claimed would "produce optical results hitherto unattainable" and specified "high speed photographic work, such as the taking of motion pictures" as one of the areas of work to which their invention might be applied.[68] Two years later, in July 1936, Kodak researchers John Capstaff and Oran Miller filed a patent outlining a type of optical system "of continuously variable focal length particularly adapted for use as a photographic objective so that the pictures taken therewith may be made to appear to have been taken from different distances or continuously changing distances from the subject, without the necessity of altering the distance between the camera and the subject."[69] Taken together, these patents offer clear evidence that organized corporate research and development took place in zoom lens technology throughout the 1930s. However, there is no surviving evidence that these zoom technologies were ever marketed or used in practice.

As this chapter has demonstrated, the late 1920s and early 1930s were the moment at which the zoom lens and zoom shot were introduced to American feature film production. Though the zoom technologies of the day were not sufficiently advanced to provide the full flexibility desired by cinematographers and camera operators, these early zoom lenses were not crude. They were "state of the art"—highly complex combinations of precision engineering and optical mathematics, constructed before laser cutting and high-speed computing. In several cases, zoom lenses were developed as the "side projects" of engineers and camera operators. Historical accounts may linger on the shortcomings of early zooms, but it is quite remarkable that they were usable at all. What is not remarkable is that the cinematographers of the day found creative and highly selective ways to use the zoom, reserving the tool's impact in order to best flatter actors and sets. Where previous histories of the late silent and early sound era have mentioned the zoom, they have tended to imagine it as a period in which there were no zoom lenses—only the aesthetic purity of the fixed focal length. Historians of the zoom know better, but they have nevertheless tended to skip across this history, seeing the zooms of the 1920s and 1930s as prehistoric curiosities unworthy of detailed consideration. In fact, the history of the zoom starts well before 1927, and there are strong links between the very first zoom lenses and those used by cinematographers today.

3 · TAKE ME OUT TO THE BALL GAME

Take me out to the ball game,
Turn the volume up loud.
With "Zoomar" lens and TV snack
I don't care if I never come back.[1]

Modern television coverage of sports fixtures, political rallies, and similar live events offers viewers a remarkable level of access. At the sports ground, powerful zoom lenses positioned high in the stadium can swoop down in seconds to pick out individual players in extreme close-up. Digital effects systems superimpose graphics on live footage in real time, highlighting the position of a hockey puck or marking out the line of scrimmage in a football game. In the highest-profile sports coverage, camera operators wearing Steadicam rigs run the touchline while cameras suspended from cables provide a top-down view reminiscent of video gaming. For the viewer at home, the impression is of complete, comprehensive, and immersive coverage. Crucially, television endeavors—through multiple angles and action replays—to show the audience at home more than the spectator on the scene could possibly discern. Coverage of the modern political event or civil crisis—fire, flood, hurricane, or earthquake—benefits from similar technological solutions.

Live television has not always been able to offer this depth of coverage. Sport on American television was, at first, an experimental addition to radio commentary. In 1939, some of the earliest television sports coverage offered only the most limited of vision. Broadcasters attempted to cover events with only one or two cameras. Commentators were not always provided with a monitor displaying camera shots, so they could only guess at the images being transmitted to viewers at home.[2] Gradually, networks added more camera angles to their coverage and devised increasingly effective ways of conveying the drama of a live event via the small screen. Techniques trialed in sports coverage were soon applied to live news reporting and the coverage of political conventions. Television's aim has always been to provide a clearer, closer picture—but this has required the development of a panoply of technological enhancements to the television camera.

In the mid-1940s, American television producers were faced with a significant challenge. In a competitive market, they were keen to provide the kind of visually appealing coverage of events that could attract significant audiences in order to deliver strong advertising revenues. Television cameras, however, were as bulky and inflexible as those used in feature film production. Their fixed focal length lenses were mounted on rotating turrets. A television camera fixed in place to overlook a baseball game or tickertape parade could not rapidly zoom in on an interesting event; a director would have to cut to a second camera while the first camera rotated over to a different lens. This procedure took several seconds and required the cooperation of the camera operator and live director. If poorly executed, the rotation of the turret would be visible to viewers at home. Early television coverage of unrehearsed events therefore often rendered unclear pictures punctuated by halting, ill-timed transitions.

The Zoomar lens offered a solution to this cumbersome, inflexible setup. Developed in New York by Austrian émigré Frank Back, it started life as a zoom lens for film cameras but was soon modified to take advantage of the fast-growing American television industry. The Zoomar is particularly remembered for its transformative effect on baseball coverage, but far from being only occasionally used for sports and news programming, it made a substantial impact on the look and feel of a wide range of American television, both on location and in the studio. The lens, a complex assembly of twenty-two optical elements arranged in a "long narrow tube," enabled television camera operators to dynamically and fluidly narrow or broaden their cameras' fields of view.[3] For viewers at home, this meant television coverage that could swoop down toward the body of a baseball star or zoom out to reveal a building among a cityscape. Sports players and politicians seemed closer to the viewer at home—studio shows more dynamic. Stations took Zoomar lenses to football fields, polo matches, and boat races. At the same time, Zoomar-equipped cameras sharpened the focus on the faces of politicians during the 1952 presidential election campaign between Dwight D. Eisenhower and Adlai Stevenson—the first to be broadcast to a mass, coast-to-coast television audience. By the mid-1950s, hundreds of television stations across the United States owned Zoomar lenses. They were used extensively in both live sports and news coverage as well as in studio-based programming including NBC's iconic children's show *Kukla, Fran and Ollie*. From humble beginnings in wartime optical technologies, the Zoomar, which was based on technology originally used to improve flight trainers and portable camera viewfinders, transformed American television. By enlarging images of distant sports players and public figures, Zoomar lenses helped create television coverage that was more immersive for audiences, while television producers benefited from the flexibility inherent in a lens that could bypass the limitations of the cameras that relied on rotating turrets of lenses. In the process, the zoom shot became a ubiquitous and unmistakable hallmark of the small screen.

THE ZOOMAR LENS

The primary inventor of the Zoomar lens, Frank Back, was a polymath. Born in Vienna in 1902, he was educated in mechanical and electrical engineering; his study of optics was, as he later described it, a "side line."[4] During the 1920s and 1930s, Back worked as a consulting engineer in Vienna. His projects and publications included the development of cameras that could take pictures inside the human body in order to diagnose gastroenterological conditions. On a trip to New York in 1928, Back demonstrated an early form of endoscope, which the *New Yorker* later described as "a swallowable camera more popular with doctors than with patients."[5] In 1938, Back, who was Jewish, fled to Paris; in 1939, he moved to the United States.[6] As the 1940s dawned, the American war effort took advantage of Back's expertise in mechanical and optical engineering. Funded by the Signal Corps and the Navy Department, Back made substantial contributions to the development of two obscure devices useful to American service personnel. For the Signal Corps, he developed a variable focal length viewfinder for use with the Bell & Howell Eyemo cameras used by battlefield cameramen. This would make it possible for those cameramen to quickly adjust their viewfinders to match lenses of different focal lengths. For the Navy Department, he developed improvements to a movie projector–based training simulator, adding a zoom lens to the device so as to increase the realism of images projected on the screen. Back's work was warmly praised by his employers; the Navy Department declared that his "cooperation and ingenuity" had made a "real contribution to the war effort."[7] It was while working on these contracts that Back first explored different ways of engineering zoom lenses. The novel optical principles of his viewfinder design were to form the basis of the Zoomar lens.

The prospect of developing an improved zoom lens for movie cameras proved irresistible to Back. From around 1943, with the help of an assistant named Herbert Lowen, he began to develop designs and prototypes for such a lens. In their workshop on Fourth Avenue, Back and Lowen experimented with different zoom lens designs. The calculations necessary were complex and time consuming. The Zoomar lens, including more than twenty separate optical elements, aligned in groups within a barrel. In order to produce a zooming movement,

Back and Lowen needed to devise a mechanism that would move some of the optical elements while keeping others in place so as to create a lens that would hold its focus while transitioning through a number of focal lengths. There were no computers to assist the process, which relied instead on books of logarithms and trial-and-error design work.[8] This meant that each possible combination of lenses in a new design would need to be analyzed to determine its optical properties. To compound the challenge, as Back noted in the eventual patent for the Zoomar lens, "the spacing of the several component parts of these varifocal lenses is so critical that even a minute deviation throws the image entirely out of focus. Normal wear in the moving parts suffices to throw the system out of focus."[9] Prototype models of the zoom lens therefore had to be accurate to the millimeter and highly robust.

When designs were sufficiently advanced, Back tested his prototype Zoomar lens by lending it to local camera operators. New York film producer Raymond B. Gamble was provided with "an experimental lens . . . before it was put on the market" and "used it to see for [himself] the operation of the lens." For Gamble, the Zoomar was "very new in the industry, very revolutionary, something we had never had before."[10] He first used the lens to film dioramas at the Museum of Natural History and later took it to the Bronx Zoo to film "a television show for Alexander Smith entitled *The Magic Carpet*."[11] In addition to working alongside Gamble, Back also collaborated with Hearst Metrotone *News of the Day* cameramen and with the Long Island Optical Company.[12] By July 1946, the lens was judged sufficiently advanced to be sold commercially. Back applied for a patent to protect the device's design; a few months later, he applied for a trademark on the name "Zoomar."[13] Designed for use with film cameras, the lens offered a 3:1 zoom ratio ranging from a wide angle of 17mm to 53mm at its longest extension. This meant that any figure in an image could be magnified by up to three times. By manipulating a lever on the lens, the camera operator moved the internal barrel forward or back, thereby zooming in or out.[14] Over the following year, Zoomar lenses were sold, leased, or loaned to a range of industrial and commercial film organizations—first to the New York film company Hartley Productions and later to Fox Movietone, the Medical Film Guild, and the Ford Motor Company in Detroit.[15] At this early stage, it is likely that the lenses were prototypes designed for field testing and promotional purposes.

Back's patent filing and trademark application coincided with a marked shift in the marketing of the Zoomar lens. While developing and testing the new lens, he came to the attention of the film producer Jerry Fairbanks and his publicist, Madison Avenue advertising executive Jack Pegler, who invested in the new technology. Under the auspices of Fairbanks's industrial film production company, which had produced long-running short documentary features including the *Popular Science* series, the trio pursued bigger customers. The newsreel giant Paramount was the first major corporate customer to buy a Zoomar lens designed for film cameras, at a cost of $12,500, in October 1947.[16] The *New York Times* reported that the studio's newsreel division had purchased the lens, known as a Field Zoomar, in order to cover the baseball World Series between the New York Yankees and the Brooklyn Dodgers. The newspaper reported Paramount's claim that the use of the Zoomar amounted to "history . . . being made," explaining that the lens "makes it possible to take close-ups of every play and player on the field with uninterrupted continuity. With a flick of the wrist the Paramount camera man, equipped with the Zoomar lens, follows the ball from pitcher to batter and from the batter to the depths of any part of the field, keeping the entire action in perfect focus."[17] Back worked closely with Paramount to ensure that the Zoomar lens performed as well as possible, zooming in and out smoothly and reliably holding its focus. Back later recalled that he had been present when the company conducted its first field tests of the lens, overseeing "almost every take because [he] was helping the newsreel men with that lens."[18]

Footage made with the Zoomar was included for the first time in a Paramount newsreel dated October 11, 1947.[19] The newsreel prepared its audience for a new way of seeing baseball on the screen, in which the camera would seem to track forward toward the action as the ball was struck into the outfield. The sequence was preceded with title cards stating, "*Paramount News* introduces the greatest innovation in newsreel coverage since the invention of sound—The Zoomar Close-up Lens!" This was followed by a series of shots showing the Zoomar lens being operated by a cameraman and a montage demonstrating the shots it could achieve. "Through this lens the eyes of the world take on third dimension [*sic*] of movement. You in the audience are brought right in on the game as it progresses on the field. Actually a player's eye view as our camera zooms with the action, every play followed to completion. Now, watch the results as this revolutionary lens is used for the first time in newsreel coverage," narrator George Putnam explained. If the audience perceived a fresh perspective on baseball, with closer and clearer highlights, then Putnam's excited commentary made it clear that credit was due to the Zoomar lens.[20]

In the highlights that followed, Zoomar shots were used on several occasions, and *Variety* reported that the "newsreel threw the house into a feverish parallel of the ballpark. Focus is so sharp players' expressions become public knowledge."[21] This was something of an exaggeration: the Zoomar lens was not sufficiently powerful to deliver true close-ups of baseball players. However, while it could not deliver the screen-filling images of players' faces that would become familiar in later decades, the lens did enable camera operators to move in closer on groups of players running to catch a ball or celebrating with one another after a successful play. It was most useful for its ability to follow the ball far into the outfield, lending an additional punch to some of the batters' more powerful slugs.

Following each successful pitch, Paramount's camera operator zoomed in, tracking the ball toward its destination, and the zoom emphasized the ball's motion. It was also used to isolate and emphasize the role of baseball stars: in the final section of the newsreel, the camera zooms toward Joe DiMaggio as he prepares to take to the field. The ability of the zoom to follow the action into the field, and to pick out moments of color or interest, led to significantly more immersive footage. The feeling of distance from the sporting action was reduced, and the zoom's pursuit of the ball into the outfield represented an early attempt to replicate the focus of a spectator in the stands.

As the newsreel progressed, the narrator continually reminded viewers of the Zoomar's role in showing each play. This overt focus on the technology used to obtain the footage continued in following weeks. Highlights of a football game between Army and Illinois, included in *Paramount News* on October 22, were again preceded by footage of the lens in operation and enthusiastic commentary on the novelty of the shots it could obtain, which would "take you right down into the line of scrimmage" with "zoom-up action."[22] Beyond the ballpark, the Zoomar lens was used by Paramount during coverage of the repatriation of the remains of more than six thousand servicemen who had fought in Europe during the Second World War. The lens enabled the Paramount cameraman to obtain closer shots of the procession of a casket carrying the body of an unnamed soldier through a crowd of mourners. The report made no mention of the use of the Zoomar lens—such promotional bluster would have been entirely out of place in a somber film sequence depicting a collective moment of public grief—but the gentle zoom, from a wide shot of the mourning crowd to a close-up of the flag-draped coffin, made for a subtle yet truly striking image. Starting from a wide shot of an indistinguishable mass of people, the zoom moves in to reveal more clearly the pained expressions of members of the crowd as the coffin and its stern-faced Guard of Honor passes them.[23]

Alongside Paramount's promotion of their new technology to the audience, the company also distributed publicity to theatre managers emphasizing the positive reaction Zoomar coverage had provoked among audience members and reviewers in the press. The material quoted a company agent in New Orleans who remarked that "everything that has been said about Zoomar Lens is more than true. One exhibitor shook his head and said he didn't see how it was possible." Another, from Connecticut, said, "Our major accounts are advertising Zoomar in the newspapers, and featuring it in the lobby."[24] Self-serving promotional accounts such as those distributed by Paramount cannot be verified, but the evidence suggests that the Zoomar remained an important tool for Paramount's newsreel camera operators for at least a decade after its introduction. Paramount chief cameraman Lou Hutt later claimed that the Zoomar lens had generated "many thousands of bookings plus many thousands of dollars in return" for the company.[25] According to Hutt, the device retained its appeal because

> there are various types of shot that we perfect with the use of the zoom lens, in some instance like a football game or a baseball game, why, we want a wide angle, [followed by] an individual shot or follow-through shot. For instance, in baseball you can take the entire diamond in from the front of the balcony in the baseball field, and as soon as the batters [sic] hit the ball, we will say, to center field, or a home run, why, we zoom right straight out and follow the ball into where it lands, giving you a terrific effect.[26]

By the end of 1947, Hearst's *News of the Day* had joined Paramount in using a Zoomar lens to enhance their sports newsreel coverage.[27] The Hearst Corporation was another early adopter of the Zoomar lens, and examination of Hearst newsreel footage made with Zoomar lenses demonstrates the significance of the device—but also highlights limitations not mentioned in Paramount's promotional material. A Hearst *News of the Day* account of an All-America Football Conference game between the Cleveland Browns and the New York Yankees—which opens with a shot of a zoom lens in operation—includes shots that start at wide angles, then zoom in to provide a closer view of the action.[28] This sort of shot is repeated several times, but only to zoom in. The range of the Zoomar lens is suggested by the footage to be somewhat limited: at its widest setting, it is able to provide a view of most of the width of the football field, the team management benches beyond, and crowds in the stands above. When zoomed in, the lens provides only a somewhat closer view of the action on the field. It is not able to zoom far enough to capture, for example, the expressions on the faces of the players or the finer nuances of their physical actions as they run the field and compete for the ball. It is also evident that the quality of the Zoomar lens was substantially inferior to the fixed focal length lenses used on other Hearst cameras documenting the same event. On Zoomar shots, there is significant distortion all around the edge of the frame, which at times is so significant that it would be more accurate to describe a circle of clarity in the center of the frame. Such distortion is not visible in static shots made of the crowd, which are of a much higher visual quality.

Hearst footage of the series-ending meeting between the Cleveland Indians and the Boston Braves during the 1948 World Series shows the Zoomar's capabilities.[29] Here the zoom is used to track down and lock on to the ball as it lands or is caught by a fielder. The newsreel also shows how camera operators used the zoom's flexible focal length to depict various elements of the sporting action—the pitch, hit, run, and reactions of the spectators—without the need to intercut images from multiple cameras. One such sequence begins with a high-angle long shot showing the home plate and pitching mound. The pitcher throws the ball and the batter hits it, whereupon the camera pans, tilts, and zooms in to capture a fielder who attempts to catch the ball. When he fails to do so, the camera—remaining at its zoomed-in focal length—pans to show the line between third base and home plate, where a player is running to safety. As might be expected, the camerawork is rough, ready, and improvised; camera operators had little practice, and received only limited training, in operating the new lens. Nevertheless, the coverage effectively captures two connected aspects of the baseball game without the necessity for editing and without compromising spatial or temporal continuity. For newsreel producers, the Zoomar lens offered two key attractions. First, it promised greater speed and efficiency of production by increasing the amount of usable footage that a single camera could capture. Second, it empowered camera operators to follow the action in front of them with greater flexibility and fluidity. No longer needing to change lenses as action receded into the distance, they could now attempt to follow it with a zoom shot. These zoom shots, it was explained to newsreel audiences, proposed an entirely new way to watch sporting highlights. They seemed to follow the action unflinchingly, satisfying the viewer's desire to see what was happening on the field. Amid a great deal of hype, newsreels' early adoption of the Zoomar lens explored new methods of capturing sport, and these methods were to be further developed by the new medium of television.

BRINGING THE ZOOM TO TELEVISION

Newsreel trials of the Zoomar lens provided an excellent demonstration of its ability to provide more immersive, flexible footage of both sports and news events, and the enthusiastic adoption of the Zoomar by Paramount and Hearst supplied substantial capital with which to produce further lenses. This enabled Back, Pegler, and Fairbanks to invest in the newly reborn and fast-growing postwar television industry. Though initially designed for use with film cameras, a television version of the Zoomar lens had been planned by Back at an early stage, and a prototype was demonstrated in April 1947 inside Studio 3H at NBC's Rockefeller Plaza headquarters. Two image orthicon cameras—"one mounted on a moveable dolly, the other stationary"—captured a test performance by "balladeer Tom Scott, ventriloquist Paul Winchell, and dancers Nelly Fisher and Jim Starbuck."[30] Camera operators demonstrated the different means of moving closer to the action: while one physically moved the camera forward, the other varied the focal length of the Zoomar lens from a fixed position. No footage of the test survives, but it is clear that the trial provided NBC technical staff with a direct comparison between the two methods while also demonstrating that the lens had as much value for studio television production as for the outdoor assign-ments that had appeared in newsreels. In optimistic publicity that followed, NBC vice president and chief engineer O. B. Hanson presciently remarked that "ultimately, the Fairbanks Zoomar lens will become standard equipment in all television cameras."[31] For engineers like Hanson, the attraction of the Zoomar lens lay in its versatility and flexibility. Whether in cramped studios or at remote broadcasts from sporting events, existing cameras relied on rotating turrets of three or four lenses of different focal lengths. Loaded with a full complement of lenses, the turrets were heavy and turned slowly. The Zoomar lens promised to reduce the need for the sluggish rotation of these turrets, resulting in more responsive and fluid television coverage. It is not hard to imagine that television engineers and creative personnel, making new aesthetic rules in a recently invented creative industry, saw exciting creative opportunities in the zoom lens. Accountants, meanwhile, saw the promise of cost savings.

Despite Hanson's public optimism about the future of the Zoomar lens, it was not easy for Back, Fairbanks, and Pegler to persuade NBC to invest in their product. Attempts to convince the company's middle managers of the value of Zoomar lenses were met initially with skepticism: NBC attempted to negotiate lower prices for the equipment and even tried to engineer an alternative form of zoom lens to avoid having to make a purchase. Once they had received the lenses, NBC's engineers were taken aback by the much-vaunted technology's limitations: images obtained through the Zoomar lens were darker and more distorted than expected. But NBC played an active role in shaping the final form of the technology, insisting that the lenses be altered and fixed where problems arose. By robustly objecting to the device's shortcomings but maintaining a posi-tive approach to the overall venture, the company's purchase of the Zoomar lens effectively became part of the device's prototyping and development process.[32]

Discussions between NBC and the Zoomar trio represented a clash between wily entrepreneurs and a larger, and more cautious, industrial broadcaster. While the Zoomar lens was a unique and much-sought-after technology, NBC's size was a significant negotiating advantage, and they insisted on trials and tech-nical modifications before purchasing the new equipment. Jack Pegler's initial aim was to tie television broadcasters into an expensive and restrictive annual leasing agreement, which would cost the network more than $15,000 a year and prohibit them from using the lenses outside of New York. NBC managers were unwilling; they expected instead to receive sample lenses free of charge for test-ing purposes before making any serious financial commitment. Resisting pres-sure from Zoomar, NBC manager Noran Kersta explained to his colleagues that he wanted the Zoomar lens "to be used on actual television operations in the field or on as many different types of shows as we can do within a one-month or two-month period. This is the only way I feel we could appraise the value of this lens." Furthermore, Kersta urged his colleagues to remain philosophical if a Zoomar lens could not be obtained on a free trial, because NBC could in any case observe trials of the lens made by competing broadcasters. "The pillars of television will not crumble," he remarked, "if we do not have one of these lenses."[33] Such a lukewarm attitude to the Zoomar lens did not reflect a lack of interest in the technology but rather suggested that Kersta was more interested in thoroughly testing the usefulness of the lens rather than making an expensive investment based on marketing bluster. Negotiations between Zoomar and NBC dragged on for two further months, with Pegler urgently lobbying not only Kersta in New York but NBC's offices in Los Angeles and Washington, DC.

When it became clear that NBC would not agree to a leasing arrangement, Jerry Fairbanks ordered a change of approach. He offered NBC the chance to order sixteen Zoomar lenses for $5,000 each. If the broadcaster insisted on purchasing the lenses outright in smaller batches, then the unit cost would double to $10,000. This audacious approach almost backfired. Instead of quickly agreeing to buy the lenses, Noran Kersta ordered NBC technicians into the laboratory, where they were to reinvestigate the feasibility of engineering an electronic zoom lens. By electronically enlarging a portion of the image field without changing the focal length of the camera lens, this technology would make Zoomar's technology irrelevant. However, the results of the tests fell heavily in Zoomar's favor. Engineers reported significant problems with electronic zooming, including unwanted image persistence and "serious geometric distortion." These problems would have led to unwatchable television images, and it would take at least six to eight weeks of effort simply to prepare an improved demonstration, which would in any case still "probably be somewhat inferior to results now being shown by use of the Zoomar lens."[34]

NBC and Zoomar ultimately compromised, and NBC bought two lenses at a cost of $7,500 each. With their eyes on the lens's application to sports programming, they urged Zoomar to deliver the new lenses in time for the World Series. The sales agreement bound Jerry Fairbanks Productions to "make every reasonable effort" to deliver a working Zoomar lens to NBC in time for the 1947 World Series "and as many of the early football games as possible."[35] By the fall of 1947, however, Zoomar's small workshop was struggling to keep pace with demand for the Zoomar lenses. NBC's order was not delivered until late November—weeks too late for the World Series and well into the NFL season. In addition to arriving later than promised, the equipment delivered to NBC was far from perfect. After testing their new lens at a football game, engineers observed a "lack of resolution"—fuzziness—in one lens. The faulty lens was immediately replaced, yet over a longer course of testing, further problems became apparent.

Concluding that the Zoomar lens was "considerably below the standard of our regular lens,"[36] technicians observed that the lenses appeared to be "slower" than promised, rating $f/6.3$ as opposed to the claimed $f/4.5$. At this time, television camera tubes required significant amounts of light in order to generate the electronic impulses required to transmit a television image. A slower lens, admitting less light to the tube, would produce dark, ill-defined images. This meant that whether used in the television studio or on remote assignments, the lens would need considerably brighter than expected conditions to provide acceptable pictures. Brighter conditions implied increased lighting; increased lighting a much higher electricity bill; a higher electricity bill a vastly augmented production cost. Noting that the Zoomar's performance improved markedly when set to a smaller aperture—an aperture that would typically demand significant increases in illumination—they concluded that the device was better suited for use in bright sunshine, not the gloom of a winter sporting event.

Aside from problems with picture, engineers noted that substantial challenges lay in the unfamiliar nature of the lens. The mere practice of operating the equipment—smoothly zooming in and out in a way that benefited a television show—was a challenge. One engineer wrote, "We have much to learn about the technique of using the Zoomar. I think skillful use can only come with experience, but assuming we can get a good picture and get our cameramen and directors used to it, I feel it can add tremendously to our coverage on field pick-ups."[37] In the following weeks, NBC and Zoomar worked together in an attempt to improve the lens, and despite the string of technical problems that bedeviled the Zoomar lens in its earliest days at NBC, the company maintained a critical but constructive approach. Concluding a long list of snags with the lens, an NBC engineer remained upbeat about the overall promise of the technology, declaring, "So far, the best use of the Zoomar lens was made on the Macy's Thanksgiving Day programs where the coverage was from ten blocks away to two blocks away. I believe the lens has great possibilities and can be improved upon."[38] There was no mention, at this stage, of the later practice of using the zoom to inject excitement into game shows or tension into drama programming. For NBC, the zoom's appeal was the simple function of moving closer to distant action to make television coverage more immersive and flexible.

Between 1947 and 1957, Zoomar lenses would be sold to more than half of the television stations operating in the United States. Because of the decentralized nature of the early postwar American television industry, it was necessary for Zoomar's marketing efforts to go well beyond the head offices of the major television networks. In the autumn of 1947, while Jack Pegler negotiated with NBC over Zoomar specifications and delivery schedules, Jerry Fairbanks embarked on a "two-week tour of Eastern and Midwestern television stations, during which he supervised the installation of Zoomar television lenses in several video stations," and Frank Back traveled to California to meet prospective customers there.[39] This was the beginning of a personal sales and promotion effort that lasted several years and saw the pair visit new television stations from coast to coast. Compared with their approach to NBC, Zoomar's marketing strategy toward local television stations was different—especially in its greater informality. Unlike the protracted negotiations and multiple tests demanded by NBC, sales discussions took place quickly and casually; Zoomar representatives visited local stations where they shared a meal with engineers and managers before demonstrating the new lens. Though often wealthy, local television stations had neither the financial heft of NBC nor the research and development capacity to attempt to develop their own zoom lenses. They simply needed to decide whether to buy a new lens. Many, clearly, were persuaded by the potential of the Zoomar. By November 1947, Jerry Fairbanks Productions reported that orders had been received for Zoomar lenses from seven television stations in Los Angeles; New York; Philadelphia; Washington, DC; Chicago; and Baltimore.[40] Commercial momentum can only have been boosted by a Television Broadcasters Association award made to Frank Back in December 1947.[41] Meanwhile, the success of the Zoomar lens continued to test the company's manufacturing capacity: *Broadcasting-Telecasting* reported that the company was forced to rush a demonstration lens to KTLA in Los Angeles so it could be used on coverage of that year's Rose Bowl game, as "one on order . . . will not be finished in time." KTLA finally received its Zoomar lens in March 1948, becoming the first West Coast station to own one.[42]

Well into 1949, Back continued to personally visit television stations that purchased Zoomar lenses. This was partially a marketing ploy: his visits would frequently be reported in the trade press. But it was also necessary to offer after-sales care because installing the lens—and learning to operate it—was not a straightforward process. The lens's zooming function was controlled by a pushrod that extended beyond the back of the lens and needed to be threaded through the body of the camera to which it was attached. Connecting a Studio Zoomar lens to an existing RCA Image Orthicon camera required engineers to take a five-inch-long drill bit and expand existing screw holes on the front and back of their camera body, permanently modifying an expensive and sensitive piece of equipment. Once installed, camera operators—most of whom would never have encountered a zoom lens—needed to be acquainted with the new technology. A twenty-two-page manual distributed with the Studio Zoomar lens reflected the versatility of the technology. Camera operators could choose to use it "smoothly, almost imperceptibly, so that the viewer is not conscious of any change of scene as he looks at the Television screen. Or so swiftly and abruptly that the impression on the screen is that of swift flight through space either toward or away from the subject, stopping, if desired, in the middle of the 'flight' and seemingly hovering in mid-air to observe a tense moment in a drama or game."[43]

Despite this versatility, the manual emphasized the importance of restraint. In block capitals, camera operators were warned to use the zooming function "ONLY WHEN NECESSARY" because "too much zooming will defeat its purpose and distract from the game being televised." Instead, operators should begin their zooms so gradually as to be "hardly perceptible" to avoid the prospect of "sudden, startling" zooms giving "an unnatural effect." This manual is likely the best document available of how television camera operators were trained in the use of the Zoomar lens. It marks the beginning of the development of stylistic conventions governing the use of the zoom. In its appeal for gentle, subtle, natural zooms, it is strikingly similar to later discussions of the "use and abuse" of lenses in *American Cinematographer*.[44] Though couched in the language of aesthetic pleasure, this advice had sound business motivations. If the Zoomar lens was to become a ubiquitous tool for television production, it would need to avoid being seen as a gimmick or special effect. Furthermore, the sensitive, complicated mechanisms of the lens were unlikely to have been sufficiently robust to withstand frequent, sharp zoom movements. What appears to be a concern for the aesthetic attractions and artistic integrity of professional television production is equally a protective measure designed to keep TV stations happy with the smooth operation of their expensive and delicate lenses. It was also an ill-fated attempt to prevent the zoom from becoming, through overuse, a derided cliché of television.

Stations did not buy Zoomar lenses only to let them gather dust in equipment stores: the lenses were immediately put to use in the production of a wide range of television programs, ranging from sporting coverage to live news reporting to studio-based discussion shows. It was baseball, however, that provided one of the key incentives for local stations to buy and use the lenses.[45] Television stations had experimented with baseball before the Second World War, and as postwar television grew, coverage of the sport became an essential aspect of local programming. Televised baseball was, at first, "a staple of local television at a time when networks provided little programming outside of the evening hours." Prewar coverage had faced a significant problem, however: too few cameras, placed too far from the on-field action without zoom lenses, left viewers struggling to follow tiny images of players pitching and striking a "speck-like" ball.[46] The Zoomar lens—first extensively tested by Paramount at the 1947 World Series—was an obvious solution to the challenges of televised baseball. While newsreel footage suggests that the Zoomar lens was unlikely to render the baseball any less specklike, it was proven to enhance the legibility of images and players on the field. Television camera operators soon took their new zoom lenses to local ballparks in hopes of improving their coverage.

While scarcely any recordings of such early coverage survive, the challenges and advantages of Zoomar lenses are clear from trade press reviews of early postwar television baseball coverage. After watching WBKB's coverage of a Chicago game between the Cubs and the White Sox, a *Billboard* reviewer concluded that the Zoomar was used "to good advantage most of the time" but created a disappointing effect when the camera operator zoomed out: this "made the viewer feel as if he had been taken away from activity." If zooming in led to a feeling of immersion in the game, then zooming out risked emphasizing the camera's true distance from the action. Baseball, the reviewer remarked, was a "tough video nut to crack," and WBKB's coverage was little better in 1948 than in 1947.[47]

By 1950, Zoomar lenses were still a novelty at many television stations, but there was increasingly widespread recognition of the advantages of the lens. In some cases, writers in the broadcasting trade press hoped that they would improve coverage of baseball and other sports. In April that year, *Variety* reported that "while there was some criticism on [sic] WNAC-TV's coverage last season, the station has recently installed the Zoomar lens, which WBZ-TV used last year, and should result in Hub [Boston] fans getting slick coverage."[48] By September, it was reported that WPTZ had increased its contingent of cameras from two to four and "also brought in another innovation—the Zoomar lens, which is attached to the new camera on the photographers' platform along the third base line."[49] Despite these innovations, *Billboard*'s review of television coverage of the early games of the 1950 season was little more complimentary than in previous years. A clear set of norms and conventions defining the grammar of baseball coverage had not yet developed, and reviewers noted "a striking lack of unified standards of lensing" in individual stations' coverage of games.[50] By now, although there was a good deal of variation in filming styles and strategies, the use of Zoomar lenses appears to have been common to many broadcasters, and the quality of coverage gradually improved. WWJ-TV Detroit placed the Zoomar behind a transparent section of the backstop screen, "a position believed to be unique in big league parks": "Camera follow-thru on the ball was very good by second telecast, and nearly all the real action was caught; the Zoomar is already broken in for swift work in special plays in most parts of the field as well as fouls into the stands," remarked a *Billboard* reviewer.[51]

In a few short years, a new set of norms had emerged, with the zoom lens at the center of coverage strategies. By 1952, television coverage of baseball appeared to be settling into a stable pattern. *Variety* observed, "For the last couple of years there has been no significant changes in technique and the current season isn't producing any innovations either. . . . Such positive advances as the invention of the Zoomar lens, now basic equipment for all the outlets, and the most strategic spotting of the cameras, are now being utilized for maximum results within a fixed formula."[52] The fixed formula, however, left room for adjustments. For games carrying particular prestige, broadcasters began to add additional Zoomar lenses to their cameras. WOR-TV used "a couple of Zoomar lenses" in its pool coverage of the 1951 World Series.[53] Both WOR-TV and WPIX, providing simulcast coverage of the 1952 World Series, repeated the previous year's double-Zoomar strategy.[54] For reasons that are not clear, it seems that no Zoomar lenses were used during the 1953 World Series, but they returned during the following year.[55] By then, the Zoomar lens had transformed baseball on television. Balls were a little easier to follow; pitches and swings were easier to interpret. Clearer views of the faces of the players meant that television could transmit not just the mechanics of a game as it unfolded but the emotions too: expressions of joy, pain, and disappointment became more readily visible. Through the zoom shot, camera operators could more fully capture the essence of the game, finally enabling television to immerse viewers in America's pastime.

While stations initially struggled to use their Zoomar lenses to the best advantage at baseball games, they quickly achieved more satisfying results in other sporting venues. A boxing match between Joe Louis and Joe Walcott was one of the first to take place under the gaze of a Zoomar lens in December 1947, to the delight of a *Billboard* reviewer, who declared that "television as a medium for sports coverage again proved itself potent" and described how "use of the Zoomar lens was effective in moving from remote shots, embracing the entire ring, to close-ups of the battle."[56] The same month, another reviewer chided CBS's coverage of a hockey game for its *lack* of Zoomar shots. Noting that CBS used two cameras to cover the games, "one for long shots, the other for close-ups," the reviewer complained that "here is one case where lack of Zoomar lenses halves the effective coverage, inasmuch as both cameras follow approximately the same action; one Zoomar-equipped camera could do the work of both CBS cameras."[57] Other notable uses for the Zoomar lens included WAVE-TV's use of a Zoomar lens of coverage of the 1949 Kentucky Derby and, later that year, a local station's filming of the Gold Cup boat race in Detroit.[58] In 1950, Zoomar lenses were used at the U.S. Open golf championship and were suggested as a means to make live coverage of polo more visually appealing, on which subject *Variety* remarked, "Live polo pickups, which had a short run on NBC television some years ago, may return this spring on CBS-TV. . . . CBS are counting on new technical developments, such as the Zoomar lens, to compensate for the faults of the NBC coverage."[59] Reviewing coverage of a Detroit tugboat race in May 1951, *Billboard* complained of "static video coverage" but mentioned that "skillful handling of the zoomar and cameras for the last third went far to make up for this."[60] Sports assignments—which were in danger of becoming dull and lifeless when covered from only a few angles—were injected with some extra excitement when a zoom lens could be used to vary the framing and magnify the action.

By the early 1950s, Zoomar lenses were used widely for sports coverage and were recognized in the industry as one means to provide higher quality and more engaging sports television.[61] But their impact went well beyond stadiums and racetracks. In addition to sports telecasting, the zoom lens offered a new solution to the challenges of news, current affairs, and live entertainment filming. As television stations increased their hours of operation, they also began to cover a greater number of local news events, and Zoomar lenses were central to such coverage. In November 1948, *Broadcasting-Telecasting* noted that a Zoomar lens enabled Chicago station WBKB to mount "the simplest remote in video history" by pointing a zoom-equipped camera in the station's headquarters toward the nearby State Street Bridge, which was to be lowered for the first time.[62] Zoomar lenses were used to produce "particularly impressive" views of General Douglas MacArthur's return from Japan in 1951, and similar coverage brought viewers close to the inauguration ceremony of President Dwight D. Eisenhower in January 1953.[63] In Cincinnati, Zoomar lenses were used by WCPO during a series of live broadcasts from a fairground in 1952.[64] In June of the following year, WCCO in Minneapolis used "two cameras, one with Zoomar lense [sic], atop a building adjacent to its studio" to provide coverage of a major parade.[65] A few months later, *Variety* described how Chicago station WBBM broke into scheduled programming "and gave the viewers a look at an attempted suicide. A woman was perched on a ledge outside a window on the 20th floor of Tribune Tower, threatening to jump. . . . The Zoomar equipped cameras were over a half mile away from the scene, but the coverage and pictures were excellent, catching all of the raw drama of a priest talking with the woman, other persons passing coffee to her as she deliberated, until the final moment when a fire marshal grabbed her and pulled her to safety."[66] In 1958, Zoomar lenses helped a Kansas CBS affiliate capture a meteorological drama when for "probably the first time in the history of the fifth estate, tv was in a position to bring viewers a first-hand picture of an approaching and terrifying tornado. . . . The tornado struck at 5:42 p.m. with the funnels hitting the ground less than 100 yards from the live cameras. The Zoomar lens of the tv cameras had them in perfect detail on live tv."[67] As these examples demonstrate, zooms were bringing home viewers closer to action that could only be filmed safely from a distance.

Broadcasters also began to find innovative ways to use Zoomar lenses in planned programming. Episodes of the NBC network show *Kukla, Fran and Ollie*, which originated from WBKB in Chicago, were shot almost exclusively via the Zoomar lens, partly because of cramped studio conditions and partly because mismatched image orthicon scanning tubes meant that switching between cameras could be a visually jarring affair.[68] In January 1950, the producers of *Super Circus,* an entertainment show originated by the Chicago station WENR and broadcast across the ABC network, began to use Zoomar lenses to obtain close-ups of trapeze artists, and by March of the same year, the lenses were used "consistently" for that purpose.[69] The earliest uses of the Zoomar lens had been for specific, and often spectacular, events. Immersing audiences in high-profile sporting fixtures was an obvious use for zoom lenses and would have been particularly attractive for television stations competing for audiences and the advertising revenues they brought. However, the examples described earlier demonstrate how quickly the zoom's ability to deliver larger images from a greater distance, and to enable flexible coverage without the need to rotate a cumbersome turret of fixed lenses, became routine. They reflect television's ability and desire to be "on the scene," bringing images—live, legible, and immediate—into viewers' homes. Over the decades that followed, zoom lenses would become the standard fitting on nearly all television cameras, and further research and development would lead to powerful zooms far in excess of the technology available to film producers.

THE ZOOM AND TELEVISED POLITICS

If baseball had been the greatest test of television's ability to cover sport, then the presidential election of 1952 offered the greatest challenge to its ability to cover news events. The Democratic and Republican political conventions of 1952 promised a combination of intricately planned, carefully staged action and unpredictable moments of political drama. Zoom lenses offered a particular advantage to the networks when planning coverage of the conventions, especially when it became necessary to overcome limitations placed on them by politicians skeptical of unfamiliar television cameras.

Political conventions had been successfully televised, to a much smaller audience, during the previous presidential election. The stations in the limited television network of 1948 had covered that year's events in a manner that impressed the *New York Times,* whose reviewer remarked that "the concerted effort of the video industry reflected thoroughness in preparation and alertness in coverage." Viewers were "rewarded with television's characteristically intimate view. . . . The searching lenses of five cameras blanketed the auditorium and its entrance, keeping abreast of the action as interest shifted from point to point."[70] There was much to show, from theatrical set-piece parades and demonstrations to earnest debates, and the simple image of thousands of delegates assembled to choose their nominee for the presidency was a televisual novelty in itself. The *New York Times* was in no doubt as to the civic significance of the coverage, claiming that "television, all at once, was bringing a new political consciousness to a sizable portion of the population, while it promised to exercise a revisional influence on the convention scene," and at the conclusion of the Democratic Convention, the paper's radio reviewer, Jack Gould, declared that NBC's camerawork was the best of all the broadcasters, "particularly in the use of full and sustained close-ups."[71] Such closeup coverage helped reveal the body language and facial expressions of politicians. For the first time, in homes and at bars, viewers could consider not only the words but also the live moving images of their would-be leaders. While radio had for many years brought the voices of political leadership to a mass audience and newsreel had offered excerpts of speeches to cinema audiences, television's clear attraction was to be its ability to provide an unexpurgated and unflinchingly "closeup" view of American political discourse. In the process, it might reveal something new about the honesty and character of political figures.

However impressive the coverage may have been, the television audience for the 1948 conventions was small. Live coverage had been carried on only six stations, all operating on the East Coast. By 1952, television stations had opened across the United States, and a network of microwave transmitters and cable relays linked them from coast to coast.[72] The year 1952 promised improved technology and—for the first time—a mass audience. As Mary Ann Watson writes, "Although television had covered both of the party nominating conventions in 1948, the 1952 Republican Convention in Chicago was the first at which television news possessed the technical resources and attracted a large-enough scale audiences to have significant political impact. . . . The introduction of zoom lenses and handheld cameras called 'Creepie Peepies' gave coverage much greater range and mobility."[73]

Prior to the convention, television had already been earning a reputation as an effective conveyor of civic drama. In March 1952, in a "report on the good and the bad of TV's six years—and a look to the future," Jack Gould highlighted the effectiveness of television in depicting sporting events, but he suggested that television's real potential was as a "major stimulus to a better informed public opinion." Approvingly citing television's coverage of sessions of the United Nations and Estes Kefauver's Senate hearings into organized crime, Gould looked forward to television "bring[ing] the full weight of its influence on the Presidential campaign, with the probable result that the public as a whole is going to be more intimately acquainted with the candidates than ever before."[74] By the summer of 1952, there was mounting optimism about the positive effect of television on the political process. "The TV audience is now nation-wide for the first time in a national campaign, and the camera is also newly ubiquitous. Television will watch the political conventions in Chicago. It will examine the spellbinders. It makes a goldfish bowl out of every rostrum. It applies the litmus test to shenanigans, phonies and plain bores. It separates the men from the boys," declared an editorial in the *New York Times* early that June.[75]

While the press was optimistic about television's role in the conventions, politicians were suspicious. Behind the scenes, network chiefs battled for permission to get enough cameras into convention halls to properly cover the crucial debates and votes. Strict limitations were placed on space for television cameras, so broadcasters pooled their resources and shared coverage. To the disappointment of the television networks, portable electronic cameras—developed in a hurry so as to cover the conventions—were at first banned. Faced with a limited number of camera positions and no clear opportunities to place cameras on the floors among the speakers and delegates, the networks turned to their zoom lenses to ensure that coverage felt as "close up" as possible. *Popular Science* explained, "All eight cameras will be equipped with Zoomar lenses. . . . This lens will make it much easier to get close-ups in the convention hall, for cameras will not be permitted to move around on the crowded floor."[76] *Variety* identified further restrictions on the television networks and the utility of the Zoomar in circumventing them: "In setting up the TV equipment, the [networks] were barred from taking direct full-face shots of the speakers on the center platform, with all cameras restricted to the side of the Amphitheatre. . . . Thanks to the Zoomar lens, however, the closeups practically give the same effect as the direct front view shots."[77] Despite the political parties' initial reluctance, portable electronic television cameras—sometimes nicknamed "creepie peepies" or "walkie-talkie-lookies"—were permitted on the convention floor.[78] However, their technical limitations rendered them unreliable and impractical, and they gave "at best a murky picture." Once again, zoom lenses mounted on static cameras provided a work-around. Broadcasters opted to combine "a radio signal from walkie-talkies carried by roving reporters on the floor with video provided by long-range lens cameras from the booths."[79] By the time of the Democratic Convention, which took place a few weeks later, broadcasters had found a further advantage to using long-range shots: their relatively shallower depth of field excluded extraneous background action. "The background is put out of focus by head-on shots with Zoomar lens, rather than often copping major attention, as was inevitable with side view cameras. Proof of the video pudding is the fact that during the initial quarter-hour of the opening session, the pair of head-on cameras accounted for over 12 minutes of screen time," a keen-eyed *Variety* viewer noticed.[80]

The significance of the Republican Convention was highlighted by *Life* magazine, which particularly emphasized the use of Zoomar lenses. These it described as the "Big Berthas of the TV convention coverage [that] ranged throughout the entire convention hall with an all-seeing eye."[81] In addition to offering a closer view of important political proceedings, long lenses also added a human touch to some of the coverage. One convention chair "slipped her shoes off. . . . She remembered to put the shoes on again before stepping away. Mrs. Howard overlooked only one detail. A powerful television lens in the gallery behind her picked up every detail of the operation."[82] Her furtive action was witnessed on the screen by a *New York Times* correspondent and written up in gossipy detail. Reports like these contributed further to a general feeling in the popular press that television coverage brought viewers closer to all sorts of action and detail. *Variety* remarked, "The iconoscope and the zoomar lens are as clinical as a surgeon's scalpel. It cuts through everything. It is the great revealer."[83] The headline over a *New York Times* article about that year's Republican convention claimed, "Video-set owners have front row convention seat, and in many ways they are closer to the action."[84]

From these accounts, it is clear that Zoomar lenses played a highly significant role in networks' logistical preparations for the conventions while enhancing the quality of the coverage provided. Archived television footage from the 1952 conventions—of which there is very little—offers an opportunity to scrutinize in greater depth the impact of zoom lenses on the televised convention. Footage of a speech by Senator Everett Dirksen to the 1952 Republican Convention shows some of the ways in which zoom shots were used both to enliven the visual appeal of television coverage and to capture unpredictable events taking place in parts of the convention hall distant from the main action of the platform speakers.[85] During Dirksen's speech, which took place as part of a "floor fight" on the seating of delegates from Georgia, the camera generally stays fixed on the head and shoulders of the speaker, panning or tilting only slightly to accommodate slight sideways movements. Occasionally—only four times in the first eight minutes of the coverage—the camera cuts away to shots of the audience. Some of these are long shots showing the size of Dirksen's audience. In other cases, telephoto medium shots focus on small groups of audience members in front-row balcony seats. The variety of shot scales of subjects, taken from various

FIGURE 3.1. Under the "all-seeing eye" of NBC's Zoomar lens, Everett M. Dirksen makes an impassioned speech at the Republican National Convention in 1952.

distances, combined with the limited number of cameras allowed in the convention hall suggests that many of these shots were obtained using zoom lenses.

The value of the zoom is most strongly highlighted by what happens when disturbances disrupt Dirksen's speech. At least two such unexpected incidents were captured by the cameras. While by this stage, broadcasters would have been well prepared for "demonstrations" and other events to take place in the audience area at conventions, the precise time, nature, and extent of such events could not always have been predicted. These occasional dramas would have been a major factor in making coverage more interesting to audiences, so broadcasters needed to be able to provide visual reporting of them as quickly as possible and in as much detail as possible. In this regard, zoom lenses evidently proved useful. Approximately twenty minutes into Dirksen's speech, a physical fight broke out among convention delegates. This momentary disorder had its roots in a verbal confrontation between Dirksen and then New York governor Thomas E. Dewey. Viewers see a lingering shot of Dewey conferring with members of his delegation while in the background, the crowd cheers its support. The director then cuts back to the convention chair, who asks security staff to "take care of the disorder in that part of the hall." This is followed by a cut to a medium shot of delegates surrounding a sign reading "Michigan." The camera zooms out, showing the position of the Michigan delegation within the convention hall and capturing the extent to which the convention seems to be in an uproar. Some delegates stand up and face away from the speaker, fixing their gazes instead on the moving crowd. As the movement of the crowd increases, a commentator describes the action: "There's a great deal of confusion out there. Here goes a fight, there's a fight up. [Inaudible] a photographer getting in trouble, I don't know who was hitting who, somebody got knocked down, but it's pretty hard to tell who it was. Officers were in the middle of it; they really are having a time here tonight." Amid this commentary, the camera attempts to capture as much of the action as possible, with the zoom lens proving crucial in providing unbroken coverage of the events on the convention floor. As soon as jostling among delegates turns into a fight, the camera pans to follow the confrontation. A zoom-in returns viewers from the wider shot of the convention hall to a closer shot that shows—albeit with poor clarity—the interaction between individual delegates and the intervention of a police officer. The pictures give some idea of the facial expressions and body language of those involved, while the zoomed-in closeup shot testifies to the chaos that the commentators struggle to describe.

The television coverage follows a similar strategy when the delegation from Pennsylvania calls for a poll during balloting to determine who will be nominated as the Republican candidate. Here again the zoom lens is used to move from a wide shot, encompassing crowds, toward individual delegates huddled around the state's signboard. From the longer shot, individual bodies are barely distinguishable and faces cannot be seen, but at the longest extension of the zoom, delegates can be seen conferring; one is seen to smile broadly, but most are listening intently to the speaker. Just about visible, though mainly hidden behind the state's sign, is the rapidly moving head of a Pennsylvania convention member who is making an impassioned speech. A few minutes pass before a new angle is obtained on the Pennsylvania delegates, during which time the camera lingers on the considerably less visually interesting image of a convention secretary calling out names. The length of time it takes to establish a new shot suggests that initial zoom-in shot of the Pennsylvania delegation may have been a last resort in the absence of better images; however, it also provides a valuable demonstration of the practical utility of the device. Here we see an early test of the zoom lens's ability to help television directors extract the personal, individual story from a mass political rally with thousands of delegates. Before portable cameras could successfully bring the audience to the convention floor, zoom lenses helped redress the balance between politicians and private citizens, ensuring that protesting delegates on the floor could be seen with almost as much clarity as elected officials on the dais.

From the point of view of mass media coverage, 1952 was one of the most significant American election years—the point at which new production practices were cemented through hard negotiations between television newcomers and the old hands of radio, newsreel, and the print media. Gould, writing in the *New York Times*, lavishly praised the coverage, arguing that the networks' "masterful" coverage had been "responsible in part for the country's interest in the subsequent campaign that brought out a record vote."[86] This was a multifaceted success, involving showmanship by political parties, entertaining commentary from familiar journalists, and the simple fact that convention coverage blanketed the networks to the exclusion of all other programming. Among all these factors, the flexibility offered by the then unique Zoomar lens played a significant role in determining the style, and therefore the success, of the coverage. Without zoom lenses, the networks would have been stuck between arguing more strongly with the political parties for floor positions—with unpredictable results, given the politicians' distrust—and retreating to the sidelines and using fixed focal length telephoto lenses. Such coverage would have been considerably more static and less varied than the combination of zooms and wireless sound. Even if audiences were captive, and even if television coverage had struck the average viewer as neither educational nor compelling, television coverage of conventions impressed at least one set of people: opinion makers working for newspapers such as the *New York Times* and think tanks such as the Brookings Institution. This was a moment at which American television demonstrated its civic worth and expressed its journalistic potential, and it was the Zoomar lens that helped create some of the most engaging and memorable moments of coverage.

In the twenty-first century, zoom lenses remain an important part of the coverage of political conventions and other similar major events, and in their ability to reach from a great distance into the space occupied by a political candidate, official, or supporter, they certainly have the ability to bring viewers "closer to the action." However, for intimacy, this approach was eclipsed by *Primary* (Richard Drew, 1960), in which a lightweight camera—as small and light as the television networks had dreamed of for their live coverage—followed John F. Kennedy as he attempted to secure the presidential nomination in 1960. This was a different form of closeness, achieved via a handheld camera operated in proximity to the candidate himself. Since then, moments of real connection between the viewing electorate and the politicians who seek their votes have tended to occur at moments of physical closeness between camera and personality, as seen in televised debates since 1960, Richard Nixon's interviews with David Frost in 1977, and Bill Clinton's televised denials of impropriety in 1998. Conventions have not produced such intimate moments: the zoom, in this context, seems limited to rendering a better view of the action, if not a sense of real intimacy.

As Zoomar lenses became more widespread, the brand name began to be used beyond the circles of television technicians. Uniquely among the case studies in this book, the Zoomar brand name itself had some impact on the broader lexicon of film, television, and popular culture. By the early 1950s, references to the use of Zoomar lenses become less detailed and more colloquial: often, the word is no longer capitalized, inviting questions about whether the trademark was becoming a generic term.[87] As the 1950s progressed, it became more common for *Variety* to refer to Zoomar in this way. From time to time, the magazine referred to "Zoomar-type" lenses or enclosed the trade name in quotation marks to signal a generic reference—such as when reporting on a Russian television station's acquisition of "'zoomar' lenses."[88] The "Zoomar" name is also occasionally used within television periodicals as a metonym for the television camera or television industry. In October 1952, a *Variety* article remarks on "enterprising music publishers who, seemingly, are not permitting themselves to be caught asleep at the Zoomar switch"; a fictional politician in a 1955 episode of *Alcoa Hour* is "a man obviously smitten by a zoomar lens"; and, as shown previously, at least one account of national party conventions included metonymical references to "television's . . . Zoomar lens."[89]

Following the success of Zoomar lenses in the 1940s and 1950s, some of the earliest models continued to be used on television cameras well into the 1960s. Frank Back remained attached to the company, working with an expanded team to develop improved models of the television Zoomar lens with greater zoom ranges and better responses to low-light conditions. During the 1950s, however, Zoomar faced stiff competition from Europe. As television dramas and sitcoms gradually shifted from live transmission to 16mm studio filming, Zoomar's dominance as the major innovator in television zoom lenses was threatened. The introduction of Pan Cinor lenses, developed in France and specially designed for film cameras, sparked fierce competition. A battle over Zoomar's patent protection ultimately ended the company's dominance of the market. Though Zoomar's leadership was relatively short-lived, its role was decisive. It had introduced the zoom shot to the American television audience, enabling television stations to bring closer views of the highs and lows of sporting, political, and civic life directly into the American home. Of all the devices required to make postwar American television successful, few can have been so critical—and so easily overlooked—as the Zoomar lens.

4 · UNLIMITED HORIZONS

In 1953, two new zoom lenses—both designed for 16mm film cameras—appeared on the American market. They were almost identical, but they came from radically different backgrounds. One was the Zoomar 16, a new lens designed by the New York–based firm Zoomar Incorporated. The other, the Pan Cinor 60, arrived from France and was marketed by a subsidiary of the Swiss camera manufacturer Paillard. In the battle to capture the market for 16mm zoom lenses, Zoomar entered the decade with the upper hand. It had been first to bring film zoom lenses to the postwar market, and the company held a patent that seemed to grant them the exclusive right to sell zoom lenses for cameras through the 1950s and 1960s. Yet despite Zoomar's advantage, it was Paillard and the Pan Cinor that won the battle to bring zoom lenses to 16mm cameras. The Pan Cinor's dominance came at Zoomar's expense. By the end of the 1950s, Zoomar's design department was a spent force. The company's patent protection was lost after a disastrous court battle, and their original research had come to an end.

This chapter explores the battle between the two zoom lenses and discusses the impact of film camera zoom lenses on television production during a decisive decade. As television production shifted from New York to California and from live video to film, zoom lenses saw increasing use. The practical and creative opportunities afforded to television producers were discussed in detail in *American Cinematographer*, and these discussions offer an opportunity to assess how the zoom benefited the production of television shows such as *All Star Golf* and *Night Court U.S.A.* Finally, this chapter examines the ways in which John Frankenheimer, Robert Mulligan, Blake Edwards, and Sydney Pollack experimented with the creative possibilities of the zoom shot when directing television shows. This reveals a complex picture that suggests a gradual development in approaches to the zoom on television, based as much on technological advances and production techniques as on novelty or economy. Frankenheimer and Edwards, working on live anthology drama in New York television studios, used the same sorts of zoom lenses as were used to capture baseball games and Thanksgiving parades. Edwards and Pollack, working a little later and making filmed television serials on Hollywood studio sets, benefited from the extra flexibility and quality of newer film camera zoom lenses. The introduction of these lenses, and especially the arrival of the Pan Cinor, played a decisive role in introducing the zoom shot to filmed American television and influenced the visual style of a generation of directors.[1] Frankenheimer and Mulligan experimented with the zoom shot only occasionally, using it to emphasize specific shots in a manner somewhat similar to Hollywood cinematographers' first experiments with the zoom in the late 1920s. Edwards and Pollack were much more adventurous, and in their television work, we see the zoom immersing viewers in the emotions of characters and articulating more complex spatial relations between characters.

INTRODUCING THE PAN CINOR

The Pan Cinor began its life in the late 1940s in the research workshops of the French industrial manufacturing firm Société d'Optique et de Mecanique de Haute Précision—more commonly known as SOM-Berthiot. The firm was radically different from Zoomar. Based in the town of Sézanne, about seventy miles east of Paris, Berthiot was a large, mature, and diverse institution. The company was founded by Louis Berthiot in 1857, and after undergoing a number of transformations, it emerged from the Second World War with substantial capacity. As in the United States, French industry embarked on a postwar program of converting military technologies for civilian use, and in addition to a wide range of camera lenses, the company also joined forces with other organizations to produce a diverse range of products, including dairy machinery and topographic instrumentation. By 1954, the company employed 1,100 people at three French factories.[2]

Unlike American inventors, who focused their research on standalone zoom lenses from the beginning, Berthiot initially directed their efforts toward inventing an attachment designed to add a zoom function to a fixed focal length lens. The Pan Cinor thus began its life as a modification to existing lenses. The first model was designed by Roger Cuvillier, who filed a patent in late 1949. Cuvillier's "auxiliary optical device with variable magnifying power" was a simple device consisting of two pairs of lenses arranged in a lens barrel. When one pair of lenses was moved forward or backward, the focal length would change by a ratio of as much as 4:1. If attached to a typical 25mm lens mounted on a 16mm camera, the patent suggested, "The device gives the [lens] a focal length which can be varied infinitely from 15 to 60mm."[3] Like the Zoomar lens invented by

Frank Back in New York earlier in the same decade, the design of the Pan Cinor removed the requirement of complicated mechanical image compensation—an advantage noted by *American Cinematographer* in a brief report about the accessory's arrival on the French market.[4]

Despite this flicker of attention in the American trade press, the first version of the Pan Cinor made little impression on American cinematographers, and no record can be found of its having been advertised in, or imported for sale to, the United States. Yet Cuvillier's invention was only the beginning of a much longer process of development. His efforts were joined by those of fellow optical designers Raymond Rosier and Lucien Reymond. In 1952 and 1953, Rosier and Reymond filed patents describing further improvements to Cuvillier's basic design. The first of these patents, filed by Rosier, described the Pan Cinor 60. This model retained the simplicity of design found in Cuvillier's device, but with a more limited zoom range, from 20mm to 60mm. This was a very similar range of focal lengths to the original film version of the Zoomar lens developed in the late 1940s, and the Pan Cinor offered a very similar degree of light transmission. Reymond's patent, which described the Pan Cinor 70, expanded the zoom range to 17.5–70mm but added additional lens elements to its design. Though this lens was faster than the Pan Cinor 60—rated at $f/2.4$—the extra lens element risked introducing unwanted optical distortion and lens flare. Whatever the design compromises of the Pan Cinor 60 and 70 models may have been, they had one substantial advantage over Cuvillier's original Pan Cinor: they were standalone zoom lenses that could be fitted directly to a 16mm camera. Between them, Berthiot's three zoom lens designers had negotiated the many compromises of zoom lens construction. Cuvillier's solution was simple and featured minimal lens elements, but it lacked convenience: rather than simply replacing a set of prime lenses, it would need to be screwed on to the front of one of them. Rosier's Pan Cinor 60 was a lens in its own right, but in retaining the simplicity of the original design, it lost important wide-angle range. Finally, the Pan Cinor 70, which offered more choice of focal lengths, could not replace the widest prime lenses.

The Pan Cinor 60 was introduced to the American market by Paillard Products, an American subsidiary of the Swiss camera manufacturer Paillard-Bolex. The lens was initially promoted to amateur cinematographers for use in the production of home movies. An early advertisement conjured an image of the amateur cinematographer liberated by the Pan Cinor and able to create footage with all the dynamism of a televised football game: "At last the amateur cameraman can *follow* action . . . *hold* action . . . *create* action—and a virtually unlimited variety of special effects—from one camera position! Yes, Pan-Cinor actually provides the equivalent of a 9-lens turret . . . without lens changes! . . . Imagine . . . z-z-zooming from wide angle to telephoto in one 'take'! Or dollying in and out of scrimmages without a lost play from one vantage point!"[5] This description might have tempted an amateur cinematographer to discard a set of prime lenses in favor of the new zoom, but Paillard's promotional magazine, *Bolex Reporter*, took care to point out that the Pan Cinor "is not intended to *replace* lenses of fixed focal length (each of which realizes a higher degree of optical quality for its own focal length)," instead promising that its diverse applications would enable the amateur cinematographer to "zoom for really professional shots."[6]

The market positioning of the Pan Cinor 60 reflects the changing status of 16mm film. While 16mm film had been more commonly used by amateur cinematographers, by the 1950s, its user base was expanding to include the burgeoning fields of industrial and educational film production and film-based television production. As this shift took place, Paillard increased imports of the Pan Cinor lens to the United States and changed its marketing language in order to appeal to professional customers. In 1953, Paillard began to tempt professional customers with the zooming capabilities of the Pan Cinor. Paillard salesmen demonstrated the lens at trade shows and by visiting local film camera operators. In a promotional article in *Bolex Reporter*, Tennessee news cameraman Sid O'Berry explained,

> I was introduced to the new Pan Cinor Zoom lens by Paillard Products' Regional Manager, Vladimir J. Wolf, who suggested that since I am a newsreel cameraman and film editor for WSM-Television, I would be interested in a zoom lens. Well of course I was—I had heard of the new lens and was eager to learn more about its features . . . I had the chance to use the Zoom lens outside and inside and the results were the same—very good. . . . Look at the many advantages it offers the newsreel cameraman where quick lens changing is a necessity, and also the studio use that it can be put to in smooth dollying.[7]

The growing relevance of the Pan Cinor to professional filmmakers was emphasized by *American Cinematographer*'s October 1953 report on the lens's introduction. At the time, the magazine included an extensive monthly section specifically addressing the needs of amateur cinematographers—and it was here that an article about the Pan Cinor appeared.[8] Nevertheless, the article quoted a professional photographer who was happy to recommend the lens for use in professional film work: "We find in practice the pictures made with Pan Cinor are consistently as sharp as those filmed with the best available fixed focal-length lenses. . . . We are using this lens almost exclusively for our work in 16mm television, industrial and promotion films, both black-and-white and color. The only difficulty we have found is resisting the temptation to zoom every shot."[9]

When promoting the Pan Cinor for TV use, *Bolex Reporter* took a different approach. The zoom lens was presented as a weight-reduction enhancement to cameras such as the Bolex. Writing in the magazine in 1955, Willis Cook, director of art and photography at WSAZ-TV in West Virginia, boasted of the lens's ability to capture all the necessary scenes from a news filming assignment from a single position. As with the Studio Zoomar of the late 1940s, Cook provided examples of the Pan Cinor in use in a wide range of exterior and studio-based settings. Pictures of the Pan Cinor depicted it in the hands of camera operators as well as on tripods. One zoom lens instead of three primes meant that for "candid, hand-held work its value is increased tremendously." With a zoom lens, Cook promised, "the old problem of not being able to move about as you would wish is now almost non-existent."[10]

The practicality of Pan Cinor lenses was later boosted by the introduction of updated Pan Cinor 70 and 100 models. The two lenses offered a higher zoom ratio than the predecessor Pan Cinor 60—1:4 compared to 1:3. Of equal significance to television camera operators was the improved viewfinder. Previous models had relied on a paired viewfinder—essentially a small zoom lens with an identical zoom lens attached to one side of the camera body. This was of limited use to the camera operator. However well matched to the zoom lens, the viewfinder could offer no more than an approximation of what was being captured on film. For the Pan Cinor 70 and 100 models, SOM-Berthiot adopted a new approach: a "highly-precise and complex optical system" that enabled camera operators to view directly through the camera lens.[11] Later, this sort of system would become known as a reflex viewfinder and would be retrofitted on film cameras before becoming standard equipment. In the mid-1950s, it was a significant innovation—and essential for the efficient use of zoom lenses because of the need to monitor the effect of changes in focal length.

Writing in *Bolex Reporter*, Robert H. Hess, CBS News manager of motion picture production, hailed the original Pan Cinor lenses as "a tremendous step in the right direction." Having bought one of the earliest Pan Cinors, Hess credited the lens with producing "excellent and eye-pleasing footage" of Eisenhower's 1952 election campaign: "Gone was the short, choppy lens changes and in its place was a smooth flow of motion." But Hess had been left unsatisfied by the Pan Cinor 60's viewfinder, which "was weak due to the time needed to correct for parallax." The coupled viewfinder of the original lens had been too fiddly for news camera operators filming unpredictable action. Hess pronounced himself delighted, therefore, with the newer through-the-lens viewfinder installed on the new Pan Cinor 70 and 100, which CBS had tested at the Geneva Summit in 1955. The new zoom lens enabled CBS to trial a new approach to filming such events that was "different from the conventional theatrical newsreel."

In describing this, Hess pointed out two very significant technological advantages to filming continuously using the zoom lens: "Instead of the stilted interview type story wherein constant lens changes are necessary, the Pan Cinor now comes to the forefront giving a complete range of focal distances easing the editing problem. Reducing the cutting also aids the editor due to the fact that the single system sound camera which we use presents the problem of a 'jump' cut in the sound whenever a splice occurs."[12] Hess mentions these advantages in passing, but they are very significant indeed. The "editing problem" in the context of news footage was a potentially significant bottleneck in the production process. If a camera operator filming with a turret had to stop the camera to change and refocus lenses, then the frequent disruptions to the film—and its associated soundtrack, when shooting sound-on-film—would need to be edited out of the rushes before transmission on television. By contrast, a camera operator equipped with a zoom lens could in theory shoot a single flowing sequence limited only by the length of the reel. If the camera operator "edited" using the zoom lens, then the resulting footage could be rush processed and broadcast to viewers at home without necessarily requiring the intervention of an editor and without further adjustment to the soundtrack.

The Pan Cinor 60 was not the only new zoom lens to appear in the October 1953 edition of *American Cinematographer*. That month's edition also included a cryptic advertisement for a new product designed by Zoomar Corporation: the Zoomar 16. This was the first Zoomar advertisement ever to appear in *American Cinematographer*. The text of the quarter-page advertisement read, "Promise fulfilled . . . Zoomar 16—Watch for details next month." The following month, no such details were furnished, but a further advertisement declared, "Next month . . . a dream becomes reality" and included illustrations of three different cameras mounted with the new Zoomar 16 lens. In December 1953, Zoomar reran the advertisement, with the text altered to read "available now."[13] At the same time, a New York industrial film company, Animated Productions Inc., prepared a promotional film "as a means of demonstrating to tv stations and producers the mobility and flexibility of the 16mm Zoomar lens-equipped camera [consisting] of a variety of motion picture shots filmed in Kodachrome by Dr. Frank G. Back . . . on his recent round-the-world-trip."[14]

It was not until January 1954 that the Zoomar 16 was fully described in a prominent full-page advertisement at the front of *American Cinematographer*. Like the Pan Cinor a few months earlier, the Zoomar 16's great attraction was the freedom it could offer the cinematographer. It would open "unlimited horizons: with a flick of your finger, Zoomar 16 zooms from normal . . . to telephoto . . . to wide angle . . . only Zoomar 16 fits all 16mm motion picture cameras." Patent and registered design numbers were prominently displayed in the advertisement, as if etched into the zoom lens illustrated. An article published

FIGURE 4.1. After transforming the market for zoom
lenses in television, the Zoomar Corporation promised
"unlimited horizons" for 16mm camera operators.

in the same edition of *American Cinematographer* detailed the Zoomar 16's heritage. "The result of more than seven years of intensive research and development in the field of varifocal lenses," the article situated the lens as descended from Back's original invention of 1946 and from "the Television Zoomar . . . now standard equipment on television cameras in over 100 TV stations throughout the country." Unlike the October 1953 report on the Pan Cinor, the Zoomar article confidently describes the new lens as capable of substituting for a suite of fixed focal length lenses, stating that "by design, it is not only a special effects lens but a high-quality, high speed all-purpose lens as well. By being capable of taking the place of all conventional lenses from 1 in. to 3 in. on the camera turret, it makes the long-dreamed of 'one-lens camera' an actuality."[15]

By early 1954, cinematographers could choose between two brand-new zoom lenses for 16mm filming. This was an astonishing burst of activity in a market that had been quiet for decades. Not since the experiments of Paramount and Joseph Walker in the 1920s, and the introduction of the Varo in the 1930s, had zoom lenses been so accessible for motion picture filming. But the simultaneous appearance of the lenses provoked a legal conflict that was to rumble for several years and, in the process, permanently change the American zoom lens market.

ZOOMAR V. PAILLARD: A COURTROOM BATTLE

Why did two 16mm zoom lenses appear on the American market within a few weeks of each other, and why were they almost identical in design and optical characteristics? Publicity material and trade press reports attempted to convince customers that the Zoomar 16 was the result of a long-planned process of innovation. Yet while there is no doubt that significant research and development had taken place since the introduction of the initial Zoomar lens in the mid-1940s, the physical appearance of the Zoomar 16 suggests that it also owed something to its competitor. In design, the Zoomar 16 was strikingly similar to the Pan Cinor 60, consisting of a short variable focal length lens coupled to a nonreflex viewfinder and controlled by a pivoting lever. The lever was itself a new feature: most previous Zoomar models designed for use in television had been controlled by means of a "rod" that was threaded through the mechanism of the television camera itself. The Zoomar and Pan Cinor lenses looked more like sibling products emerging from the same research and design process than lenses developed by radically different companies on different sides of the Atlantic Ocean.

It is almost impossible to determine which of the products was the "original." The similarity in physical appearance and technical capabilities of the two lenses, as well as their near-simultaneous appearance on the market, provokes a number of questions—most notably about the degree to which Zoomar and Pan Cinor could have known of their respective research and development plans. There was at least some level of informal discussion between the two companies: Zoomar employees regularly met with their Paillard counterparts to discuss products and other matters of business interest. If the Pan Cinor came first, then the long trail of teaser advertisements by Zoomar in *American Cinematographer* may suggest that Zoomar found out about the French lens and Paillard's plans to import it. In this scenario, Zoomar accelerated research and development to make a competing lens but could not bring it to market in time to "spoil" Paillard—leading to three months of advertising about a product that was not yet ready for sale. Alternatively, it may be the case that Paillard somehow became aware of Zoomar's plan to launch the new product and struck a preemptive importation deal with SOM-Berthiot. This would offer an explanation for Zoomar's apparent decision to commence marketing the Zoomar 16 several months before it was to be made commercially available: the premature advertisements were the symptoms not of a rush to beat a competitor to market but of a desire to avoid having a long-planned product spoiled by a patent-infringing intruder from Europe. Two further options remain. It is possible, though unlikely, that Zoomar's advertisements in *American Cinematographer* were published significantly after the Zoomar 16 was actually brought to market. Another slim possibility is that the simultaneous appearance of the two lenses was due entirely to coincidence. Either way, by late 1956, the Zoomar Corporation, still under the direction of Frank Back and Jack Pegler, had decided that Paillard's marketing of Pan Cinor zoom lenses infringed Back's patents. They resolved to defend their intellectual property in court.

Lawyers, witnesses, and expert witnesses for Zoomar and Paillard faced each other in New York's Southern District Federal Court over the span of several days in February 1957.[16] This was, according to the optical patent law historian Joseph Gortych, the first court case involving a zoom lens.[17] Zoomar accused Paillard of infringing their patents by selling Pan Cinor lenses; Paillard, in turn, argued that Back's patents were invalid and therefore unenforceable.[18] For Zoomar, the court hearing went disastrously wrong. Zoomar's lawyers were repeatedly criticized by the judge for using inappropriate and outdated legal methods to defend their patents. Back was an awkward witness who gave evidence while suffering from a heavy cold and was at times reticent and excessively soft spoken. Zoomar's lawyers, Shereff Brothers, commanded a methodologically flawed case that meandered from one subject to another, drawing frequent expressions of exasperation or bewilderment from the judge, Irving R. Kaufman.[19] The flow of argumentation was broken—twice—by the need to gather further material. As the company's president and leading inventive light, Back should have been a star witness. Instead, he was uncommunicative, uncooperative, and at times inaudible. Furthermore, given that Zoomar was the initiator of the case, their arguments might be expected to form a robust and cogent attack against a trespass upon their intellectual property rights. Instead, their case had the qualities of a weak defense.

During the proceedings, Zoomar's counsel portrayed Back as an expert in his field—a member of ten learned societies who had published articles in scholarly journals and trade periodicals and who had researched optics and worked in the optical industries throughout his professional and educational careers. Back testified that he held "over twenty" American patents, mostly "in optics." He stated that he started working on variable focal length lenses "during the Second World War . . . in 1943" and explained that after two or three years of trial and error, he settled on the design described in the first of his Zoomar patents.[20] Responding to questions from his own counsel, Back gave a detailed description of the construction of the lens described by the patent and invited the judge to look through a model of the Zoomar lens, which had been partly disassembled and colorized for ease of understanding. Though a legal expert,

Kaufman was a layperson as far as optical engineering was concerned. The aim of Back's color-coded zoom lens model was to communicate, in simple terms, the basic principles of the operation of the Zoomar lens. It failed to do so. After hearing testimony about a particular part of the Zoomar lens—the "erector" element—Kaufman was unable to conceal his disgruntlement:

KAUFMAN: I am sorry, I don't follow it. Do you, Mr. Shereff?
SHEREFF: I happen to know it. I lived with this for a year. But I can see the difficulty. It took me a long time to get it. . . . Dr. Back, take it easy, please, and perhaps—
BACK: It is hard to explain.
KAUFMAN: Since it took you a long time, you should have been able to really elucidate this so that I would understand it.[21]

Kaufman was forced to allow Shereff to ask questions that led Back to give a clearer explanation. Zoomar encountered more problems relating to technical details again later in the case, when Back attempted to describe the concept of a nonlinear linkage. Back offered a densely technical description of his design, leading a frustrated Kaufman to interrupt his testimony and demand a "simple and mechanical" explanation. Back, apparently unprepared to do so, instead promised to return to his workshop and craft a demonstration device to bring to the hearing's next session.

Zoomar's case was further hindered by the inadmissibility of much of the evidence they had hoped to use in order to prove the originality of the Zoomar lens. An attempt to introduce into evidence an article from the *Proceedings of the Physical Society* to demonstrate the state of the art of zoom lenses was challenged by Paillard, who objected that the article constituted hearsay evidence. Kaufman agreed, asking, "What is the relevancy? You don't prove prior art that way. And this is a man's interpretation of the prior art—a man who will not be a witness and not be subject to cross-examination." Shereff attempted to prove the point with precedent but failed to convince the court and withdrew the evidence. Paillard also argued against the introduction of material such as journal articles and awards as evidence of the significance and novelty of the Zoomar lens. Back testified that in 1948, he received "a gold medal award from the American . . . Broadcasters Association."[22] Substantial argument ensued regarding the admissibility of evidence such as this. Paillard argued that articles in periodicals—whatever their scientific reputation—could not be valued above the hearsay of a single individual, and the court largely agreed. The transcript suggests that Shereff had hoped to use numerous such items of evidence to prove the originality of Back's invention and reinforce the validity of his patent. This tactic, like the others, failed. Paillard's defense was successful, and Kaufman's judgment ultimately invalidated Zoomar's patent protection.

The significance of the *Zoomar v. Paillard* decision was soon recognized by both the press and the industry. Upon the publication of the judgment in June 1957, the *New York Times* reported that "the effect of [the] decision will be to open wide the field of manufacturing such lens system [*sic*]."[23] This was no exaggeration. Had Zoomar's patents remained unchallenged, they could have remained valid well into the following decades. As long as these patents remained in place, and Zoomar Inc. was prepared to warn competitors away from the marketplace, it seems likely that the marketing of a competing zoom lens in the United States would have been somewhat limited. Furthermore, it is possible that investment in innovation, or in the importation of foreign-made zoom lenses, would also have been curtailed. Instead, some of the effects of the judgment had already taken effect; for example, Pan Cinor lenses were already being marketed in the United States by Paillard. Nevertheless, the judgment against Zoomar was a significant moment in the development and marketing of zoom lenses. *Zoomar v. Paillard* and its subsequent appeals (also failures) were the final acts in the market entry of the Pan Cinor zoom lenses. Paillard was now free to continue distribution, and with the Zoomar patents no longer valid, there was less to discourage other inventors and importers from attempting to introduce new and different zoom lenses to the U.S. market. As an increasing number of zoom lenses became available to the American television industry, zoom shots began to be used in filmed television serials, while innovative directors including John Frankenheimer and Robert Mulligan began to experiment with the creative possibilities and practical challenges of the zoom in the context of live anthology television.

16MM ZOOMS: THE IMPACT

The corporate and legal battle between Zoomar and Paillard was fierce, but it had little immediate practical impact on television stations, film studios, and professional cinematographers. Though Zoomar sent a number of letters to Paillard customers warning them of the potential legal consequences of Paillard's perceived patent infringement, the sale of Pan Cinor lenses was never formally restrained. From the perspective of film and television production, therefore, the parallel availability of the Pan Cinor 60 and 70 and the Zoomar 16 simply meant more zoom lenses, which in turn led to more opportunities for cinematographers to familiarize themselves with the technology, as their colleagues in live television had done during the 1940s. Zoom lenses did not upend stylistic conventions and production practices, but they increased the efficiency, flexibility, and spontaneity of filmed television production.

This opportunity arose during a significant shift in television production away from live broadcast and toward filming. During the 1940s and early 1950s, the majority of television production took place on the East Coast. Anthology drama and variety shows dominated the schedules. They were broadcast live as they were performed, using bulky electronic studio cameras of the sort for which the Studio Zoomar had been designed. As the 1950s progressed, increasing numbers of television drama serials and comedies were shot on film, while 16mm—once reserved for amateur use—became the dominant recording medium. As Erik Barnouw explains, "By the end of 1957 more than a hundred series of television films . . . were on the air or in production. Almost all were Hollywood products, and most were of the episodic series type. They came from majors and independents alike. The films processed by film laboratories were now mainly for television."[24] William Boddy has accounted for this shift in cultural terms, discussing television networks' antipathy toward the perceived "carbon-copy" approach of Hollywood studios.[25] But this shift had an equally significant technological dimension: it meant a movement from television broadcast equipment (iconoscope cameras fitted with lenses calibrated specially for them) to more conventional celluloid film equipment. Zoom lenses designed for television—including the Field and Studio Zoomars and the RCA Electra-Zoom—were unsuitable for use on film cameras. It was in this context that Pan Cinor lenses, alongside the similar Zoomar 16, were introduced.

By the late 1950s, 16mm zoom lenses were provoking significant levels of debate among film and television cinematographers. Indeed, it was at this stage that Joseph V. Mascelli began to regularly consider the aesthetics of the zoom lens in various articles in *American Cinematographer*. In his earliest article, "Use and Abuse of the Zoom Lens," Mascelli had urged cinematographers to be restrained, cautious, and consistent in their use of the zoom.[26] Yet despite such ideals, there is little evidence of consistent zoom usage at this point—even within individual programs. Mascelli wrote at length in 1958 about the production of a new series, *All Star Golf*, and gave the zoom lens great credit for reducing shooting time to a single day. In *All Star Golf*, the zoom was used as a substitute for a fixed telephoto lens; it was also used to "bridge continuity gaps" and execute the complex camera movements that track golf balls from tee to hole. Mascelli describes how "variety in camera angles, lens choice and zoom effects are injected as the game progresses in order to keep the camera work from becoming a monotonous recording. . . . The zoom lens is effectively, and often dramatically, employed not only as aid to editing. [Producer-director Sidney] Goltz insists that zooming should be restrained and justified by the action or editing. 'After all,' states Goltz, 'that zoom lever isn't a pump handle!'" Despite these varied applications, Mascelli claims that the zoom is used "with discretion, variety and good taste. *All Star Golf* sets a very fine example of the proper use of zooming techniques for filming this popular sport." Mascelli's article demonstrates the flexibility and fragility of newly developed conventions for the zoom lens. In the context of a real example of industrial television production, the earlier insistence on slow, steady zooms gives way to a far more flexible and pragmatic approach. The article embraces the production economies of the technique while emphasizing that its use causes no loss in esteem for the production's visual style. Mascelli quotes *Variety*'s praise for the show's camerawork, which, the reviewer concluded, "could hardly be better. Cameras zoom in for extra curricular color, facial expressions of the players, their measuring of the green and attitudes of the onlooker."[27]

Another television production that was described in detail by Mascelli and made comprehensive use of a zoom lens was *Night Court U.S.A.* *Night Court* originally appeared "as a live local programme from the Los Angeles studios of KTLA" in April 1958.[28] Each episode of the show followed a simple pattern: a series of fictional legal cases were brought before "Judge Jay Jostyn," played by the actor Jay Jostyn. Plaintiffs would generally either protest their innocence or plead guilty with mitigating circumstances. After hearing their arguments, Jostyn would decide on an appropriate punishment. In each episode, the overwhelming majority of the action takes place on the courtroom set, though the camera occasionally ventures to side corridors. The extant version of *Night Court* is not the original live series of episodes but a version reshot by Banner Productions for national syndication. The title was changed to *Night Court U.S.A.*, and episodes were produced to a thirty-minute format—the original had been an hour. For this second version, the restrictions of live television programming—notably the necessity of a flexible setup of cameras to provide continuous coverage with minimal opportunities to change setups—were replicated in the form of cost-saving filming strategies. As Erickson notes, "Episodes were hastily shot on an assembly-line basis, using multiple cameras and lengthy, uninterrupted takes."[29] *Night Court U.S.A.* therefore offers an opportunity to analyze how new zoom lenses for film cameras aided the efficient production of a television series.

The Pan Cinor zoom lens was central to both the efficient production and the unique "unrehearsed" atmosphere of *Night Court U.S.A.* In a detailed account of production practices on set, Joseph V. Mascelli explains in some detail how the show achieved its level of spontaneity and realism: "While almost everything that is done in producing *Night Court* has been done before, in part, the successful combination of the various elements that go into filming a television show have never been so perfectly coordinated. . . . Live television technicians cite the show's free-flowing movement—the genuine 'live' quality of the show. And vast numbers from television's nightly audience have extolled the shows' [*sic*] 'believability.' 'It seems so real,' many have said, 'it must be filmed in a real courtroom during actual litigations.'"[30] As Mascelli points out, the techniques used to produce the show were not in themselves novel. The strategy of filming from multiple angles to later edit into a consistent narrative is based on the most fundamental principles of classical continuity. The introduction of the zoom, however, must not be overlooked, for it added a substantial degree of flexibility to the setup. Three Mitchell BNC cameras were used to film the action on *Night Court U.S.A.*'s single main set, each taking advantage of a different form of mobility. Camera 1 moved backward and forward on a dolly and was tasked with capturing close-ups of the judge during cases. Camera 2 was mounted on a crane, with a wider lens to "cover the courtroom audience and to follow defendants as they are brought in." The Pan Cinor zoom lens was mounted on Camera 3, behind the judge's position.[31] Mascelli's article quotes one of the show's cinematographers, William Whitley, who explains how the cameras work together to achieve the desired sense of "reality": "Lighting, camera angles and camera movement all contribute to the spontaneous, sometimes hesitant, action of the person on trial. Cameras 1 and 2 are at the far end of their track, and the zoom lens is at its widest position, at the beginning of a sequence so that the courtroom can be re-established and the defendant brought to the bench in a wide-angle sweeping motion. As the case progresses the cameras move in, and the zoom lens is adjusted to telephoto position for a more intimate view of the proceedings."[32]

The significance of *Night Court U.S.A.* lies in the contribution the Pan Cinor zoom lens makes to this sense of unrehearsed documentary coverage. The conceit of "reality" is reinforced by the structure of each episode, in which an apparently random selection of cases is heard before the judge. A typical episode begins in medias res, during a brief break between the cases (the same mechanism is used to accommodate commercial breaks).[33] A whispered voiceover introduces the audience to the seemingly ongoing action: "Ladies and gentlemen, this is Night Court, taking place as it actually happens, with real people appearing in true cases. This session of Night Court is already under way. The next case to appear before His Honor Jay Jostyn is momentarily to be called by the court clerk, Henry Scott." As each defendant is called, the camera pans, tracks, and sometimes zooms to pick him or her out of a group of defendants and members of the public seated in the courtroom. As each defendant approaches the bench, the main pattern of shooting for the exchange among the judge, lawyers, and defendant is established: typically, the defendant is shot from a high angle approximating the view of the judge, while the judge is shot from a lower angle representing the position of the defendant. Occasional shots from the side show the clerks' bench, the door to the courtroom, and those assembled in the public gallery.

The shooting arrangement for a typical "case" featured in a first-season episode of *Night Court U.S.A.* offers a vivid example of the production efficiencies of the zoom lens. The defendant, Frank Muller, has been summoned before the court on a charge of assaulting his neighbor Arthur Harrow. Muller wishes to plead guilty but offers an explanation: he claims that his children had been upset to see Harrow attacking his pet dog, and after a great deal of provocation, he had attacked Harrow for this reason. A few minutes into Muller's detailed account of his offense, there is a disturbance in the courtroom: somewhere behind Muller, someone sitting in the public gallery appears to lunge across the seating area. The camera that has been fixed on Muller zooms back to capture a wider view of the courtroom, showing two men confronting each other and being restrained by court officers. After a cut to a side-on shot of the courtroom, the fracas dies down. The camera tracks back toward Muller, and the questioning resumes. In the meantime, the original camera returns to its position fixed on Muller's head and shoulders, and after a few seconds, this shot returns.

Here the zoom provides a quick and flexible reaction to a change in the narrative, helping create a sense of spontaneity in the ostensibly unrehearsed proceedings. Though the disturbance is obviously scripted and is resolved as part of the next case to be brought before the judge, a combination of zoom lenses and camera movement enhances the appearance that the disturbance has taken the court by surprise. Achieving the same coverage simply by cutting between two cameras would have been highly consistent with standard practice in rehearsed drama, defeating *Night Court*'s quest for an appearance of extemporaneity. If the impression of an unrehearsed outburst had been created by having one or both cameras pan or tilt in search of the action, the impression created would be of an unprepared or incompetent camera operator. By contrast, and because of its familiarity from news and sports coverage, audiences would arguably have had less trouble in "reading" the zoom-out as a reaction to unexpected activity happening out of view of the cameras.

In the "case" that follows, two comedians—the men who caused the disturbance mentioned earlier—plead guilty to breaching the peace at a comedy club the previous night and enter into a comedic dialogue with Jostyn in which they each blame the other for the conflict. Whereas during the previous case the zoom is used to articulate the surprise of the "unexpected" disruption to an otherwise straightforward two-way conversation between Muller and Jostyn, in this part of the episode, the zoom lens is used more comprehensively. It creates a wide and flexible range of camera positions, thereby accommodating a dynamic conversation among the two standing defendants and the single seated judge. When intercut with shots from the other two cameras, the zoom lens creates the appearance of a larger number of camera positions than actually exists and allows for smoother editing of the final sequence. On the face of it, the sequence is an uncomplicated treatment of an undemanding dramatic situation. But the combination of zoom lens, moving camera, and multiple-camera technique results in a more complex and visually impressive sequence than might otherwise be expected. On the set, the flexible zoom saved time by reducing the need for changes in camera position or lens setting while creating more variety and a greater sense of spontaneity in a show for which the greatest attraction was the feeling of being unrehearsed and true to life.

Night Court U.S.A.'s zoom is never "unmotivated" or used for "shock" effects. Instead, it is used in conjunction with a number of other techniques. Shots are taken from various angles, and one camera physically moves within the set. Thus the zoom shot does not dominate the show's visual style; it efficiently enables a number of distinct and discrete shots to be created from the position of a single camera. The zooming action also adds an immersive form of movement that is further distinct from that seen from the crane-mounted camera. A high-angle zoom over the shoulder of Jostyn places the viewer firmly into the judge's perspective and makes the defendant seem small and powerless, thus articulating the power relations within the court and highlighting the paternalistic and authoritarian nature of Jostyn's position. Finally, the zoom enables rapid and apparently spontaneous reframing of the profilmic at times of apparently unpredictable drama. This evidently had the dual benefit of allowing faster and less error-prone production, but to the viewer at home, it was a further restatement of the zoom as a tool that was especially suited to the capture of actuality, spontaneity, and believability.

Night Court U.S.A. and *All Star Golf* are but two examples of the growing use of the zoom lens for routine television production during the 1950s. They cut against the story of the zoom as a tool limited to use in live news and sporting applications. These shows were made not only with Hollywood production efficiency but also with care as to their aesthetic appeal to the viewer. By the end of the 1950s, this approach to the zoom—as a tool to be used creatively—was also being cautiously embraced by some of the most prominent figures active in live and filmed television drama.

THE ZOOM AND 1950S TELEVISION DRAMA

The tidal wave of zoom shots that appeared in feature films from the mid-1960s onward has often been attributed to the introduction of the Angénieux 10:1 zoom lens. Central to this development, say many accounts, were the "TV Generation" directors who began their careers on the small screen before shifting to the feature film industry. Historians including John Belton have noted that some of the most adventurous uses of the zoom during the 1960s may be found in the work of directors who cut their teeth in television, including John Frankenheimer, Robert Mulligan, Sydney Pollack, Blake Edwards, and Robert Altman.[34] By the time these directors made the transition from television to film, so had the zoom lens, and this—the theory runs—accounts for their readiness to use the zoom in feature films. This notion, however logical, is somewhat limited. As the following discussion demonstrates, while some uses of the zoom

FIGURE 4.2. The Pan Cinor zoom lens, in use on the set of television serial *Night Court U.S.A.*, tightens the composition on a young hoodlum.

shot prefigure those later seen in Hollywood features, the TV Generation cannot easily be regarded as the progenitor of the zoom in 1960s Hollywood film. This is because uses of the zoom lens by TV Generation directors evolved in a complex manner. Zoom lenses were available to the directors of live anthology drama in the middle to late 1950s, but their application was severely limited. The studio anthology work of Robert Mulligan and John Frankenheimer, for example, was defined by adventurous blocking and camera movement; zoom shots, likely made with Studio Zoomar lenses of the type developed in the late 1940s, were a rarity. Adventurous zooms, of the sort that may be observed in features in the 1960s, are not a stylistic feature of live television drama. However, they may be found slightly later in filmed television work directed by Blake Edwards and Sydney Pollack. In the work of Edwards and Pollack, we see early examples of emphatic zooms, which often signal the psychological disruption of characters. The remaining pages of this chapter examine these differing uses of the zoom in the various contexts of 1950s and early 1960s television.

The difference between the application of zoom shots in television and their application in film is starkest in the work of Robert Mulligan and John Frankenheimer, whose television careers were both spent almost exclusively in New York–based live anthology drama. Mulligan's early work offers only a few unambiguous zoom shots. The most interesting of these appears in "Time of Delivery," a *Philco Television Playhouse* episode first aired in October 1954.[35] At one point in the narrative, the zoom lens is used to create an extreme close-up on a young couple whose relationship has been central to the narrative. Each act shows disruption caused to the protagonists when a postal worker falls ill and fails to deliver a bag of mail. In the second act, the inconvenienced parties are a young soldier named Willy and his sweetheart, Pamela. Willy's delayed letter to Pamela would have informed her that rather than marry her and take a job in her family's business, he had decided to extend his enlistment and would soon be redeployed to Germany. Because the letter does not arrive, Willy is forced to impart this news to Pamela in person. After much discussion, he decides to follow through with his reenlistment. But as he is heading to catch his train, Pamela rushes (offscreen) onto the station concourse, meeting Willy just as he has walked through the latticework platform gate, which is closed behind him. The lovers meet. A close-up shows their faces, separated by the gate. They kiss, and as they do so, the camera zooms in for an extreme close-up, isolating their lips and eyes. After they kiss, the camera zooms out, and Willy's army buddy Eddie says, "You missed the train." The camera zooms in again, settling on an extreme close-up of Willy and Pamela as the screen fades to black for the conclusion of the act. This is a fairly concealed use of the zoom, which in this case might easily be mistaken for a tracking shot. We cannot know exactly why a zoom was used at this moment: it is possible that it was a more practical way to move into such an extreme close-up from an already tight camera position. The effect, for the viewer, is to emphasize the lovers' kiss, which caps their narrative arc within the episode. However, this device is the exception, not the rule in "Time of Delivery" and, apparently, in Mulligan's anthology television work in general. Zooms can be observed in the *Alcoa Hour* play "President," but only in simulations of television coverage of a political convention that provides the backdrop for the drama.[36] The episode opens with a shot ranging across delegates on the floor of a fictional party convention, gently zooming in, mimicking "real" convention coverage. The same technique is then used in simulated television coverage, which is shown on a monitor within the mise-en-scène. The combination of zooms in the opening scenes and on the television monitor immerses the viewer in a sense of reality: by emphasizing stylistic conventions familiar from television news coverage, the drama is made to feel more immediate. Again, these shots are exceptional within the episode: they establish the setting, but the rest of the scenes are covered in more conventional style. The cameras and the players move, but coverage is from a range of fixed focal lengths.

Television productions directed by John Frankenheimer are more striking in their visual style, making particularly adventurous use of the wide-angle compositions for which he would become known. He later described his camerawork on *Climax!* as featuring "extreme wide-angle, extreme depth of focus, a lot of camera movement. Really, really complicated stuff."[37] Frankenheimer's earliest extant television work demonstrates precisely these sorts of compositions. Of the few zoom shots that can be identified, the most striking appears in a *Playhouse 90* adaptation of the children's book *Eloise*, first aired in December 1956.[38] "Eloise" includes numerous complicated and dynamic action sequences but only one zoom shot—a set-piece camera movement delivered shortly after Eloise (Evelyn Rudie) discovers that her parents are seeking a divorce. As the tearful girl is comforted by her nanny and an acquaintance, the camera finally tilts up and zooms toward Eloise's face. Rudie appears to hesitate a moment for the zoom to complete before delivering—directly to the camera—the scene's final line: "Everything's not all right! I want to see my lawyer!" In contrast to the dynamic, fluid camerawork in the episode in general, this combined camera movement is inelegant and jerky. Its halting execution draws attention to itself and to Rudie's direct performance style. Like Mulligan's isolated zoom into the kissing lovers in "Time of Delivery," Frankenheimer uses the zoom to deliver a moment of emphasis. As the scene-ending line, the zoom functions to draw attention to the episode's young star. Her precocious demand for legal representation is important in two ways: it sets up the drama of the next act (to continue following commercials) and defuses the emotional charge of scene. This approach to the zoom tells us something about how Frankenheimer may have regarded it at this moment: rather than using it to shape the narrative or alter the framing from one moment to the next, he reserves its impact for one powerful and carefully rehearsed moment within the drama. In its isolated and calculated use to focus on a central character at a moment of highest drama, this zoom is strikingly redolent of some of the more complex zooms found in late 1920s silent films.

Frankenheimer also uses the zoom during the opening scene of the *Playhouse 90* drama "Days of Wine and Roses" (1958).[39] While the opening credits roll, the camera zooms onto the shadow of a man drinking wine outside an Alcoholics Anonymous meeting, setting the tone for a drama that takes alcoholism as its main theme. In common with the example in "Eloise," the zoom appears as an isolated special effect, manifesting itself as the only movement visible on the screen at this point. What both of these examples have in common is that they are neither mixed with dialogue nor fluidly integrated into a camera pan, tilt, or track. Nor are they cut into or out of at the beginning or end of a scene. The zoom is isolated from the rest of the camerawork and treated as a special effect. "Eloise" was evidently an ambitious and challenging production featuring a great deal of camera movement around complex, relatively fast-paced blocking on various sets. Yet for all this adventure and experimentation, barely any zoom shots can be observed. For Frankenheimer, as for Mulligan, the evidence is clear

FIGURE 4.3. An early example of a zoom emphasizing a dramatic point at the end of an act, under John Frankenheimer's direction, the lens movement makes plain the distress of Eloise (Evelyn Rudie).

that zoom lenses were available when shooting anthology drama episodes. However, the directors' use of dynamic zoom shots was minimal, especially when compared to dramatic wide-angle compositions. It may be the case that Frankenheimer's preference for wide-angle lenses is itself a reason zoom shots are not prevalent in his television work: in the cramped conditions of a television studio, wide lenses allow for close-ups more readily than longer lenses. Furthermore, zoom lenses designed for electronic television cameras were larger and more unwieldy than later models designed for film use. They required bright lighting in order to work effectively, and they were often awkward in operation. Live television drama required nimble production practices; technical failures had the potential to ruin the drama. In live television, the zoom was a risky choice and precious commodity, and Frankenheimer and Mulligan both treated it as such, limiting its use to specific and well-rehearsed moments that would best emphasize the dramatic peaks of the teleplays they were directing.

While Mulligan and Frankenheimer directed dramas within the limitations of live television in New York, filmed television serials—produced in Hollywood—offered an entirely different means of production. Sets could be larger, and location filming was feasible in some cases. Filming multiple takes with a single 16mm camera, which could be stopped and restarted during scenes, meant that more complex camera movements could be planned and executed. As the examples of *All Star Golf* and *Night Court U.S.A.* demonstrate, these factors in combination made the zoom lens an irresistible tool for directors of filmed television serials. Consequently, the television work of directors such as Blake Edwards, Sydney Pollack, and Robert Altman is rich in early examples of the zoom shot. Unlike the reserved and limited uses of the zoom in live anthology drama, these examples really do prefigure the ways in which the zoom was to be used in Hollywood features from the mid-1960s onward.

The examples of Blake Edwards and Sydney Pollack, in addition to illustrating typical uses of the zoom in filmed television, emphasize the diversity of the broad group of directors who have been described as the "TV Generation." Though Edwards and (for example) Frankenheimer went on to work within the same feature film industry, the beginnings of their careers were completely different. Frankenheimer, as we have seen, was New York based and worked largely in live anthology drama; Edwards's career was more focused on television and entertainment shows produced on film in Hollywood. Meanwhile, Sydney Pollack did not start his directing career until the early 1960s. Both Pollack and Edwards show somewhat more willingness to use the zoom lens than their live-television contemporaries, but like Frankenheimer and Mulligan, they also initially saw the zoom as a technique to be used sparingly. As the early 1960s advanced, however, their works show a more adventurous and more complicated approach to the technology.

In the *Peter Gunn* episode "The Comic" (October 1959), Edwards uses a particularly long and striking zoom shot when adopting the point of view of the episode's villain of the week, a paranoid stand-up comic.[40] As the comedian performs his act, we see the audience from his perspective, fixating on two audience members who appear to be talking to one another. Whispers, imagined by the comic, flood the soundtrack while the camera zooms in for an extreme close-up on the conversing audience members. In another *Peter Gunn* episode, "Wings of an Angel" (April 1960), Edwards uses the zoom to creep from a medium close-up to an extreme close-up as a character delivers a menacing line of dialogue.[41] In these moments, the zoom serves a similar function to the isolated zooms seen in "Time of Delivery" and "Eloise," emphasizing for the audience particularly important aspects of the narrative. However, Edwards also finds more prosaic uses for the zoom: for example, "The Comic" opens with a zoom onto a poster that displays a picture of him performing. From this point forward, we increasingly see zooms used in establishing shots and at other moments of lesser dramatic significance.

On a different show, Edwards performed bolder experiments with the stylistic potential of the zoom. The *Mr. Lucky* episode "The Brain Picker" (February 1960) opens with an establishing long shot of the protagonist's floating restaurant, moored underneath a bridge with its neon sign flashing.[42] A long, slow zoom—lasting about eight seconds—tightens the framing on the restaurant. This is followed by a cut to the inside of the restaurant for the scene's dialogue, after which the opening zoom is repeated in reverse—on this occasion, signaling the passage of time, as the next shot returns to the interior of the floating restaurant later that evening. Here the zoom acts more traditionally as a stylistic technique than in the previous examples. But it is important to note that not all establishing and reestablishing shots in this episode are made using the zoom lens; the zoom is also not used to accentuate other camera movements in, for example, a fight scene.

Sydney Pollack's television work shows uses of the zoom that are substantially similar to those described earlier. But he too advances more complicated and stylish uses of the zoom, the earliest of which appear in "Diagnosis Danger" (March 1963), an episode of *The Alfred Hitchcock Hour*.[43] The episode concerns the spread of anthrax, emanating from an animal-hide drum imported from Africa. Sharp zooms appear four times in the episode. On the first occasion, it "tags" the drum as significant and draws the audience's attention to it. On subsequent occasions, it reinforces the significance of the object as it moves around the city. These zooms are motivated by narrative alone, but those that appear in "The Dark Labyrinth" (March 1963), an episode of *Alcoa Premiere* that follows a group of tourists into a fabled underground cave, have a more psychological motivation.[44] Here, Pollack combines zooms with abrupt handheld camera movements to simulate both the physical perturbations caused by an earthquake and the fear and anguish of the tourists trapped underground. A sharp zoom onto the face of a screaming male character is followed immediately by a matching and intensifying zoom onto the face of his terrified female companion. The visceral sense of terror this combination of devices creates is quite unlike anything seen in the aforementioned examples.

Pollack again uses the zoom to imitate psychological disruption in an episode of *Breaking Point*, "Solo for B-Flat Clarinet" (September 1963).[45] The attention of a troubled character, a clarinetist named Jason Landros, is depicted through a long zoom to the profilmic artifact on which he is fixated—in this case, the nameplate on the consulting room of a doctor whom he wishes to visit. This demonstration of Landros's interiority is matched to an immediately preceding scene in which he appears to suffer a breakdown and interrupts a church service by playing his clarinet from the balcony. The shock of the congregation at the disturbance is conveyed by a sharp high-angle zoom from their perspective onto Landros, high above on the balcony. Thus in these scenes, zooms stand for Landros's mental disturbance. One conveys others' shock at witnessing it, while the other conveys Landros's disrupted patterns of thought.

One of Pollack's most interesting uses of the zoom shot, which differentiates itself from the isolated examples described previously, can be seen in an episode of *Ben Casey*.[46] In "A Cardinal Act of Mercy, Part 1" (August 1963), "Dr. Casey tries to help a woman lawyer kick her morphine habit, but encounters resistance, lies and manipulation when she gets a young man, who is unaware of what is going on, to smuggle some dope into her hospital room. The young man is visiting his mother, who is in the hospital for treatment of injuries received in a beating."[47] Pollack uses the zoom shot to articulate a key moment during the episode that reestablishes the link between two characters and focuses attention simultaneously on the lawyer's professional skills and the vulnerability of the elderly patient in the next bed. The two women are separated by a curtain. As a police detective enters the ward, the camera moves from the lawyer's side to the elderly lady's side. We see the detective question her. Then as she begins to give her account of the assault she suffered, we cut to a shot from the side of the bed. At first, this takes in both the victim and the detective, but the camera immediately begins to zoom forward, enlarging the characters before ultimately zooming "past" them, filling the screen with the curtain that separates them from the lawyer in the next bed. As soon as the curtain fills the screen, Pollack cuts to a shot of the lawyer sitting up in bed and eavesdropping on the conversation. Here, the zoom serves to reinstate the spatial connection between the two women, transgressing the physical boundary imposed by the curtain. For the viewer, the zoom "through" the curtain emphasizes that although the scene features two actors who barely interact with one another and are separated by a curtain, the action takes place within a single space. Pollack's use of the zoom here is representative of how, in the early 1960s, television directors increasingly used zoom shots in combination with other forms of camera movement in order to convey emotional and psychological effects. In both their complexity and their integration with other forms of camera movement, these zooms are entirely different from the tentative experimentations occasionally seen in live anthology drama.

Most accounts of the development of the zoom lens describe the 1960s as the decisive decade in its adoption, but as this chapter has demonstrated, there is a strong case to be made that the crucial developments—both technological and stylistic—were made during the 1950s. It was during that decade that the market for zoom lenses was disrupted by the introduction of serious transatlantic competition. For the first time, inventors in the United States and Europe offered to the market designs that competed within the same range of technical characteristics. At the beginning of the 1950s, the market for zoom lenses had been dominated by Zoomar, which offered a narrow product range of bulky zoom lenses for studio cameras used on live television broadcasts. By the end of the decade, cinematographers could choose from more compact and flexible lenses produced by multiple manufacturers and designed for 16mm filming. The intervention of Paillard, and their marketing of SOM-Berthiot lenses, broke a de facto monopoly that might otherwise have stifled innovation and competition throughout the 1960s. Yet the introduction of Pan Cinor lenses must not be seen in exclusively technological terms. Every Pan Cinor imported to the United States offered another director or cinematographer the opportunity to become acquainted with zoom lens technology and to experiment with the stylistic attractions of the zoom shot. Zoom lenses designed for 16mm cameras meant that the zoom was no longer a tool of necessity, useful mostly in live news or sports: zooms began to appear in the growing volume of television drama and comedy originated on film. Filmed television could be rehearsed, and film zoom lenses were smaller and easier to manipulate than those designed for television. Shows like *All Star Golf* and *Night Court* are only two of a great many shows that benefited from the efficiency, spontaneity, and flexibility of the zoom, while more ambitious directors of filmed television dramas began to explore the device's psychological and spatial opportunities, often zooming to immerse audiences in the psychological torment of their characters. From the audience's perspective, however, the most striking experiments with zoom lenses lay ahead. As the next chapter explains, it was the introduction of the Angénieux 10:1 lens in 1962 that ultimately enabled truly dramatic zoom shots. Yet without the enabling developments of the 1950s, the "zoom boom" of the 1960s could not have taken place.

5 · CREEPERS AND NECK-SNAPPERS

A low-key announcement in the September 1962 edition of *American Cinematographer*, which noted that the camera manufacturer Arriflex was selling "a new zoom lens for Arriflex 16—the Angénieux Model 120—which zooms from 12mm to 120mm focal length," gave little clue of the transformation that was soon to take place in the zoom lens market.[1] Though the zoom was an increasingly well-established technique by the beginning of the 1960s, especially in television, until December 1962, the promotion and discussion of zoom technology in *American Cinematographer* had been relatively inconspicuous. Throughout 1963, by contrast, the magazine was full of articles and advertisements promoting the arrival of the zoom. Subscribers opening the January 1963 edition were met with a full-page advertisement covering the magazine's first page, with large lettering proclaiming the arrival of a "10 to 1 zoom!" The rest of the page consisted of a prose description of the benefits of the new lens, including "dramatic focal length range . . . double that of any lens previously available, at any price"; "superb optics . . . a lens of unparalleled utility and perfection"; and "gear-driven zoom movement [which] gives the cameraman precisely controlled, exceptionally smooth zooms."[2] Not since the appearance of the Varo in 1932 had zoom lenses attracted such hype in the cinematography trade press.

During the 1960s, a broader, more active market for zoom lenses and associated technologies led to more creative uses of the technology. The French company Angénieux introduced a zoom lens that was longer and more versatile than any that had come before. Meanwhile, engineers and camera operators developed ways to operate zoom lenses electromechanically, creating smoother, more precise zooms. Gradually, using a zoom lens on a feature film set was becoming an easier and more familiar option. As a result, zoom shots—which had rarely been seen in 1950s features—became an increasingly common sight in feature films and a mainstay of filmed television. In turn, this provoked an intense debate over how the zoom should and should not be used. There was a conflict between those who wished to use the zoom more extensively and those who felt that it was contrary to traditional forms of visual storytelling. Many directors and cinematographers made extensive and creative use of zoom shots, but when talking about their techniques in the trade press, they generally discussed the practice in disapproving terms—as evidenced by the frequency with which words and concepts such as *misused, overused,* and *zoom-happy* appear. By the late 1960s, there was an increasingly wide gulf between how creatives described their zoom shots and how these shots appeared in films. As this chapter discusses, films like *Planet of the Apes, Camelot,* and *The Thomas Crown Affair* reflect Hollywood's confused and often contradictory approach to the zoom. These examples are symptomatic of the friction that occurs when changing technologies begin to disrupt stylistic norms, and in the 1960s, few technologies were more disruptive to visual style than the zoom lens.

The roots of the adoption of the zoom lens for feature films lie in the late 1950s. As the previous chapter demonstrates, this was the decade in which zoom lens technology spread from television to film. The arrival in the United States of French-made Pan Cinor zoom lenses broke Zoomar's dominance, creating a more diverse and competitive market for zoom lenses. In 1957, the introduction of a 35mm version of the Pan Cinor 60 further broadened the potential uses of the zoom lens in both television and feature film production. By the end of the decade, feature films such as *Odds Against Tomorrow* (Robert Wise, 1959), *-30-* (Jack Webb, 1959), *Studs Lonigan* (Irving Lerner, 1960), and *Hell to Eternity* (Phil Karlson, 1960) were making substantial use of the technology. *Odds Against Tomorrow,* in particular, broke ground by using the zoom in an adventurous and creative manner that had not been seen before in feature production. "We used the zoom lens quite often, not as an instrument to obtain magnification or to approximate traveling shots, but as an editorial medium corresponding to a progressive fast or slow switch of image format, or as a rythmic [*sic*] element in combination with sound and dialogue," explained Joseph Brun, the film's director of photography.[3] Brun's description accurately reflects the zoom shots that appear in the film, which show significant variety in their style and motivation. Zooms that "switch . . . image format"—by which Brun means shot scale—gradually close in on targets, including a messenger making a cash delivery to a bank and a moving bus. Several times, the zoom is used as part of an eyeline match shot to demonstrate that a character's attention has been drawn to an object or subject, anticipating similar techniques found in film and television produced late into the following decade.[4] These zooms are performed at a relatively slow pace, but as the film's narrative intensifies, zooms become more rapid—quickly moving toward one of the bank robbers as he is discovered by a

FIGURE 5.1. Lavishly used in *Odds Against Tomorrow* (Robert Wise, 1959), in this scene, the zoom emphasizes a doorway that has caught the attention of Johnny Ingram (Harry Belafonte).

police officer and zooming down toward the face of Johnny Ingram (Harry Belafonte) as he climbs a ladder in the film's climactic scene.

Zoom lenses were also used on the set of *-30-*, which was shot by *Dragnet* cinematographer Ed Colman. Zoom lenses helped overcome some of the limitations imposed by working on a single set with few moveable walls: "A zoom lens was employed in conjunction with the dolly-mounted camera to 'lengthen out' some dolly shots where it was not feasible to dolly past a certain point. For example, a scene would start with a long shot and the camera would then dolly-in a far as possible, until blocked by a desk or other object. As the dolly eased to a stop, the zoom lens operator would take over, picking up the forward movement and continuing to push in to a big closeup. A sharp camera crew was essential to achieving such a transition with smoothness and subtlety."[5]

American Cinematographer's account of the film's production contains revealing hints about ways of using the zoom lens that, by this time, had become normal practice: "In other instances the zoom lens—which had a range from 38mm to 170mm—was used in the conventional manner. At several points in the story the camera is framed on a group. A particular story point is made and the lens is zoomed in for a closeup to show the expression on the face of a player reacting to some action or passage in the dialogue."[6] Nevertheless, the article is not

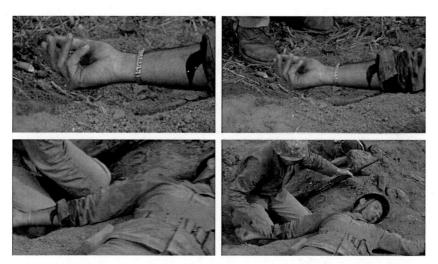

FIGURE 5.2. The zoom moves toward the wristwatch of a slain soldier in *Hell to Eternity* (Phil Karlson, 1960).

unequivocal in its appreciation of the zoom. In common with the cautious tone set by Joseph V. Mascelli in 1957, the author warns readers of the drawbacks of this technology: "Despite the notable results achieved with a zoom lens on this production, Colman is well aware that a zoom is no panacea for photographic problems on the set. He points out that most zoom lenses are tricky to operate smoothly, have several unfortunate technical shortcomings, and are often misused. A major disadvantage, he says, is that zooms have an inherent 'flatness' which produces an effect on the screen very much like that of zooming in on a still photograph."[7]

Zoom shots continued to make brief appearances in feature films in 1960—sometimes used for momentary special effects shots; at other times, they made more substantial contributions to visual style. In *Studs Lonigan*, a zoom shot follows "a struck ball across the table and into a corner pocket,"[8] while in the Pacific-theatre-set war drama *Hell to Eternity*, the zoom provided for flexible and mobile filming of action sequences. In addition to two standard cameras, a "third camera, mounting a 'zoom' lens, followed Hayakawa and his men as they moved about the set. Three men manned this camera: an operator, one assistant controlling the 'zoom' handle and the other pulling the focus."[9] *Hell to Eternity* applies the zoom to one moment of particular dramatic significance—a zoom out from the hand of a dying soldier—in addition to occasionally using the zoom to demonstrate spatial context around large groups of Japanese soldiers. The occasional, tentative uses of the zoom lens echo those seen in the late 1920s: in both instances, directors and cinematographers were cautiously finding their way with a new and relatively unfamiliar technology for which creative norms were not yet established.

THE ANGÉNIEUX 10:1 ZOOM

Despite the arrival of the Pan Cinor zooms for 35mm cameras, the zoom shot remained a relatively rare sight in features in the late 1950s. This was soon to change dramatically, thanks to the arrival in the United States of a 10:1 zoom lens manufactured by the French firm Angénieux. This lens was to become the first zoom used extensively in feature production work. Its arrival heralded the "zoom boom" of the 1960s, with which the zoom became most closely and notoriously associated.

Angénieux was founded in 1936 by Pierre Angénieux, a veteran of the film industry whose career began with collaborations with camera manufacturer André Debrie and director Abel Gance.[10] Though Angénieux's first major contribution to the zoom lens market did not occur until 1963, when their new 10:1 lenses for 16mm and 35mm filming were introduced, the firm had been developing zooms since the mid-1950s. Their first model, a 17–68mm lens designed for 16mm cameras and distributed in the United States from around 1958, was a direct response to, and competitor for, existing Zoomar and Pan Cinor lenses.[11] This 4:1 lens had been under development since 1953 in a process that overlapped a major technological change in lens design practice: computers were becoming small enough and affordable enough for medium-sized businesses to own. In the United States, Zoomar—where Frank Back and his colleagues had previously toiled with slide rules and tables of logarithms—had benefited from the purchase of a Burroughs E101. In France, Angénieux's research and development efforts were boosted by the purchase of a Gamma 3 computer. For Angénieux, the ability to perform complex calculations at high speed opened the door for a new approach to lens design. Angénieux zoom lenses were mechanically compensated, relying—like Joseph Walker's zoom lens in the 1920s—on precision assemblies of cams and gears to manipulate the glass elements within the lens barrel.[12] The underlying calculations were fearsomely complex, but computers helped make them feasible. The payoff was faster, more robust zooms that were cheaper to design and manufacture. The 17–68mm zoom lens—the first zoom lens to be brought to market by Angénieux—was a commercial success. Thousands of copies were sold, despite its slightly inferior optical performance when compared with its Pan Cinor competitor.[13]

From around 1962, after eight years of research and development, Angénieux began to manufacture a new zoom lens in two versions: a 12–120mm model for 16mm filming, with a maximum aperture of $f/2.2$, and a 25–250mm model for 35mm cameras, with a maximum aperture of $f/3.2$. The versions were identical in their basic design, consisting of fourteen optical elements arranged in ten groups. This was far less glass than the Zoomar lenses of the 1940s, enabling greater light transmission and higher optical quality. The new lens was to have a transformative effect on the zoom's place in cinematographic technique, but the timing of its introduction was somewhat serendipitous. When Angénieux began to develop the lens in the 1950s, the firm had the amateur 16mm filming market in mind. By the time the project came to fruition, 8mm cameras had largely replaced the larger gauge in the amateur market. "The result was that our plan to make a great many zoom lenses for the 16mm amateur market never materialized. However that was probably the best thing that could have happened to us, because now we are essentially involved in supplying optics for the professionals," Bernard Angénieux later explained.[14] For 16mm cameras, the lens was produced in two essential designs. One had an integrated reflex viewfinder enabling a camera operator or director to monitor framing and focus even if the lens was mounted on a nonreflex camera. The other, without the additional weight and expense of a viewfinder, was designed for reflex cameras. For both film formats, the lens was produced in a range of further variations to make them compatible with the various cameras already on the market, including variations to fit Paillard, Bell & Howell, Auricon, Cineflex, and Cameflex cameras as well as for vidicon television cameras.[15]

Cinematographers were now able to use a zoom lens with a far longer range of focal lengths, but devices designed to make zooming smoother and more convenient were slower to appear. Zoom motors had been developed, but they were of limited sophistication and versatility. In the mid-1950s, Zoomar had advertised a zoom lens "with two flexible shafts attached which can be connected to remote manual or electric controls"; the company also sold "miniature D.C. motors" to accompany the lens.[16] RCA's Electra-Zoom could be also controlled by electric motor. Meanwhile, Arriflex developed a similar product to provide operators with "finger-tip convenience of zoom operation that results in smooth, readily duplicated zooms." The unit permitted operators to set a zoom speed in advance and then zoom in and out at that speed, but the device did not allow changes in zooming speed during operation.[17] The need for electronic zooming was recognized by at least one major studio. In late 1962, MGM had announced that after fourteen months of research and development, it had created an "electric motor drive with remote control ... for [35mm] zoom lenses." The device, developed by camera assistant Paul Koons, was designed to automate the rendition of zooms based on presets, with multi-take Hollywood production processes in mind. Koons described how "it is mistake proof. . . . After initial pre-setting, it repeats its 'custom' operation for as many takes as desired."[18] Koons's invention initially found use in the production of films including *The Courtship of Eddie's*

Father (Vincente Minelli, 1963) and *It Happened at the World's Fair* (Norman Taurog, 1963). This advance, however, was not mirrored in the products available outside of the studio.

Despite the shortcomings of zoom motors and other similar controls, advertisements for Angénieux's 10:1 lenses nevertheless encouraged their buyers to be adventurous in their zooming. The earliest advertisement for the lens in *American Cinematographer* paid particular attention to the dramatic focal length range and smoothness of the zooming action, suggesting an intended use for zooms that would be visible to the audience rather than purely as a substitute for a range of fixed focal length lenses. This advertisement was typical of the content of zoom lens advertisements in the earliest days of the Angénieux 10:1 lenses. The central illustration of a Bach Auricon advertisement featuring the lens is a row of three stylized "frames" showing the progressive enlargement of a model holding a camera with Angénieux zoom lens mounted, again implying the dynamic usage of the lens. Equipment companies started to develop more complex ways to make zooming easier. An advertisement placed by the Camera Equipment Company showed an operator looking through the viewfinder and using a handle to operate the zoom movement, noting that "all lenses come equipped with a zoom crank for slow travel effects and a zoom lever for rapid zoom effects."[19] The same company also marketed a motorized accessory enabling zooming at various preset speeds.[20] Another firm advertised a "dramatically new 12mm/120mm zoom lens with [Camera Service Center] zoom control knob" and also offered "support brackets and zoom correlators," which "line up the mechanical and optical lens axes so they coincide to produce perfect zooms."[21] By 1964, General Camera Corporation had developed a more sophisticated zoom motor, which "allows 2 second neck snappers or 50 second creepers. Just preset your zoom range and speed and make the exact same zoom time after time—or—use the variable speed rheostat and change speeds while zooming with complete control. 'V' belt drive gives smooth starts and zooms to a glide stop with no end slowdown or bump."[22] Thus zoom lenses, which had barely been discussed in *American Cinematographer* before 1963, were suddenly thrust into the center of the trade discourse. Most of the suggestions about their use came in the form of paid advertisements, which unsurprisingly painted a rosy picture of the value of the zoom lens and encouraged filmmakers to enliven their images with zoom shots. Professional cinematographers, by contrast, were more wary about the attractions of the newly potent zoom lens.

ZOOM STYLE IN THE 1960S

The "buzz" created by advertisements may have been somewhat artificial, but it provoked a genuine debate about the value of the zoom shot. At the exact midpoint of the 1960s, in July 1965, *American Cinematographer* printed a highly unusual article—a lengthy and almost entirely positive essay on the creative potential of the zoom lens. Written by Panavision cofounder Richard Moore, the article—titled "New Uses For Zoom Lenses"—painted an optimistic picture of the future of film and television cinematography, calling attention to "a wealth of new ideas and techniques with which to help recapture the theatre-going audience" and advocating that "the cinematographer, as the most important man on any movie set, must be the leader in accepting these new ideas and techniques." Making a case study of the zoom lens (of which Moore reported hearing "a distressing amount of adverse criticism . . . from first cameramen down through film loaders"), Moore argued, "The zoom lens is a rather exotic piece of equipment, which must be understood to be used effectively. The most common complaint lodged against them is that zooms, in the hands of an unsophisticated director, are over-worked. Certainly, in the tv commercial field, the zoom effect is used to the point of being ridiculous. . . . But when used with discretion, a zoom shot can produce sensational effects." Moore makes the case for zooms of all speeds, from low-speed zooms combined with helicopter shots, to "medium speed zooms . . . to gain an effect that no amount of dolly track or cranes could produce," to the "undeniably startling effect" produced by fast zooms. He dismisses concerns about changes in perspective caused by zoom shots and reassures his audience about the resolving power of modern zoom lenses—drawing particular attention to the "remarkable degree of acutance" of Panavision and Angénieux zooms, which he describes as so sharp that "they can be left on the camera permanently and used as a lens with an infinite number of fixed focal lengths." As evidence for the versatility of the zoom, Moore cites the "countless tv commercials, a series of half-hour tv shows, and numerous features" on which he has used it, giving a particularly detailed account of the zoom's utility as a substitute for a set of prime lenses during the production of *Operation CIA* (Christian Nyby, 1965): "Fully 20 per cent of this picture was shot with the Arri and the Angenieux zoom, yet there are only three actual zoom shots in the entire film. I found that leaving the zoom lens on the camera at all times was of tremendous value since it facilitated grabbing shots that would otherwise be lost. With the zoom lens I could get just the right framing or image size with a simple turn of the wrist rather than shifting lenses or moving and re-leveling the camera." Moore concluded his article with a plea to cinematographers unconvinced by the value of the zoom: "Don't close your mind to the zoom. It opens up terrific opportunities for exciting and dramatic photography, and anything that does that is worth the best effort on the part of any cinematographer."[23]

This was not a position shared by all in the film industry. In a letter published in the next edition of *American Cinematographer*, Hal Mohr—American Society of Cinematographers (ASC) president from 1963 to 1965—responded to Richard Moore's article:

> [He] has presented some very cogent and valid suggestions for extending the usefulness of zoom lenses, but I don't think that the zoom's inherent dangers can be dismissed with a simple "So what?" For whenever focal lengths of lenses are changed at a fixed camera position, there will be a compression effect between the foreground subject and background. . . . This is particularly annoying in the case of definable background, such as a row of building columns, and it is more obvious to the viewer when done continuously with a zoom, than when the same thing is done with a series of cuts.[24]

On top of these problems, Mohr described as "disastrous" the visual effects caused by camera operators who chose to use the full range of recently introduced 10:1 zoom lenses. Another article, published a year after Moore's, complained that the use of zoom lenses as a substitute for physical movement of the camera reduced the "fluidity" of cinematography: "Zoom lenses, while extremely useful in certain situations and for specific effects, should not be used as a lazy man's substitute for dolly or trucking shots. When misused in this way the effect is much like that of progressively cropping in on a still picture and there is a certain sterile flatness to the result that the more dramatic cinematographer finds unaesthetic."[25]

In common with the industrial debates highlighted throughout this book, these articles reflect a range of attitudes toward the zoom. For the first time, however, we begin to see the degree to which directors of photography were flexible in their attitudes toward the zoom—and not always honest in their descriptions of how they used it. Decisions about whether to use the zoom were finely balanced between considerations of practicality and stylistic effect. They were also subject to the—often contrasting—opinions of directors, directors of photography, and other personnel working in film production. Dogma in the trade press gave way to pragmatism on set. An isolated example of this can be seen by drawing a comparison between two films: *Hud* and *The Outrage*, both directed by Martin Ritt and both shot under the supervision of James Wong Howe. Despite having senior creative personnel in common and being produced in quick succession, each film adopts a different approach to the zoom shot. In *Hud*, the technique is not used, even where there is a clear practical justification for doing so. As Howe told *American Cinematographer*,

> Some of [the] interiors were so small that we had to use a wide-angle lens to get any sort of establishing shot. We didn't use too many dolly shots inside—nor did

the director want to use a zoom lens as a substitute, which may seem surprising since he comes from live TV. He simply has found that the zoom lens has been overworked. I don't care for it either because it produces just a flat frame coming toward you. In a zoom shot the perspective is static—the camera doesn't pass anything and you have no sense of true movement. It is just a set composition being blown up larger by degrees.[26]

However, only eleven months later, after serving as Ritt's cinematographer on *The Outrage*, it seemed that Howe had changed his mind. As *American Cinematographer* observed, "While both Howe and director Ritt normally dislike using zoom lenses because of the perspective they create, there are several sequences in *The Outrage* where the zoom lens was used in combination with dolly and pan movement to create certain desired visual effects."[27] Despite Howe's justification for the appearance of the zoom in *The Outrage*, the effects he mentions do not seem carefully chosen with a consistent motivation in mind. In stark contrast to *Hud*, the zoom appears at least ten times during the course of the film, most often as a convenient means of altering shot scale, with occasional "shock zooms." The "appropriate" use of a zoom was a flexible notion that depended on the circumstances surrounding shooting and the nature of the relationship between director and cinematographer.

By the late 1960s, zooms were increasingly used as the standard lens on a camera, and we see an increasing number of accounts of their use in the production of high-profile films. Caught between the competing interests of efficiency, artistic integrity, and industrial norms, directors and cinematographers performed myriad rhetorical contortions in an attempt to justify their uses of a

FIGURE 5.3. A dramatic zoom rushes toward Colonel Wakefield (Laurence Harvey) as he takes his own life in *The Outrage* (Martin Ritt, 1964).

novel and controversial technique. Reports of the production of *Camelot, Planet of the Apes, The Thomas Crown Affair*, and *Mirage* demonstrate how industrial descriptions of the application of the zoom sometimes diverge from the evidence of the films themselves. In 1968, an *American Cinematographer* article about the filming of *Camelot* (Joshua Logan, 1967) remarked approvingly that "although the camera seems to move fluidly throughout the production, there are only four actual dolly shots in the entire roadshow-length film."[28] Describing the shooting, Herb Lightman explained, "First up were the Forest sequences . . . to be filmed in a man-made woodland glade. . . . It was a magnificent set—with only one serious drawback: there were no 'wild' trees. They were all more or less permanently anchored in the floor, leaving no place to lay dolly tracks. Here again [cinematographer] Kline was forced to manipulate the zoom lens in lieu of genuine moving camera shots, but the method worked so well that he continued to use it throughout the filming—which accounts for the fact that there are only four genuine dolly shots in the entire picture."[29] As in the early 1960s, the zoom remained a device whose use must be justified by personnel, but zoom shots and "fluid" camerawork were no longer seen as mutually exclusive. By the end of the decade, creative personnel had developed more nuanced ways of discussing their use of zoom shots. The film's director of photography, Richard H. Kline, reported to Lightman that "on almost every shot we made, with the exception of close-ups, there was some shift in image size called for and we were able to execute this smoothly with the zoom lens. I like using it this way as an 'adjustment' lens, rather than for shock value—as it is often mis-used. . . . the best usage of the zoom is in conjunction with the movement of actors in the scene. The adjustment of image size and the movement of players 'synchronize'—so to speak—so that the audience is unaware of the technique being used."[30]

Similar logic was applied to location shooting of *The Thomas Crown Affair* (Norman Jewison, 1968), where zoom lenses were used to film a scene in which the protagonists flee a bank robbery. The director of photography, Haskell Wexler, explains how a camera "equipped with zoom lens, was located in a doorway across the street. With that camera we were able to get the movement of cars and people walking close to the camera in the foreground and, as the robbers came out of the bank, the operator was able to tighten the composition with his zoom—thus maintaining the feeling of the street, while concentrating interest on the action."[31] Similarly, Leon Shamroy describes zoom shots in *Planet of the Apes* (Franklin J. Schaffner, 1968) in terms of their careful and discriminating selection. Shamroy utilized a "simple, clean and direct style—with no obvious tricks to mar the realism of what is essentially an unreal subject. . . . He did use a 10-to-1 zoom lens in a few selected scenes, but he even has certain reservations about that often-convenient instrument."[32] *American Cinematographer's* approving account of Shamroy's restraint emphasizes the value of the zoom as a time saver but restates once more the perils of attempting to use it as a replacement for real camera movement.

Edward Dmytryk expresses a similar view in the course of an extensive interview about his relationship with various directors. Dmytryk said, "I wish we'd had the zoom lens a long time ago, actually. I consider it an extremely effective piece of equipment. However, I believe it should probably be used very infrequently. People are going 'zoom lens-happy' as they always do with any new technique, and it's kind of silly." Dmytryk used the zoom in *Mirage* (1965) to simulate a camera move across a street that could not be closed to allow for the laying of dolly track. This "move," the director maintained, was concealed from the audience and thus different from other more "dramatic" zooms that appear in the film: "Since [Gregory Peck's] image remained constant you weren't really aware of the difference in perspective as far as the background was concerned, which is, of course, the difference between a zoom and a dolly shot. Then when he got to the other side of the street, we were able to pan with him and follow him down the street. It made a very effective shot which I couldn't have got in any other way, except by putting my camera on wheels. That's one valid usage."[33] In these reports and interviews, Kline, Wexler, Shamroy, and Dmytryk all emphasize the continuity, appropriateness, and concealed nature of the zoom in the films they work on. These cinematographers are attempting to wrest control of the zoom from colleagues in television, news filming, and industrial production. With no authority over newsreel cameramen and no direct influence over amateur cinematographers, they attempt to define what might be described as a "quality," or "Hollywood," zoom. This would be a smooth, cautious zoom. It would be used not as a shock effect but as a tool of efficiency and convenience, justified by the professionalism, restraint, and finesse with which it was employed. As described in the pages of *American Cinematographer*, these films ought to offer a style guide for the director of photography newly possessed of a zoom lens but unsure of how to use it.

However, the films in question show very different applications of the zoom to those described by their chief cameramen: they were more obtrusive and less adeptly concealed. *Camelot* includes some quite abrupt zooms that—though they coincide with camera or actor movement—are made more noticeable through this coincidence. An early scene in which Arthur (Richard Harris) jumps off a tree is a case in point, as are some of the zooms in the May Day dancing scene, and the extreme zoom toward Lancelot (Franco Nero) on his first introduction. *The Thomas Crown Affair* includes scenes in which the zoom does not simply "tighten the composition" but radically alters the space depicted by the camera. For example, a shot of a police interrogation room begins with a close-up on the face of a witness wearing a green dress before zooming back to reveal progressively more of her surroundings, placing her on an intermediate image plane, and finally—in conjunction with a tilt and pan—decentering and marginalizing her. The zoom is similarly handled in *Mirage*: the dolly substitute that Dmytryk describes is present (though not as smoothly executed as he would wish his colleagues believe), but so are a number of sharp, high-ratio, emphatic zooms at a number of key points during the narrative. While Dmytryk desires to stress the skill with which he accomplished the difficult task of integrating the zoom into his camerawork, its latter appearances are far more significant to the overall style of the film. The substitute zoom serves the needs of the mobile frame; the later zooms connect with the troubled mind of David Stillwell (Gregory Peck), the apparently hallucinating protagonist.

But it is in *Planet of the Apes* that the most substantial difference between the cinematographer's account and the final film can be found. Shamroy claims to have had "reservations" about the zoom and complains of its overuse. The article that reports these views describes "a few selected scenes" in which the zoom is used. Yet *Planet of the Apes* contains numerous prominent zoom shots. It opens on a zoom and closes on a series of zooms. As the narrative progresses, zooms appear in the service of a variety of effects: to articulate shock (the discovery that Stewart has died during the voyage), to introduce new characters (the entrance of Dr. Zaius), to adopt the perspective of other characters (Zira's viewpoint as Taylor shaves his beard), and for less "motivated" reframings such as the zoom toward the plant and the repeated zooms toward trees during the initial chase scenes.

In the later years of the 1960s, the zoom shot was thus a technique fraught with contradictions. For more than a decade, zoom lenses had been improving in quality and utility. After a slow start following the introduction of Pan Cinor lenses, which offered a zoom ratio of only 4:1, Angénieux's 10:1 zooms captured the market. Like no zoom lenses before, they were able to reach from a wide angle to telephoto and stop at every focal length in between. This enabled unprecedented transformations of the image captured on film, and advertisements for Angénieux's lenses encouraged camera operators not to use their new equipment merely as a variable prime but to create visual impact via dynamic zoom shots. This, however, was hardly conducive to the self-effacing mode of direction and cinematography traditionally preferred in Hollywood features. Cinematographers found unfamiliar zoom shots self-conscious and gimmicky and did their best to circumscribe their use. Yet even films made by cinematographers who professed to dislike the zoom—or insisted on using it with subtlety or restraint—inflected their cinematography with unmistakable zoom shots. It was as a result of these films that some filmmakers began to suspect the emergence of a cinematic style that was too reliant on the zoom. However, if this change had been the responsibility of directors of photography, they managed to escape some of the blame. Instead, much of it fell onto the shoulders of a different group: young directors whose careers had begun in television and, during the 1960s, migrated to work on features.

TWO DIRECTORS, MANY ZOOMS

As Warren Buckland has argued, the landscape of influences on 1960s and 1970s filmmaking was complex, encompassing European "New Wave" art cinemas, the New York school of filmmaking, and technological developments relating to handheld filming. But foremost in his account of the period is the observation that "a number of directors . . . exchanged TV directing for Hollywood feature filmmaking in the 1960s and, by doing so, transformed its aesthetics and working practices."[34] The growing use of the zoom shot was one such transformation, and TV Generation directors such as John Frankenheimer, Robert Mulligan, Sydney Pollack, and Robert Altman were among the most important figures in this development. When accounting for their own artistic influences, some of these directors have given significant credit to their television careers. Interviewed in 2000, Frankenheimer claimed, "Everything I've ever done in film is directly a result of my live television experience. The way I move the camera, the way I frame the shot, the way I work with actors, the way I work with writers, and the rhythm at which I work. Everything. I owe everything to live television."[35] The previous chapter examined the ways in which prominent directors used the zoom in their television work; this chapter now considers their application of the zoom in film. Looking at their film work during the 1960s in the broader context of the decade, but with their previous television work in mind, we see a complex picture. While critics and cinematographers alike have attempted to argue that the zoom's rise in film can be attributed to the influence of television, the lack of clear continuity between these examples suggests that television's influence was not quite as direct.

John Frankenheimer was initially as cautious about using the zoom in filmed features as he had been when directing for television. Over the course of the 1960s, Frankenheimer's adoption of the zoom lens was gradual and tentative, but by *The Gypsy Moths*, he was using the technique in a manner unrecognizable from his television career. The application of the zoom shot at this point in Frankenheimer's career is more suggestive of a gradual organic development in style than of a sudden affectation, and there is little evidence to support the assertion that Frankenheimer imported tried-and-tested zoom techniques from television to feature films.

Frankenheimer's approach to the zoom begins in a fashion similar to his work in television. In his second feature, *The Young Savages*, the zoom lens is used to adjust the framing of a sequence of images seen through binoculars. As in

Frankenheimer's *Playhouse 90* episode "Eloise," discussed in the preceding chapter, this is a solitary use of the zoom shot: the film is otherwise limited to shots of static focal length. Frankenheimer is little more adventurous in *All Fall Down*, in which the zoom appears twice, purely for framing reasons during a brief bowling alley sequence. A series of jump cuts from different focal lengths, in which Beatty's position relative to the background barely changes, suggests that a zoom lens may have been used as a substitute for prime lenses during the production of the film. *Birdman of Alcatraz* continues the limited approach, adopting the zoom on a few occasions to obtain close-ups of the protagonist's birds, but otherwise avoids the technique.[36] It is not until *The Manchurian Candidate* that dynamic zoom shots begin to make meaningful and more frequent appearances.

In *The Manchurian Candidate*, zoom shots take a form not noted in Frankenheimer's earlier television work, and in the films that follow, they are used in increasingly adventurous ways. The first zooms in the film, a pair of high-ratio but moderately paced zooms onto the faces of wounded soldiers as they are being loaded onto military helicopters, are straightforward emphases of profilmic significance. However, Frankenheimer subsequently zooms twice to reflect the perception of characters: once onto the face of Bennett Marco (Frank Sinatra) when he appears at the door in search of Chunjin (Henry Silver), and once again from Marco's perspective as he attempts to prevent the climactic shooting in the convention hall. The frequency and nature of the zoom shot in this film represents a subtle but significant departure from Frankenheimer's earlier practice: it is, apparently, his first use of the technique to represent the interior thoughts or perceptions of a character.

Seven Days in May adopts a similar approach to *The Manchurian Candidate* in its use of the zoom to simulate television footage and other forms of intradiegetic actuality—including, for example, surveillance footage of President Lyman (Fredric March) at his lake retreat. However, *Seven Days in May* is not stylistically identical to its precursor, as it is here that Frankenheimer first adopts the technique of zooming to "tag" significant people and items. Frankenheimer zooms twice onto the license plate of a car carrying General Scott (Burt Lancaster), once onto a note regarding the economy, and once onto a cigarette case. The identification of significant props and moments via the zoom is repeated in *The Train*, which features repeated zooms onto coins later used to block the oil pipe of a locomotive and subsequently onto timepieces to emphasize the "ticking clock" narrative device used to create tension during an early sequence. The film's narrative portrays the attempts of a French resistance agent (Burt Lancaster) to prevent a trainload of priceless artwork from being evacuated to Germany in the final days of the occupation of France. Much of the action takes place in and around the French railway system as weapons and human resources are moved out of the country amid Allied air raids. Constant physical movement of the camera is augmented by zooms that are used for a variety of purposes. One shot in particular, of Burt Lancaster scrambling up a hillside to escape from pursuing German soldiers in one of the film's final action sequences, has been isolated for comment by Kaminsky, who notes that this zoom "emphasise[s] smallness in relation to nature, then picks [Lancaster] out of that nature by [his] very movement to elevate [his] meaning in the landscape in one emphatic movement."[37]

This shot is arguably anomalous in the context of *The Train*, as the zoom in this film is more often used as a narrative device to call attention to significant objects or moments in the course of the narrative. This technique is particularly noticeable in the form of long zooms toward significant items in the narrative—in the most significant instance, a coin in the hand of railway engineer and resistance saboteur Papa Boule (Michel Simon). This zoom shot transforms the profilmic from a wide two-person shot to an extreme close-up on Boule's hand and cues the audience to understand that the coin will be significant. Later, a matching shot returns to the same coin, which has been jammed into the oil pipe of a Nazi train. Despite the zoom's prominence in this shot, the scene otherwise follows familiar and established editing conventions. In the second of these shots, an establishing wide view of the damaged train grinding to a halt at Rive-Reine station is followed by shots of a German officer running down the length of the train, followed by Papa Boule observing the broken pipework. Next a conversation between Boule and a German officer is shown using a standard shot/reverse shot editing pattern. Following the German officer's departure, a new three-quarter-back shot of Boule is introduced. Within this shot is interposed a close-up of Boule as he checks whether anyone is watching him. We return to the three-quarter-back shot to witness Boule removing the obstruction from the pipework, and a long rapid zoom to the franc piece in his hand transforms the composition. The earlier coin shot is part of a less complex piece of editing in which we cut to a moving camera shot that follows Boule to the bar counter; he receives his change, and we cut to the next scene. In both of these scenes, the zoom operates as the functional equivalent of cutting to a close-up, differing from the standard close-up only in the means of arriving at that position; furthermore, it is very clear that this scene adopts the classical convention of "'planting' and foreshadowing, of tagging traits and objects for future use."[38]

This example provides an initial demonstration of how zooms can be integrated into narrative convention and serve a function common to classical cinema and independent of the zoom itself. Here, the zoom's effect is to provide a more prominent and enhanced form of cut. By reserving its use for such moments and presenting a matched pair of zooms, the lens becomes a device capable, through its visual specificity, of structuring the audience's understanding

of the wider narrative. Rather than merely pointing out the momentary significance of an item or character, such shots refer more insistently to what has
come before and/or what is yet to come. After the first instance of such a paired
shot, the audience is cued by subsequent long zooms to understand that what
is being zoomed toward will have significance later. The film becomes, on one
level, a series of events bookended by zoom shots in which items of significance
take their place in the linear order of the narrative. Cuts, unless they are combined with some other visual or auditory manipulation, cannot easily achieve
this function. The zoom is therefore able simultaneously to replicate an existing
technique (the cut) while distinguishing itself from that function and carrying
wider meanings.

The Train offers one of the earliest examples of how the zoom lens can be a
technology that simultaneously conforms to, and offers a departure from, established modes of directing the attention of the audience as the cinematic narrative
unfolds. One opportunity to do so arises when the zoom is called on to articulate "a device in what's come to be called the classical Hollywood tradition . . .
the 'ticking clock.'"[39] Though the overall narrative is one of subterfuge and eva-
sion, an early episode of action depends for its drama on a "race against the
clock" in which Labiche must ensure that an important train is held up at a station that is due to suffer an air raid at precisely ten o'clock. The "ticking clock"
formulation is taken entirely literally by Frankenheimer, who shows the passing
of time through a number of deliberate shots of timepieces. The last of these, a
comparatively slow zoom-in on the wristwatch of a German officer as ten o'clock
strikes and the air raid commences, uses—and gains from—the extra dynamism
of the zoom action. The image in the frame expands slowly and steady, imitating
the advance of a third hand around a clockface, weighing out the last few
moments of orderly time before the air-raid siren and ensuing chaos. The profilmic result differs qualitatively from what may have been produced had the
shot been made by performing a dolly-in: it magnifies, rather than becomes
closer to, the subject, and it provides a contrast to the restless dynamism of
the earlier film. Here the zoom offers a different sort of dynamism, one that is
smoother and more controlled than physical movement, one that is editorial and
evokes an authorial choice about what action to pay attention to, rather than—as
in the film's other shots in busy moving environments—seeming to follow the
flow of the action. As in the previous example, the zoom-in overlaps and inter-
mingles with established modes of classical narration. In addition to substituting
for the close-up, it also reinforces the finality of the moment: communicating, in
another way, that the deadline has been reached.

Seconds, which has been retrospectively identified as forming a "paranoid
trilogy" along with The Manchurian Candidate and Seven Days in May, shows a

further gradual progression in Frankenheimer's adoption of the zoom shot. In his critical biography of James Wong Howe, Todd Rainsberger points out that the film's visual style was the result of a creative partnership between Howe and Frankenheimer, in which the cinematographer "took credit for the visual concept of the piece [and] Frankenheimer selected most of the camera positions."[40] What is not clear is under which of these categories the zoom shot might have fallen, though Howe's interview with Scott Eyman suggests that Frankenheimer pressed Howe to use the zoom.[41] And even though, as Rainsberger details, Howe and Frankenheimer fell out badly over "'gadgets' and camera trickery" during the filming of The Horsemen (1971), Howe was never averse to trying new techniques. In Seconds, "tagging" zooms remain in evidence (e.g., to the base of a tennis trophy on which the phrase "Fidelis Eternis" is inscribed and onto a significant newspaper report), but they are joined by frenetically edited scenes of a wild naked party and are punctuated by rapid zooms, which are further intensified by cutting close to (whether before or after) the zoom shots. This technique departs from Frankenheimer's previous style but is similar to applications by other TV Generation directors working at the same time—it also appears in festival scenes in What Did You Do in the War, Daddy? and party scenes in Pollack's The Slender Thread (1965, discussed later on).

"Tagging zooms," in the sense that they are used in The Train, Seconds, and Seven Days in May, are absent from The Gypsy Moths, but psychologically motivated zooms make brief appearances. They reflect the mounting concern of Mike Rettig (Burt Lancaster) as he notes blustery conditions prior to his parachuting display, and later, spectators' shock as he plummets to his death. At least part of the purpose of the earlier series of zooms is to suggest that Rettig may be in some peril. These zooms, like those used during the "naked dancing" sequence in Seconds, are punctuated by rapid cuts between Lancaster's stolid face and increasingly wild panning/zooming shots of the audience and a fluttering windsock. The sequence mixes overt intrashot dynamic zooms with Rettig's gradually increasing scale in the frame. Bingham describes this sequence as a "series of French New Wave–style jump cuts of [Lancaster], broken up by a succession of shots that in effect stare off into space,"[42] and it is important to note, as Bingham does, the pacing of this brief sequence of shots: thirteen cuts between Rettig and his point of view in approximately twenty seconds, and the frequency of cutting intensifies as the sequence progresses.[43] The result is an arresting sequence out of keeping with the visual style of the rest of the film, which ties the zoom shot firmly to Rettig's concerns about the risks associated with parachute jumping. Having established this connection, Frankenheimer exploits the zoom at subsequent moments of crisis. After a series of successful jumps, Rettig's attempt to make a descent while wearing a complicated wingsuit ends in failure, and Frankenheimer uses a series of sharp zooms onto horrified spectators as Rettig free-falls onto the grass in front of them. This technique is further repeated as his colleague Malcolm Webson (Scott Wilson) hesitates before unfurling his parachute during the subsequent memorial display.

That there were very few zoom shots in Frankenheimer's early features is entirely consistent with the television style that he had developed in New York, where striking wide-angle compositions were far more common than zooms. It was in features, not television, that Frankenheimer developed a confident and carefully planned approach to zooms: by *The Gypsy Moths* (1969), he was using the technique in a manner unrecognizable not only from his television career but also from his earliest feature films. Despite this, he did not embrace the zoom lens in the manner of Altman or of early 1970s television. The application of the zoom shot at this point in Frankenheimer's career is more suggestive of a gradual organic development in style enabled by increasingly versatile zoom technology. Frankenheimer did not acquire a habit for the zoom in television and transplant it wholesale to film.

In the case of Sydney Pollack, the picture is different. Pollack's feature career began in the mid-1960s, several years after Frankenheimer's. Unlike those directors, Pollack's feature work contains numerous zoom shots from the get-go, and there is little coherence in their use from one film to the next. By the end of the decade, Pollack uses the zoom in a manner typical of that seen in mid-late 1960s cinema. In *This Property Is Condemned* and *They Shoot Horses, Don't They?* Pollack zooms in a calculated and thoughtful manner to express the internal thought processes of subjects; however, and in common with the majority of Frankenheimer's work throughout the decade, zooms also appear frequently in fulfilment of a wide range of functions—occasionally standing in for camera movement, sometimes evoking shock, and sometimes intensifying the pace of a sequence.

In Pollack's first feature, *The Slender Thread* (1965), which concerns the hunt for a suicidal Inga Dyson (Anne Bancroft) after she calls a telephone hotline manned by a volunteer (Sydney Poitier), zooms are most frequent in the opening titles and during the film as action becomes more frenetic. Particularly striking are a wild series of fast zooms during a nightclub scene, matching the brash drum-and-electric-guitar soundtrack and enthusiastic whooping of the crowd. Zooms also appear during a search sequence, purely to flag significant material to the audience, and again for the same reason when a character's attention is drawn to a newspaper headline. In common with examples from his television work, Pollack also uses the zoom to reflect the perception and/or location of Dyson, who while contemplating suicide on a beach is emotionally affected by the discovery of a small sand castle. The camera zooms to the sand castle when she first spots it before following Dyson to the sand castle, where she falls on her knees and empties a bottle of alcoholic drink over it. Later, a long zoom shows Dyson standing on a dockside as, in voiceover, she describes how she "even tried to get arrested, but everyone looked the other way." The zoom closes in on an isolated Dyson, but cinematography and context conspire to prevent the audience from feeling in any way closer to her. Though Dyson seems close, and we are not "looking the other way" as "everyone" did, the distancing quality of the telephoto zoom means that even in looking closely at her, we are unable to maintain any sense of proximity.

Pollack's approach to the zoom is somewhat different, and at its most interesting and complex, in *This Property Is Condemned*. The film was shot by James Wong Howe, teamed once more—as Rainsberger points out—"with a neophyte director." As with Frankenheimer's *Seconds*, Rainsberger detects a "schism" between cinematographer and director. Howe, he suggests, controlled the camera placements—but probably not its movement. As a result, Rainsberger suggests, "the film is filled with numerous short tracks and zooms which do not reveal anything new or even improve the composition."[44] But this seems to underestimate the subtle impact of the film's zoom shots. In *This Property Is Condemned*, zooms contribute significantly to the retrospective mood of the film. That the story is told in the past tense is clear from the outset: the narrative begins with a meeting between Willie Starr (Mary Badham) and a young boy, Tom (Jon Provost), during which Willie begins to recount the film's main narrative. But the retrospection is more organized, and inheres more deeply, than in this simple expository device. It can be seen in the opening scene in the form of Willie's dress and jewelry—an ill-fitting, poorly maintained red dress that she declares "belonged to her sister," and it further emerges when Willie's sister Alva (Natalie Wood) visits the cinema with Owen Legate (Robert Redford), where they watch *One Way Passage* (Tay Garnett, 1932). As the pair leaves the cinema, they discuss the film, and though framed as a reminiscence of the show, the narrative purpose of the conversation is to prefigure Alva's death, which the audience (and Alva herself) must already know is a potential resolution to the narrative:

OWEN: Crybaby.
ALVA: But it was so sad. You know, sometimes when I see a sad movie, I want to see the end again—just hoping it'll come out better the second time.
OWEN: No use. No matter how many times they show it, she dies in the end.
ALVA: Wouldn't it be wonderful if she didn't? I mean, what if you went to see it again, and the end was totally different? I mean like, if folks did like her, and she didn't die?
OWEN: Think how unhappy you'd be, though. You couldn't cry in the end.

In the final scene, Willie also recalls the film—though she does not mention the title—and compares the manner of Alva's death to what she saw in the film. Retrospection is therefore a key device, and as a result, it is notable that Pollack's most significant uses of the zoom in this film animate moments that reinforce or reinscribe the sense of retrospective telling.[45]

The zoom first appears in this manner about four minutes into the film. After the opening credits and expository dialogue between Willie and Tom, in which Willie explains her personal circumstances and those of her absent sister Alva, the film cuts to a shot of the pair sitting on the railroad track. Willie gestures toward a derelict building in the distance and says, "Boy, you see that house over yonder? We used to have some high old times in that big yellow house." As she delivers this line, the zoom advances, first retaining its focus on the characters in the foreground before refocusing to make legible a broken sign reading "ROOMS." This is followed by a lap dissolve into shots of the house filmed at closer range while Willie continues, "Musical instruments going all the time—piano, Victrola, Hawaiian steel guitar—everybody playin' on something. It's awful quiet now, though." The camera investigates the shuttered windows and finds a poster that reads, "This Property Is Condemned." After another cut, and while Willie describes how she now lives alone in the house, the camera moves inside, finally zooming (at a more moderate pace than the initial zoom) through a broken screen door, back toward Willie and Tom on the railroad track. A further cut returns to the initial position close to the pair, and Willie's dialogue completes the transition to the present: "Sure is empty now, though."

FIGURE 5.4. A motif that reoccurs throughout the movie, in *This Property Is Condemned* (Sydney Pollack, 1966), the zoom evokes a wistful past-tense mood.

This sequence forces a series of disorienting changes of position and perspective. During the second zoom, which returns to Willie and Tom, the camera moves from an extreme long shot to a long shot (through a zoom), then cuts to a further low-angle long shot and to a level-angle medium shot. This mirrors the series of shots that take place after the first zoom, which initially moves the perspective from a frontal-medium shot of the house to a closer, oblique shot. This may disrupt the scene's spatial continuity—still delicate because the film is only minutes into its running time—but the payoff is the establishment of the zoom as a clear visual motif for retrospection. Pollack returns to this motif occasionally as the film progresses. When Alva finally leaves Dodson, she sees through a train carriage window the house that the audience first encountered in the opening scene. Her lingering glance is emphasized through a zoom-in, and as in the opening scene, it is a zoom of sufficient ratio to transform the rough shape of *a* house into a clear vision of *the* house around which the narrative is based. Like the earlier zoom, this one makes legible the (intact) sign advertising rooms for rent. The house is maintained in this zoomed-in view until it disappears behind the window frame, and we cut back to see Alva, who looks back, troubled: we are invited to infer that Alva is considering her past in Dodson. The next cut—to an exterior of the train via a transitional shot of the railway track—is accompanied by a change of pace, both musical (up tempo, and the increased volume of the clattering railroad) and visual (a static shot of Alva is replaced initially with a shot of the track racing past). Yet Alva's attitude is unchanged: in the next shot, we see her looking with furrowed brow out of the window, and the gradual zooming out of a helicopter shot reveals that the train has traveled to a dramatically different location—away from dry, dusty Dodson to the Mississippi coast. This zoom, somewhat like the one that returned to Willie and Tom in the opening sequence, removes us from Alva's retro/introspection and begins to indicate the context of the scene that is to follow.[46]

The zoom is called on for the final time during the closing scene, where it is one device among others (track, crane, and helicopter) that remove the camera from the action and signal the conclusion of the narrative. Here again the zoom is part of a mixture of techniques that denote retrospection. The concluding conversation restates Alva's demise, contrasting it with that in *One Way Passage*. Willie, finally, predicts, "I'm gonna live for a long, long time. Like my sister. When my lungs get affected [*sic*], I'm gonna die like she did, with all my rings, my gold charm bracelet from Marshall Field, then I guess somebody else'll inherit all my beaus. Sky sure is white. Well, so long." At the end of this line, Willie turns to walk back along the railway track, in the opposite direction to the start of the film. In this final shot, the poor state of her dress, which used to belong to Alva, is clearest to the audience: for the first time, we see clearly that it is haphazardly pinned at the back, and we see the extent of a tear that reveals Willie's undergarments as she walks away from the camera. While Willie preoccupies herself with how her death might mimic Alva's, the audience is left considering the life that Willie faces. As she makes her way down the railway track, she is also on track toward the same exploitative fate as Alva. In a final reference toward the spectatorship that is another running theme of the film, Tom stands silently and watches as Willie walks into the distance. He remains still for several seconds before swinging his arms and retreating from the railway track. A zoom carries out part of the initial movement away from Willie, but this turns within seconds into a retreating tracking shot before ascending, by helicopter, into the air and away from the railway track. The zoom is at its most conventional here, as a signifier of withdrawal from the diegetic world, but because of the close link throughout the narrative between the past tense and the zoom, this final lens and camera movement has an added power and significance.

While *The Scalphunters* contains many more zoom shots than *This Property Is Condemned*, it does not build on the former film's psychological complexity. Instead, the zoom is used as a routine tool for directing attention through framing, with some particularly long, deliberate zooms—often from extremely high angles. On many occasions, these shots adopt the perspective of the film's characters—including two shots that appear to adopt the perspective of Joe Bass's (Burt Lancaster) horse. Pollack uses the zoom less often, but for similar purposes, in *Castle Keep*. The two films contain numerous examples of what may be called unmotivated—though not necessarily self-conscious—zooms, which inject focal length movement into a scene that might just as well be covered with a series of static shots or with physical camera movement.

Despite this apparent change of direction, *This Property Is Condemned* was not exceptional in terms of the psychologically motivated zoom, for in *They Shoot Horses, Don't They?* the two approaches can be seen to blend somewhat. There are many zoom shots in the film, but while they often seem merely to be reframing space, they are also frequently psychologically significant.[47] Like *This Property*, *They Shoot Horses* is temporally complex, consisting of three components: a main narrative—the dance marathon in which Robert (Michael Sarrazin) and Gloria (Jane Fonda) participate—interweaved flashbacks to what Janet Meyer describes as an "imaginary scenario with a horse . . . employed to inform the metaphorical meaning of the film," and flash-forward to Robert's arrest and questioning.[48] The flashbacks remain temporally disconnected from the main narrative, which ultimately catches up with the flash-forward. In *They Shoot Horses*, the zoom straddles the boundary between routine mobile frame function and special psychological effect related to the film's temporal complexity. It is loosely tied to the character Robert, and this connection is established from the outset, with the introduction of three motifs that are repeated throughout the narrative: the memory of a galloping horse, the isolated interiority of

Robert, and the contrastingly brash showmanship of the dance marathon's (as yet unseen) emcee—represented by the first utterance of the phrases "around and around they go" and "yowzah, yowzah." Each of these is emphasized by a zoom shot in the film's first ten minutes.

Pollack's first use of the zoom associates the child in the horse sequence with Robert, leading the audience to infer—though it is never explicitly confirmed—that the boy is "young Robert." The final shot of the opening montage is physically immobile, unlike those that precede it. A long shot shows a young boy almost lost among tall grass and in front of a muted backdrop. The zoom closes in to a medium shot, slipping out of focus before cutting to a well-focused medium shot of Robert standing on a beach, beside the pier that is to be the film's primary setting. The two shots are meticulously symmetrical: Pollack positions the pair—identically dressed in a hat, dark coat, and light-colored shirt—as if in conversation with each other, the boy's right shoulder foremost in the first shot, the man's left shoulder foremost in the second. The zoom-out mirrors the zoom-in, drawing back from Robert and bringing his background into focus. The only breakdown in symmetry, the mismatch in focus between the final frame of the first shot and the first of the second, is accounted for by the soundtrack, which changes on the cut from dreamlike, nondiegetic music to the loud crashing of the waves behind Robert. The simultaneous cut back into focus and change in sound suggest a sudden return to the narrative present: we sense that we have shared Robert's memory or (as Meyer suggests) his daydream.

As the narrative proceeds, the zoom shot maintains its attachment to Robert. It is the zoom that reestablishes him skulking on the margins of the dance hall, unsure of whether to take part. This zoom occurs shortly after the emcee draws Claudia's attention to Robert, but it does not directly adopt her gaze; it is not a point-of-view shot. (Indeed, not long after, once the dance is under way, Claudia points one of the other competitors out to Robert. Pollack cuts to a static shot of another dancer to indicate Claudia's point of view.) As in other parts of the narrative, the zoom remains broadly objective: the camera moves to centrally frame Robert before the emcee calls to him, drawing him to Claudia's attention. On being hailed as "cowboy," Robert looks about himself, pats his chest, and raises his eyebrows in a Chaplinesque pantomime of uncertainty. The zoom, however, leaves the audience in no doubt that we have apprehended the correct target, and its decisiveness of movement leaves even less room for ambiguity because it restates the connection forging first established in the fantasy/memory opening sequence.

Once Robert and Claudia are united as dance partners, the zoom shot remains more interested in him than in her. Early in the marathon, during a slow dance, Pollack moves restlessly from couple to couple, establishing the ensemble

FIGURE 5.5. A perfectly symmetrical pair of zooms introduces us to Robert Syverton (Michael Sarrazin) in *They Shoot Horses, Don't They?* (Sydney Pollack, 1969).

cast. The starlet and her partner and the sailor and his partner are picked out in relatively short focal lengths, through cuts and camera movement. Robert and Claudia, by contrast, are approached via the zoom. Yet we are as uninterested in them *as a couple* as they are in each other. The two couples we see prior to Robert and Claudia maintain some level of physical attachment—whether embracing or holding hands. When we see Robert and Claudia, they are barely touching: framed from the waist up, we are left to guess that they may be holding hands out of view of the camera. And when the soundtrack joins Robert and Claudia, their dialogue directs attention not to *them* but to *him*: Claudia irritably asks, "What are you looking at?" and Robert explains that he is trying to see the sun through a window in the roof.

Despite its attachment to Robert, the zoom is not reserved for him. A contrast is created late in the film by a zoom toward Claudia, picked out in a spotlight, walking the dance floor alone. The zoom, we might speculate, highlights Robert's absence. But the symbolism of this moment is not entirely clear, for throughout the film, Pollack uses the zoom for a variety of purposes that have no direct bearing on Robert. Pollack also uses the zoom as a diversely functional reframing device, applying it variously to approximate the gaze of a character (Claudia's

"God, check that one"), to accompany and emphasize a sudden change of tempo (a snap zoom to "Mr. Rhythm" at the start of the Ten-Minute Derby), to smooth the transition between an establishing shot and the action that follows, or to emphasize (as a sharp zoom-out) shock when one of the female competitors wakes, screaming.

These zooms, complementing those used for more psychologically motivated purposes, reflect typical uses of the zoom shot found in the films described in the preceding chapter and in much of Frankenheimer's work during the 1960s. In films, Pollack builds on approaches to the zoom shot first tried in television—a combination of emphasis of characters and their interior thoughts (as in *Breaking Point*) and occasional negotiations of the profilmic space (as in *Ben Casey*). Pollack largely limits his use of the zoom to occasions on which there are specific meanings to that particular camera movement—in which the zoom offers something that other techniques cannot. However, Pollack's zooms perform this function more obtrusively and more stylishly than similar functions in Frankenheimer, and Pollack begins to experiment with zooms that structure space.

The 1960s was a decade of transformation. Angénieux's 10:1 zoom lens was not the first to be introduced, but with a longer range than any lens before it, it transformed the impact that zooms could have. In parallel with the widening availability of reflex cameras, the influence of freer New Wave styles, Direct Cinema, and vérité, the zoom shot flourished. This was not an isolated, technologically determined cause and effect. Cinematographers attempted to claim authority over the zoom's uses and debated its pleasures and pitfalls. At the same time, the infusion of directors from television, where the zoom had been established—and often essential—for far longer undoubtedly helped normalize it in feature production. But directors like Frankenheimer and Pollack developed ways of using the zoom in features that diverged and developed from television; thus the small screen can be neither entirely blamed for nor fully credited with the development of the zoom shot.

6 · THE ZOOM BOOM

In the 1960s, the zoom lens had been a new tool that enabled stylistic innovation. Directors and cinematographers experimented with zoom shots, bringing a fresh new energy to filmmaking. Though many in Hollywood expressed concerns about the often abrupt, self-conscious nature of the zoom shot, by the end of the 1960s, the Angénieux 10:1 zoom lens was well tested and had become standard equipment. As the 1970s dawned, the zoom was no longer novel, but its attractions remained significant. As well as its ability to create a unique visual impression, the zoom created time- and money-saving opportunities for film and television producers. As a result, during the 1970s, zoom lenses were used more and more in both feature films and television series. While lens manufacturers such as Angénieux and Canon strived to develop zoom lenses with a longer reach and improved optical quality, other manufacturers developed secondary systems that made zooms more useable. Programmable electronic zoom controls made changes of focal length smoother and more consistent—and when added to gyroscopic helicopter mounts, zooms could be used to make more ambitious and practical use of aerial cinematography. Meanwhile, zoom lenses increasingly found their way into the hands of amateurs thanks to their presence on 8mm cameras. Far from a momentary stylistic trend, the zoom became increasingly embedded in film style. As this chapter discusses, by the 1970s, the zoom lens was exerting its broadest influence on the American moving image. The influence of the zoom could be seen in varied films, from disaster movie blockbusters to the creative excursions of Robert Altman. In the hands of feature directors, amateur moviemakers, and television cinematographers, the zoom shot ultimately became synonymous with 1970s film style—as closely associated with that decade as "flared jeans or sideburns."[1]

ZOOM STYLE: PROFESSIONAL AND AMATEUR

About one-third of the way through the paranoid space fantasy *Capricorn One* (Peter Hyams, 1977), an astronaut transmits a cryptic warning that he has been taken hostage by NASA in a conspiracy to fake a manned landing on Mars. In a video message from "space," the astronaut, Charles Brubaker (James Brolin), tells his wife to promise their son a trip to Yosemite National Park, "like last summer." Watched by news reporter Robert Caulfield (Elliot Gould), who has already caught a whiff of the subterfuge, Kay Brubaker (Brenda Vaccaro) hesitates for a moment before promising to pass the message on. Her hesitation—she knows the family made no such trip—sets in motion the conspiracy's exposure. Questioned later by Caulfield, Brubaker dismisses her husband's strange message as distracted forgetfulness. When Caulfield pushes a little harder, she reluctantly explains that the family went to Flat Rock, Arizona—not Yosemite—that summer. Temporarily satisfied, the reporter leaves, only to return sometime later to ask more questions about the family's trip. Brubaker shows Caulfield a home movie shot by her husband on their trip to Flat Rock. As the projector whirrs and shots of a gunfight scene from a Western movie illuminate the screen, Brubaker explains, "They were making a movie the day we were there. Bru got a big kick out of it. He never knew it took so much time to just do one simple scene. . . . Bru was fascinated with the detail. He couldn't get over how something so fake could look so real. He kept on saying that with that kind of technology you could convince people of almost anything."

Capricorn One is a film filled with cameras. The rocket launch at the film's outset is scrutinized from multiple angles by closed-circuit cameras, their images relayed to screens and consoles at Mission Control. The astronauts, extracted from the launch vehicle moments before blastoff, are hurried to a distant studio where television cameras stand ready to film a theatrical Mars walk. While the empty rocket travels toward its destination, the kidnapped crew waits in the desert, and the media assemble outside their family's homes. We watch as Caulfield and his television reporter colleagues set up for a doorstep interview with Kay Brubaker; film and electronic cameras are prominent in the mise-en-scène, as they are when the astronauts and their wives take place in the film's crucial interplanetary video conference and Charles Brubaker slips his wife the cryptic message about Yosemite.

Thus as well as a paranoid sci-fi fantasy, *Capricorn One* is also a documentary, not of its own making, but of what it meant to make moving images in the late 1970s. The film is a snapshot of the media production technology of the time: we see TV news camera crews and electronic studio television cameras, and we see footage, apparently shot on an 8mm cine camera, of a 35mm feature crew at work. Given *Capricorn One*'s genre and era, we might imagine (or misremember) it as being filled with zoom shots, moving in and out of framings and emphasizing moments of greatest melodrama. This would be in keeping with the contemporary cultural imagination of the zoom as a marker of seventies style. In fact, the film offers remarkably few dramatic zooms. Those that can be observed tend to be sedate, well concealed, and specifically motivated, as in the striking zoom-out that reveals the bleak expanse of desert into which the astronauts flee from their NASA captors. Meanwhile, the most important zooms in the film are the most easily overlooked. When television crews crowd around astronaut Brubaker's wife, nearly all the cameras have an Angénieux 10:1 zoom lens mounted on them. For a few moments, we stand back from the rabble of news reporters, a cool observer from a fixed focal length. The audience, literate in television style, knows that the footage captured by these cameras will be close up and hectic and that the mobility of the zoom will capture whatever is placed in front of them.

Cameras are a central motif of *Capricorn One*, but the film's most important camera is never seen. Brubaker's home movie footage of Flat Rock, Arizona, depicts a fully crewed 35mm film shoot. We see flashes of heavy-duty film cameras on cranes, lit with Hollywood lights. The footage itself, however, implies an amateur camera in the hands of a nonprofessional. Though Brubaker is at the peak of his own profession, he does not know how to use a camera with skill and finesse. His 8mm Kodak camerawork bears the hallmarks of amateur cinematography: jerky, handheld motion; uncoordinated panning; and rapid zooms. The zooms are no accident; this is a professional cinematographer's pastiche of amateur style. Brubaker's footage, it seems, has neither style nor aesthetic strategy: he points, shoots, and zooms toward whatever grabs his attention. From Brubaker's camerawork, we infer an amateur cinematographer uncertain of his equipment and overreliant on the zoom. These few moments of ersatz amateur footage are a counterpoint to the film's own cinematography, and they quietly indicate a key context for the development of the zoom lens and the changing articulations of professional attitudes toward it.

Amateur cinematography—candid videos of children's birthday parties, days at the beach, and the more earnest efforts of cine-club enthusiasts—seems far removed from the highly professionalized craft of the feature cinematographer. However, the two are more closely linked that may at first appear.[2] Until 1959, *American Cinematographer* had included an "Amateur Section," delineated from the rest of the magazine. Most professional cinematographers, when interviewed about their careers, describe formative experiences in amateur cinematography and photography. In turn, mainstream feature film and television provide an aesthetic blueprint to which amateur filmmakers may aspire or from which they may diverge. Camera advertisements may have been designed to appeal to specific audiences—amateur or professional—but filmmaking equipment was never clearly split between the two groups. Rather, it occupies a continuum of cost,

FIGURE 6.1. In *Capricorn One* (Peter Hyams, 1977), a zoom-out reveals the lonely expanse of desert into which astronauts Brubaker, Willis, and Walker must flee.

complexity, and format. There is little to prevent the wealthy amateur from renting or purchasing professional-grade equipment. Equally, some professionals have made films using amateur equipment (8mm, camcorders, smartphones), valuing the simplicity of consumer technology and relishing the creative challenge posed by less-sophisticated equipment.

When it comes to the zoom, however, the relationship between amateur and professional camera operators slides toward antagonism. While cinematographers argued over how best to use the zoom, away from film sets—on streets, in backyards, and on beaches—amateurs forged their own style. Operating the camera themselves, often pointing and shooting at action they had not planned, amateurs tended to use the zoom more than professionals. Their unsophisticated use of the zoom became a naïve style against which professionals could contrast their own skill and judgment. It is worth, therefore, looking briefly at how zoom lenses were marketed to amateur, small-scale, and informal users.

As an importer of the French Pan-Cinor zoom lenses, Paillard-Bolex was one of the first camera firms to market zooms to amateur cinematographers. However, it would be several years before the company would directly address home-movie makers. In the early 1950s, Paillard-Bolex had marketed its zoom lenses primarily to "small producers"—including television stations, commercial and industrial filmmakers, and cine clubs. The company trumpeted the flexibility of the Pan Cinor lens, promising that it would be compatible with more than ten varieties of 16mm film camera.[3] Semiprofessional filmmakers were thought likely to overuse the zoom, and so early articles introducing the lens included clear instructions on its use. One such article, contributed by a college tutor at Temple University, related the owner's delight in borrowing a Pan Cinor lens to aid his filming of a television series showcasing the work of his college students. Like many articles about the Pan Cinor, his was a cautionary tale with a happy ending: "I am afraid my reaction was like that of a six-year-old with his first electric train, because the early sequences zoomed back and forth like a pendulum. However, I settled down, and shot what I feel is the best film in the entire series using the Pan Cinor lens alone."[4] When *Bolex Reporter* offered guidance on the zoom, it took the form of authoritative and unambiguous edicts on "correct" zooming: "Success in filming with the Pan Cinor depends on the scrupulous observation of certain important rules: Always use a tripod to keep the camera steady; this is a 'must.' Move the 'zoom' (focal length) control slowly and gently, without jolting it," urged an explanatory article published in 1953.[5] In articles like these, *Bolex Reporter* functioned in much the same way as *American Cinematographer*, strongly encouraging its customers to conform to industrial norms in their use of the new technology.

Toward the end of the 1950s, as greater numbers of amateur filmmakers acquired 16mm equipment, and as zooms were provided with 8mm cameras, *Bolex Reporter* began to address home-movie makers in their marketing. In 1957, one article urged readers to "add a Pan Cinor-70 to your H-16 Leader," offering the example of "a movie of your youngster riding his tricycle" as the sort of subject that customers might be attempting to capture. The same article included a series of photographs of a mother and baby, taken through the zoom lens from a distance, promising that "zooming gives a special feeling to candid movies. . . . While the unwary subjects continue their action, the audience moves in on them." Here, perhaps, was a vision of a father filming his wife and child from a distance without their becoming self-conscious in the face of the whirring clockwork camera. Amateur users, like their professional colleagues, were pro-vided with clear rules about their new zoom lens, with minor adjustments to take account for tighter budgets: a tripod was *preferred* for home movie makers, but "the camera can be set on any solid surface. . . . Don't jolt when you zoom."[6] In this way, *Bolex Reporter* made allowances for the relatively limited resources of casual filmmakers.

By the early 1960s, *Bolex Reporter* was focusing its greatest energy on the amateur film market, where zooms were quickly becoming standard equip-ment. "The result," an article by Merrill F. Sproul declared, was that "more and more Sunday movie makers are zooming into everything from the Fourth of July parade to daughter's freckles." Like the professional trade press, the article suggested that there were appropriate, and inappropriate, uses of the zoom lens. However, here the categories were rather differently constituted. Sproul urged home-movie makers to use a zoom lens to make a "dramatic point," to catch action that would otherwise be missed ("Wouldn't it be wonderful to see your one year old son taking his first step and then to zoom in for a close up of his face and capture that proud expression just before collapse?"), or simply to replicate a "dolly" or "crab." Sproul could think of only two reasons *not* to use a zoom lens. The first was that *sometimes* a zoom might not be appropriate to a scene; the sec-ond was that prime lenses, being more suited to lower-light conditions, might be more appropriate for shooting in darkened conditions.[7] The zoom—an expen-sive add-on to a luxury toy—would be the default choice for the home-movie maker who followed these recommendations, thus satisfying the filmmaker in the value of his or her investment.

At this stage, Paillard-Bolex was engaged in an energetic campaign to per-suade its customers that zoom lenses were now of equal optical standard to primes. While articles still discussed the relative merits of zoom and turret cameras, in 1961, Bolex introduced an 8mm camera that removed this choice. The Bolex Zoom Reflex P-1 featured an integrated zoom lens that could not be swapped for a prime lens. The design of the lens used had been subtly modi-fied when compared to earlier versions: the zoom lever, which protruded from the bottom of the lens, was thick and stubby. This was quite unlike the long, slender levers of earlier lenses—and a completely different design principle to a hand crank or barrel twist. The new lever, an illustration accompanying one promotional article suggested, could be manipulated with just the thumb and forefinger of one hand.[8] While *Bolex Reporter*'s articles encouraged amateur cin-ematographers to feel creatively confident in their use of the zoom, the design of the Zoom Reflex P-1 encouraged users to feel physically comfortable when operating it.

Paillard-Bolex was not the only firm to encourage its customers to zoom as freely and as often as they liked. Advertising copy for Kodak's Zoom 8 Reflex

NEW:
BOLEX ZOOM
REFLEX P-1

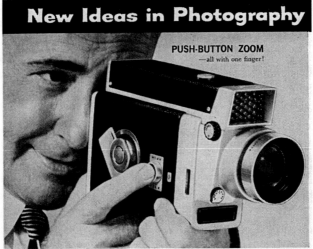

New Ideas in Photography

PUSH-BUTTON ZOOM
—all with one finger!

Look! A single button operates the camera and zooms your movies, too!

Z-0-0-0-M! Push button zooms your movies, electric eye
sets the lens—new Kodak Zoom 8 Reflex Camera

FIGURES 6.2 AND 6.3. As details from advertisements for Bolex
and Kodak 8mm cameras show, by the 1970s, camera manufacturers were developing simpler and more practical methods for controlling zoom lenses on consumer cameras.

camera rhapsodized about the simplicity of the camera's most novel feature, a motorized zoom lens that could be operated at the push of a single button: "A push button brings you the most marvelous thing that's ever happened to movies—the zoom! You look through the finder and before your eyes people and objects suddenly swoop close and fill the scene. Or, starting with a close-up, the scene suddenly widens like opening the curtain on a gigantic stage."[9] Mounted on the side of the camera, conveniently controllable by a single finger, the zoom button was a precursor to the rocker switch design that later became common on camcorders. Advertising materials included illustrations of the camera's user holding a finger on the zoom button, emphasizing ease of operation.

By the beginning of the 1970s, however, this facility to zoom had begun to rankle with serious amateur filmmakers. In a few short years, the zoom lever began to disappear from consumer cameras. Kodak's Instamatic M20 Super-8mm camera, introduced in 1968, featured a "power zoom . . . with fingertip control on top of the camera"—one of the first examples of a portable movie camera with zoom easily controlled by a more intuitive rocker switch.[10] Manuals written for amateur cinematographers expressed grave concern about home-movie makers overusing their zoom lenses. Henry Provisor's *8mm/16mm Movie Making*, published in 1970, identified the zoom as a new technology that "in the hands of the inexperienced film-maker . . . become lethal weapons that produce out-of-focus images and a dizzy display of bad sequences that destroy an effect he may have wanted to produce."[11] Jerry Yulsman's *Complete Book of 8mm Movie Making*, published two years later, complains that "[Super]-8 camera owners, proud of their smoothly operating powered zoom lenses, ranging all the way to 12-to-1 ratios, treat them as toys. It is so satisfying, so effortless to operate that little rocker switch. It can be terribly exciting."[12]

Manufacturers and distributors of amateur equipment communicated similar aesthetic ideals to their customers as writers in the professional trade press, but they were more flexible about the use of the zoom. Recognizing that amateur cinematographers would be more interested in capturing the action in front of them than creating an aesthetically pleasing production, they made zooming both a convenient facility of their cameras and an acceptable stylistic device. Despite the qualms of writers like Provisor and Yulsman, the zoom's ability to capture spontaneous moments of family life without rehearsal made the zoom a key marker of the aesthetic of the home movie. This would only be magnified in the 1980s as the cine camera gave way to the camcorder. As professional equipment developed, often "catching up" to the achievements of home-movie technology, amateur style lurked in the background, subtly influencing the expectations of film and television audiences and coloring the attitudes of professional cinematographers.

IMPROVING THE ZOOM

In the 1960s, the Angénieux 10:1 lens became the "standard" zoom lens with which cinematographers equipped themselves. As a result, the Angénieux zoom was the standard against which future lenses would be compared. During the 1970s, while Angénieux's groundbreaking lens remained popular, a plethora of new zoom lenses became available to cinematographers. Panavision's Panazoom lenses found favor on some film sets, and for the first time, lenses designed and manufactured in Japan by Canon became available in the United States. These new lenses offered a variety of advances over earlier equipment. New ways of coating glass resulted in zoom lenses that required less light and offered clearer, sharper images. Longer zoom ranges became possible—up to 50–500mm by the end of the 1970s. In addition to direct improvements to lens equipment, other technologies advanced in ways that made it more practical or more economical to use the zoom. While lens coatings and improved glass compounds reduced the amount of light needed to shoot with zoom lenses, increasingly sensitive color film stock—notably Kodak 5254—made older or slower zoom lenses more feasible.[13] The development of miniature, low-power, integrated circuits led to increasingly compact and sophisticated electronic zoom controls. Over time, these developed from relatively simple servo motors designed to provide smooth zooming to programmable devices capable of repeating zoom movements multiple times. This technology in turn benefited one of the most significant new technologies to emerge in the 1970s: the Steadicam offered an unprecedented degree of control in "handheld" filming, and the utility of the device was significantly increased when it was combined with an electronically controlled, remotely operated zoom lens.

Lens designers and engineers increasingly spoke of the zoom as a mature, stable technology—but some worried about the potential for further progress. In a paper presented at a technical conference in Hollywood in 1971, British lens designers G. H. Cook and F. R. Laurent remarked that "optical specifications and levels of performance have improved to the point where zoom lenses can perform as the prime tool, rather than the accessory." However, Cook and Laurent feared that the rate of improvement seen during the 1950s and 1960s could not be sustained. "It becomes apparent," they warned, "that many of the types of zoom lenses in use today may have reached the limits of further modification and improvement."[14] The sense of a plateau was shared by a new entrant to the zoom lens market. In Tokyo, Canon's optical engineers recognized that zoom lenses had been greatly improved by computer-aided design and the introduction of "precise image evaluation criteria" intended to enable the objective comparison of competing lenses. Despite these advances, Canon felt that the limits of trial and error had been reached, and a radical new approach—the construction of lens elements from synthetic calcium fluorite crystals—was the way forward. Canon developed the ability to not only make high-quality lenses from calcium fluorite but also manufacture the material in bulk.[15]

Canon's entry to the American market was rapid and well planned. Previous companies had seemingly blundered into the market by striking lucky with one particularly valuable or innovative lens—as in the cases of the Studio Zoomar or the Angénieux 10:1 lenses. Canon, by contrast, carefully researched potential gaps in the market and worked in partnership with industry bodies before offering their lenses for export and distribution. As a result, a succession of new Canon lenses appeared on the market in rapid succession in the early 1970s. The K-35 Macrozoom lens, introduced in 1972, was designed to a specification produced by the Motion Picture and Television Research Center. The lens was particularly fast and produced high-quality images, but with a 25–120mm (4.8:1) range of focal lengths, this came at the expense of the flexibility of longer zooms. Nevertheless, the lens won Canon an Academy Award in 1973.[16] K-35 lenses were distributed in the United States by the Cinema Products Corporation, which offered customers the opportunity to use the lens in conjunction with its own electronic zoom controls.[17] At the other end of the format spectrum, the Canon Scoopic DS8, introduced in 1970, followed the form of earlier 8mm cameras by including a built-in zoom lens.[18] The Scoopic was well timed to catch an increasing market for professional film production on the Super-8mm format. Aside from these innovative lenses, Canon also hedged their bets by producing a 12–120mm zoom lens for 16mm cameras, matching the standard range of focal lengths defined by the market-leading Angénieux zoom.[19] However, it is difficult to gauge how popular this lens was: compared to the more popular and acclaimed K-35, it was scarcely advertised or discussed in the trade press.[20]

While most manufacturers focused on lenses with ranges of focal length that would be most useful for "routine" assignments, high-powered telephoto zoom lenses were also developed. Panavision's 50–500mm zoom lens offered an unprecedented ability to reach from a "normal" focal length to an extreme telephoto setting. This made it possible for camera operators to zoom from a "face in the crowd" to an entire landscape, or to do the opposite. Zooms with this reach were particularly effective for spectacular camera movements. The final shot of Hello Dolly (Gene Kelly, 1969) pulls back from a shot of Dolly Levi (Barbra Streisand) and Horace Vandergelder (Walter Matthau) on the steps their wedding chapel, ending on an extreme long shot of the church, the wedding guests, and the Hudson River and its valley snaking into the background. The shot was achieved by mounting the camera on a "giant Chapman Titan boom" and zooming out from 500mm to 50mm, creating "a panorama of spectacular scope," visually capping the narrative and complementing the film's final orchestral flourish.[21] The 50–500mm lens was also particularly useful for aerial cinematography—airborne sequences of *Capricorn One* were filmed with it—and the same lens was used frequently by the second unit on *A Bridge Too Far* (Richard Attenborough, 1977).[22]

Lens coatings became an increasingly important technology as zoom lenses became more complex. By the 1970s, high-range television zoom lenses could include more than sixty glass elements, almost three times as many as in the Zoomar lenses of the 1940s. As the number of lens elements increased, so did the number of microscopic flaws and imperfections contained within the glass used to manufacture them. These flaws scattered the waves of light traveling through the lens, contributing to a murkier picture and exacerbating lens flare. Manufacturers adopted diverse techniques to avoid these problems. The success of Canon's K-35 lens lays partly in the company's development of lens elements made out of synthetic fluorite crystals, which offered better light transmission and clearer images when compared with traditional optical glass. Meanwhile, new coating techniques such as Fuji's, which used an electron-beam gun to apply multiple microscopic layers of coating to glass surfaces, made highly complex zoom lenses a more practical technology by further reducing lens flare.[23]

Technological innovation was not, however, the only way to deal with the "problem" of lens flare. Some directors and camera operators accepted the distinctive visual qualities of the zoom lens and began to make them part of a gritty documentary aesthetic. Such an embrace of imperfection was anathema to traditionalists. Speaking at a trade show, cinematographer Charles G. Clarke blamed lens flare on the impossibility of attaching matte boxes to the end of zoom lenses and complained about flare as a marker of an emerging documentary style: "It's not 'cinema vérité' to have a flare in your eyes, because if that did happen you would shut your eyes or change your angle. So, it is absolutely foreign to have a flare in the lens—but, because they haven't been able to avoid it when using zoom lenses, they've invented an excuse for it and said: 'This is the new film; this is "cinema verite" this is something great!' They've made up an alibi to cover a thing that never occurs in nature."[24] Clarke's unequivocal antipathy toward lens flare was by no means universal. The younger Vilmos Zsigmond, speaking at the same event, defended lens flare, declaring himself "proud" of the flares he and director Steven Spielberg had permitted in *Sugarland Express* (1974). Zsigmond's view prevailed: lens flare remained acceptable in documentary films and became increasingly visible in features. Eventually, lens flare was not just tolerated but seen as desirable in some contexts.

As well as new lenses from new manufacturers, innovative enabling and enhancing technologies made zoom lenses more practical than ever before. Improved optical quality and longer zoom ranges combined with freshly developed electronics to provide potent combined products: powerful, fast zoom lenses that could be precisely and smoothly controlled. For some professional filmmakers, it was a source of frustration that such improvements had first been available to amateurs and home-movie makers. As a television news camera-man complained in 1971, "It is the amateurs who have made less complicated, more portable gear with such innovations as automatic exposure systems, power zooms, lighter weight, electrically operated gear, while newsmen still have spring-driven cameras that give them only a 20- or 30-second roll."[25]

Motors and remote controls for 35mm zoom lenses and professional cameras had existed before the 1970s, but these inventions were tentative and idiosyn-cratic and tended to rely on simple mechanical motors, allowing for little finess-ing of the zoom movement. The relative lack of commercial products designed to make zooming easier was one aspect of a "vacuum" that, in 1967, provoked electronics engineer Ed DiGiulio to leave a job as director of engineering at the Mitchell Camera Corporation and set up a company that would develop and manufacture improvements to existing camera technology. DiGiulio's firm, Cinema Products Corporation, made its name by "reflexing" Mitchell BNC cameras, enabling camera operators to look directly through the viewfinder while the camera was in operation. This was in itself useful to camera operators who might want to use a zoom in 35mm feature production, but the company's next product, the J4 joystick zoom control, had even greater utility. As DiGiulio recalled, earlier zoom motors had been as unrefined as "clock motors."[26] Replac-ing them, the J4 consisted of a "powerful motor geared to the zoom ring of the lens" coupled to a "highly sophisticated Servo control circuit." The J4's key advantage was in its flexibility. The speed of the zoom could be adjusted so that zooms could be exceedingly fast or creepingly slow—from a snap zoom lasting only a second to an inch-by-inch push-in or pull-out lasting up to six minutes. The mechanism was designed with the operator in mind: the J4's control box featured a joystick that enabled the cinematographer, or an assistant, to control the zoom with a single thumb. It was almost completely silent in operation.[27] At the Academy Awards presented in April 1972, Cinema Products Corporation won a citation for their development of a "control motor to actuate zoom lenses," which praised the company for its provision of "accurate, smooth, and propor-tional lens movement" via a "convenient hand control unit."[28]

Though not unique, the J4 was one of the first electronic zoom controls to be mass-produced and offered on the open market to any producer or camera operator who might want to use it. The oft-discussed and exceptionally overt zooms in Stanley Kubrick's *Barry Lyndon* (1975) were made using a modified Angénieux 20:1 zoom lens.[29] But it was the joystick control that, according to the film's cinematographer John Alcott, made the film's zoom possible. Alcott's account made the joystick's attractions clear: "It starts and stops without a sud-den jar, which is very important, and you can manipulate it so slowly that it almost feels like nothing is happening. This is very difficult to do with some of the motorized zoom controls. I find that this one really works."[30] Precise, silent, electronic controls renewed the appeal of zoom lenses by expanding the range of circumstances in which they could be easily be used.

The story of Cinema Products and the J4 was exemplary of the growing influence of advanced electronics on film and television production technology.[31] In the 1970s, electronics-based technologies became increasingly available to television and feature crews. Cinema Products played a highly significant role in bringing automation and convenience technologies to professional 16mm and 35mm cinematography equipment. Indeed, the J4 control unit was an essential part of making the Steadicam a feasible technology. From the outset, the Steadicam had a remote-controlled zoom, which was essential to avoid the unbalancing effect of direct "hands-on" interaction with the camera.[32] The mobility of the Steadicam spurred Cinema Products to further develop remote-control devices for zooming, focusing, and other lens operations. By the late 1970s, Steadicams were supplied with wireless zoom controls, enabling an assistant to manipulate the various functions of the lens while the Steadicam-wearing camera operator performed the physical movements required for a scene.[33]

Aside from electronic zoom controls, video assist began to gain popularity among directors and cinematographers. These systems added a video camera to the reflex viewfinder of the film camera, enabling the action being filmed to be shown, live, on a separate monitor. Early video-assist systems were marketed and promoted with the challenge of zoom shots in mind. A description of a Panavision video-assist system in *American Cinematographer* in 1970 described how the system was "built right into the door of the Panavision camera for through-the-lens viewing, thus eliminating all parallax and making possible the accurate monitoring of zoom shots."[34] A similar video-assist system—Samcinevision, developed by the British firm Samuelson Film Service—helped cinematographer Álex Phillips capture scenes during location shooting for *The Wrath of God*. Phillips remarked,

> It's almost like watching dailies. I've found out that it can also be helpful to the cameraman in several ways. For example, it gives the cameraman complete control of his operator—really total control. I've always had trouble on zooms, trying to get the assistant to do it exactly the way I visualize it—to zoom it very slowly, to speed it up there, and not let it go all the way when he hits the end. Now I don't have that trouble any more. I have the Panavision pistol-grip control that zooms the lens in and out, but I'm watching the video monitor as the camera is running. So I control these moves completely, which is fantastic.[35]

While reflex cameras made it possible for one person at a time to monitor action through the lens, video assist meant that a wider creative team could scrutinize how camera moves, lens settings, and lighting setups were affecting what could be seen within the frame. The zoom shot, which had until now been the responsibility of a camera operator or cinematographer, often in consultation with a director, could now more easily be debated on set by a creative team huddled around a video monitor.

DEBATING THE ZOOM

Despite—and to some extent because of—the zoom's increasing popularity, some directors and cinematographers were ready to revolt against the zoom shot by the beginning of the 1970s. That the zoom had been overused was a persistent theme in cinematographers' complaints. Interviewed about the production of the comedy musical *Hello, Dolly!* (Gene Kelly, 1969), Harry Stradling remarked, "People zoom in and out for no logical reason, and I think this is very distracting. The zoom lens can be used once in a while very effectively, but I think that in future films we will be getting away from so much use of the zoom—because it's too much of a mechanical device and it usually shows up like what it is."[36] Stradling's prediction, made at the end of 1969, was both correct and incorrect. The zoom was not abandoned in the 1970s, but a rising chorus of voices criticized its use. Their reasons for doing so were as diverse as the films they produced. Some were anxious about the zoom's seemingly anachronistic qualities. Oswald Morris, when shooting *Fiddler on the Roof* (Norman Jewison, 1971), imagined that Tevye's family had shot the film themselves on 8mm: "They wouldn't have a zoom lens—I shouldn't imagine they could afford one—but they would keep things basically simple and very honest, because they'd know no other way of approaching it."[37] For Philip Lathrop, shooting *Wild Rovers* for Blake Edwards, the zoom was one device in a suite of "slick mechanical gadgetry" that would seem "very false in relation to a period Western."[38] Others invoked the memory of their forebears to explain why the zoom, among other "showy" techniques, should not be used. Speaking in 1972 during the production of *The Last Picture Show*, Robert Surtees reported that Peter Bogdanovich "won't even allow a zoom lens on the set. He detests zooms, even when they're used just to follow someone. Orson Welles had told him that a zoom creates artificial movement and, technically, he's correct. A zoom shot is merely a magnification of an object."[39] Karl Malkames, writing in 1974, invoked the films of Charlie Chaplin, Eisenstein, and Griffith to argue that zooms should have no place in theatrical motion pictures. Showing a striking faith in the ability of cinematographers to transcend trends in technology, Malkames suggests, "Even if the excellent variable focal length lenses of today had existed during the 20's and 30's it is doubtful that many of the top cameramen or directors would have employed the zoom while the camera was rolling. It would have remained a time-saving convenience to have but one lens for all angles."[40] Each of these cinematographers co-opts the stylistic strategies of the past in order to make an argument against the wider use of the zoom lenses, but here Malkames goes even further. Such is his keenness to banish the zoom from the feature screen that he creates a counterfactual narrative that ignores—or is unaware of—daring experiments made with the zoom in the 1920s and 1930s.

Despite strident declarations such as these, senior cinematographers remained flexible in their opposition to the zoom. This was the position maintained by James Wong Howe until the end of his life: though never entirely comfortable with the zoom lens, Howe managed to use it to meet the requirements of directors while simultaneously criticizing its use. Filming *Funny Lady* (Herbert Ross, 1975) prompted Howe to recall his youth when, he remembered, he had shot *Transatlantic* (William K. Howard, 1931) "with only two lenses—a 25mm and a 35mm." In the zoom, Howe saw a threat to a key aspect of a cinematographer's skill—namely, the ability to find the "right" focal length for the required shot scale or mood. Nevertheless, Howe conceded that Ross "uses [the zoom] very well."[41] In Howe's view, it was directors, not cinematographers, who used—and therefore "abused"—the zoom.[42] Toward the end of the 1970s, this was a view shared by *Godfather* cinematographer Gordon Willis, who described "machine-gun shooters [who] arbitrarily cut closeups with a zoom lens" rather than carefully choosing an appropriate focal length.[43] If cinematographers could not contain the rising appeal of the zoom—and they certainly could do little to fight its obvious economic efficiencies—they could at least transfer a portion of their creative responsibility to the director.

Taken in isolation and at face value, these comments might suggest that highly artistic films, and those with the highest production values, shunned the zoom lens (or insisted on their use only in a limited or specifically motivated fashion), while television producers and personnel working on adventure, disaster, and exploitation movies used them without hesitation. But the facts describe a more complex history. Two main attitudes to the zoom can be detected in the films of the 1970s. Some directors used the zoom without hesitation, zooming as frequently and as obviously as they wanted to. Others did their best to conceal its use—using zoom lenses as an alternative to a set of prime lenses, coordinating zoom moves to take place at the same time as pans, or simply zooming as little as possible.

In the early 1970s, it became increasingly common for zoom lenses to be used as a substitute for a set of primes. Shinsaku Himeda, for example, used a 50–95mm Panafocal lens exclusively during parts of the shooting of *Tora! Tora! Tora!* (Richard Fleischer, 1970).[44] On some multicamera shoots, zooms and primes were combined for optimum flexibility. During the location filming for *Lost Horizon* (1973), two identical Arriflex cameras were fitted with a prime lens and a long zoom so as to provide "matching action for inter-cutting."⁴⁵ A Panavision Panafocal zoom lens was used for most of the shooting of *Chinatown* (Roman Polanski, 1974), but variation of focal length was strictly limited. The cinematographer, John A. Alonzo, explained how this handling of the zoom lens was part of an overall vision for "subtle" cinematography designed to mimic human perception: "I told [Polanski] about my feeling—which is strictly my own concept—that in the anamorphic format, the lens that best reproduces what the human eye sees in the 40mm—just as in the 1.85 format the 25mm lens serves that purpose. So I said to Roman: 'I have an idea that if we shoot the remainder of the picture with a 40mm, 45mm or 50mm lens, whenever possible, this will give the picture a very subtle look—not a distorted look. It won't be *A Clockwork Orange*.'"⁴⁶ In many cases, the utility of a zoom lens was limited by its interaction with other technologies. The use of a relatively slow film stock or the need to film in low ambient light conditions often meant that a zoom lens could not easily be used. When shooting *The French Connection* (William Friedkin, 1971), Owen Roizman avoided using zoom lenses as much as possible because of their poor performance in lower-light conditions. When zooms were used, they caused as many problems as they solved. The softness of the zoom lens limited Roizman's choices when filming through the window of a restaurant, making it impossible to cover the window with a gel and forcing a change in lighting strategy.⁴⁷ Conversely, other new camera technologies provided a degree of flexibility and mobility that took the place of the zoom. Steven Spielberg and director of photography Vilmos Zsigmond were the first to experiment with the Panaflex, a lightweight 35mm film camera, as they filmed *The Sugarland Express* (1974). The compact size and low weight of the camera encouraged adventurous shots and camera movements. The zoom, by contrast, was concealed. As Spielberg explained during the production,

> Vilmos is the only cameraman I know who thinks like me in terms of lateral dolly moves and in terms of hiding the zoom. I hate to see unmotivated zoom shots, and I see them so often on TV—zoom in, zoom out! Vilmos feels the same way about it, so we disguise all of our zoom shots. You don't notice that the camera has gone from close to far. By the time you would normally become conscious of the zoom a cut has been made and you are only faintly aware that the scene has assumed a different look.⁴⁸

By the later 1970s, it was increasingly acceptable practice to film almost exclusively with zoom lenses. After shooting *Rocky* (John G. Avildsen, 1976), James Crabe explained,

We used zoom lenses on all of our cameras and I don't believe we ever took them off. Nowadays that's more or less standard technique, since the quality of zoom lenses is evidently approaching that of hard lenses. I'm aware that statement is debatable and probably refutable in terms of sheer mathematics, but what actually worked out in practice was that it was very expedient to use 10-to-1 zoom lenses on our cameras, so that during the course of a scene we could easily change focal lengths. For example, if Camera A were covering the main pattern of the action, Camera B could zap in for a closeup, much as a documentary unit might shoot.[49]

Despite these advances, there was no genre with which the zoom could be most closely associated. A clutch of mid-1970s disaster movies, for example, show great variation in their use of the zoom. A Panazoom lens was used both during the shooting of *The Poseidon Adventure* (Ronald Neame, 1972) and by the unit filming action sequences for *The Towering Inferno* (John Guillermin, 1974).[50] Both films feature the constant use of extreme and unmistakable zoom shots. Yet in *Earthquake*, a film that is very similar in tone and content and identical in genre, the zoom is scarcely seen. This was the choice of cinematographer Philip Lathrop, who felt that zooms "just wouldn't have fit this picture." He used an interview about the production of the film to develop a broader, and by now very familiar, point about the show-off zoom: "I'm not against zoom lenses. There are times when a zoom shot can be very effective, but there are a lot of people who don't quite understand how a zoom lens should be used, and they use it incorrectly. It's a tool like any other camera tool. If it's used right, it's terrific—but to use it just because you've got a zoom lens and say: 'Look what I did. I zoomed into a closeup!' . . . Who cares?"[51]

THE ZOOM IN 1970S FILM AND TELEVISION

Just as the 1970s was the decade in which the zoom became truly ubiquitous in the American feature film, it was also the point at which the zoom began to exercise film critics and interest film historians. While the development and use of the zoom lens up to the 1970s has been rather neglected by historians, from this point forward, there is no shortage of critical and historical accounts on which to draw. Often, they refer to a similar set of films in mapping their territory, paying attention to the influence of Direct Cinema and cinema vérité, the work of directors of the "TV Generation" and the later American New Wave, as well as provocative New Wave films emerging from Europe. Hence John Belton's account of the zoom's history is energized by the examples of Roberto Rossellini and of Claude Chabrol, whom he describes as "the grand master of the zoom" for his "emotionally turbulent yet paralytic zooms," alongside discussion

FIGURE 6.4. Numerous zoom shots appear in *Towering Inferno* (John Guillermin, 1974), especially in the film's action sequences.

of the work of Robert Altman, Robert Mulligan, and (for its "best known zoom in avant-garde cinema") Michael Snow's *Wavelength*.[52] A similar set of films and cinematic influences is highlighted by Bordwell in *On the History of Film Style*.[53] David A. Cook also highlights television directors, New Hollywood, and Europe—and singles out, for more detailed analysis, the work of Robert Altman and Stanley Kubrick.[54] Cook also associates the zoom with 1970s "youth-cult films" that, he suggests, attempted to find novelty in the "conspicuous abuse of rack-focus composition and the zoom lens."[55] All of these accounts agree on a similar canon of films that were important to the development of the zoom in the 1970s, and all agree that Altman was particularly important. But none examine what was taking place simultaneously in television. Therefore, rather than discuss in detail well-worn examples of 1970s films, this chapter concludes with a closer examination of a less frequently discussed television history. In contrast to the career trajectory of Robert Altman, the work of Walter Strenge—a senior and well-respected cinematographer who crossed from feature cinematography to television—provides a provocative alternative history of the development of the zoom during the 1970s.

There is no doubt that Robert Altman was innovative and unusual in his use of zooms. No director has inspired as much critical discussion of the zoom. Altman's body of work in the 1970s has provided the raw material critics needed to work through their views on the zoom lens. However, in the context of the longer-run history of the zoom, the continual focus on Altman as the primary example of an American film director who used the zoom is not entirely helpful. Too many scholars and serious critics overstate the novelty of the zoom by the mid-1970s and isolate Hollywood features from television production. By strategically overlooking the porous border between television and features, and by ignoring the fact that movie audiences and television audiences are not mutually exclusive, some historians have reduced the landscape of 1970s film to the films of a few pioneering auteurs working in an otherwise barren wasteland of run-of-the-mill studio productions. By virtue of his auteur status, Altman is seen to use the zoom exceptionally, and with exceptional skill; under this analysis, most other directors fall by the wayside. However, a serious examination of the many other uses of the zoom in film and television during the 1970s suggests that Altman's approach to the zoom may not be quite as exceptional as has been traditionally argued.

It is therefore worth directly comparing what Altman was doing with the zoom in the early 1970s with what his colleagues were doing in television at the same time, where the zoom lens was making just as significant an impact as in film. Network television producers, filming at a faster pace and with lower budgets than many features, eagerly adopted the zoom lens. Increasingly, entire episodes of major network drama serials were shot using the zoom, and some directors experimented with replacing dolly moves with zooms. A few weeks before production of *MASH* began, the ABC television network screened a two-hour *Movie of the Week* drama pilot titled "A Matter of Humanities" (March 26, 1969) and subsequently commissioned the series *Marcus Welby, M.D.* By the time the final episode of *Marcus Welby*'s first season had screened on April 14, 1970—a few weeks after *MASH* had opened on general release—the series cinematographer, Walter Strenge, had developed a visual style that also used zoom lenses liberally in order to structure space and attention. Yet while *MASH* made an impression on critics, it was Strenge's work on *Marcus Welby, M.D.*, that was seen, over the years, by a larger television audience and made an impact on the trade discourse surrounding the zoom.

Walter Strenge was one of the leading figures of the first generation of television cinematographers. Long before the TV Generation migrated to feature films, Strenge's career had progressed in the opposite direction. After twenty years as a director of photography on features, after 1950, his career was dominated by television work. Meanwhile, Strenge developed a significant voice within Hollywood's community of cinematographers. In the late 1950s, he served two terms as president of the ASC, and during the 1960s, he wrote the "Question and Answer" section of *American Cinematographer* and edited the *American Cinematographer Handbook*. Thanks to Strenge's privileged position within the ASC, *American Cinematographer* published two substantial articles on his work toward the end of his career, as he filmed episodes of *Marcus Welby, M.D.*, and *Owen Marshall, Counselor at Law* for ABC. These articles provide a detailed snapshot of television production practices, and they describe a cinematographer who uses the zoom as a standard tool. Strenge's career and work complicate the notion that a trailblazing TV Generation developed new ways of using the zoom that were particular to feature film production. An examination of his earlier work reveals hints of a gradual stylistic progression similar to what can be found in the television and film work of the TV Generation—and shows that his later television directing was as reliant on the zoom as any contemporaneous Altman film.

Filming television episodes on Hollywood studio sets, Strenge made use of the zoom from the early 1960s onward. "Journey into Darkness," an episode of *Arrest & Trial* shot by Strenge in 1963, shows the zoom lens in occasional, but relatively complex use.[56] Early in the episode, the murderer at the center of the narrative, Paul LeDoux (Roddy McDowell), is picked out with a zoom that reveals him to have been loitering around the murder scene. The scene opens on a shot that shows a pawn shop with part of the road in front of it visible, in addition to a car and a crowd of people. A detective leaves the shop, climbs into the car parked in front, and drives away, leaving the crowd of bystanders dominant in the frame. Once the car is out of frame, an individual begins to leave the crowd, taking a few steps toward right of frame and toward the camera. He raises his hand to block the sun, and as he does so, the camera zooms to a closer shot that isolates him against the crowd in the background. A later scene performs the opposite: the zoomed-in camera isolates LeDoux amid a dockyard setting, then zooms out and pans to show more of the surrounding environment. Starting from a medium long shot, a slow zoom introduces assorted dockside paraphernalia—mooring posts, lifeboats, and so forth—before moving farther out through a long shot and into an extreme long shot. As this takes place, the contrast changes, leading to a composition in silhouette as LeDoux walks slowly through the dockyard, once again alone in the frame. Despite these moments, the zoom does not dominate the visual style: physical camera movement is often used to establish closer shots and cuts to close-ups for conversations between characters. A similar approach is evident in "The Jar," an episode of *The Alfred Hitchcock Hour* in which the zoom appears as a substitute for tracking—notably during a sequence in which a Charlie Hill (Pat Buttram) hunts a man who he believes has stolen his property.[57] This is in addition to at least one striking zoom shot used to show that the man has found the jar propped up on a log: a short series of eyeline match cuts move between Hill's face and the swamp before a long zoom-in to the jar signals that he has found what he sought. Up to this point, the television episodes on which Strenge served as director of photography used the zoom in strictly functional ways—namely, to adjust framing and simulate tracking.

By 1968, Strenge had become considerably more adventurous in his use of the zoom. "A Dangerous Proposal"—an episode of the action-drama series *Run for Your Life*—shows the zoom used to its fullest extent both to deliver quick shocks and also to gradually alter framing.[58] It is most strikingly used early in the episode as Gillan Wilmont (Judy Carne) sits at an outdoor café table with Sir Henry Hiller (Albert Dekker). In a movement that lasts for less than two seconds, a long, sharp zoom draws the audience toward a car in the distance, where the show's principal character, Paul Bryan (Ben Gazzara), is standing. As the zoom takes place, and after it is completed, Wilmont leaves the café table and walks to the car to start a conversation with Bryan. In other scenes, the zoom is used in a less dramatic fashion, apparently both as a substitute for prime lenses (suggested by the appearance of numerous different focal lengths from a fixed camera position) and as a dynamic zoom. Halfway through the episode, during a scene in which Hiller paces forward and backward, gradual zooms maintain him at roughly the same size in the frame. On other occasions, the zoom is used to the full extent of its range, zooming in for a close-up of Wilmont's face at a bedroom doorway before zooming out rapidly to capture the entire room. This is performed as a single movement without accompanying panning or other camera movement. Smooth, rapid zooms are then used to change the framing as Wilmont takes measurements of pictures on the bedroom walls. A final zoom, the reverse of that which opened the sequence, bookends the scene and removes viewers from the space of the bedroom. Although there is no "psychological" zoom to be found here, these examples show Strenge and the episode's director, Barry Shear, use the zoom in complex and creative ways that shape and emphasize key moments in the episode's narrative.

In the early 1970s, Strenge's work in television was examined in two highly detailed observational articles published in *American Cinematographer*. In the first article, Robert Kerns observes the shooting of part of an episode of *Marcus*

Welby, M.D., and in the second, he observes the production of the feature-length pilot episode of *Owen Marshall, Counselor at Law*. Kerns's account of the production of *Marcus Welby, M.D.*, describes how the production used a Mitchell and an Arriflex camera, the former fitted with a "motor driven Angenieux 25mm-250mm zoom lens."[59] The centrality of the zoom lens is emphasized by Kerns's description of a complicated action sequence shot in the studio backlot and involving three characters, one of whom approaches the scene astride a motorcycle. This intricate sequence is filmed "in one continuous take," without any camera movement; it is left to the zoom to maintain the framing of the actors. This is very much the sort of zoom shot often criticized for its "laziness"; rather than move the camera, the zoom's change in focal length fully accommodates the changing scale of actors within the frame. However, Kerns' account indicates that using the zoom was not an easy, much less a lazy, solution for the crew of *Marcus Welby, M.D.*: "It took every member of the camera crew—including Strenge—to make this shot. Hoffberg physically controlled the camera. Bluemel worked the motorized zoom and Wolk pulled the focus. As the camera panned back and forth, there was an exposure change so Strenge handled the lens stop. Four pairs of hands were on the camera but the scene went smoothly."[60]

Occasionally, prime lenses were used to shoot singles, and some camera movement is evident in the completed episode, but it is generally limited to short, oblique lateral movements, apparently along dolly tracks—as Kerns notes, "The set was quite small with very little room to move about in."[61] At all other times, the zoom dominates. Where significant alterations of scale or depth are called for, they are performed using the zoom lens. During the episode's precredit sequence, the first shot of a cramped apartment depicts a child playing with a baby on a low bed. A zoom out brings the rest of the apartment into view, showing the girl's father opening the door to Welby. At the end of the precredit sequence, another zoom works in the opposite way, moving in from a medium close-up encompassing a hospital bed to a close-up of the priest, Father Hugh, who is suffering an asthma attack. As is frequently the case on *Marcus Welby*, the scene ends with a sharp zoom. The zooms are not always "perfect": on occasion, they are performed hastily and "adjusted" at the end of the zoom.

Subsequent scenes show the zoom generally used in the same way—that is, not to replace camera dollying, as the technique is not imitative of it, but to pick out subsections of an overall scene for closer attention. In the scenes that immediately follow the precredit sequence, zooms—alternatively in and out—move between two pairs of key framings, showing a wider view of a waiting room and a closer shot of the receptionist's desk. In the next scene, involving the examination of a teenager's tennis injury, and consistent with Kerns's description, this opening master shot is followed by a shot/reverse shot sequence through the ensuing conversation, from camera positions ostensibly perpendicular to the master shot. At the conclusion of the conversation, the master shot returns. Welby's nurse enters through a door, and the camera simultaneously pans and zooms to show her inspecting an X-ray; when she has finished doing so, the zooms extends further to an extreme close-up of the X-ray itself. On another occasion, a character—a teenage girl (Ronne Troup)—gets out of a chair and walks toward the camera, which zooms out to keep her consistently framed. The camera then tracks the teenage girl to another more distant part of the set, zooming in as she sits down in another chair, to establish the beginning of another shot/reverse shot sequence depicting her conversation with Father Morley. Zooms transport the viewer from one setup to the next. While evidently saving time in production, one of the consequences of this approach is a curiously uneconomical treatment of movement through space. Tracking a character's movement across space with the zoom deprives the editor of the opportunity to abbreviate a scene through a well-concealed jump cut. Instead, the entirety of the actor's performance across the stage is preserved. The highly theatrical context of the one-hour drama removes entirely the "documentary" connotation from the panning and zooming camera. If anything, the zoom's preservation of

FIGURE 6.5. In *Marcus Welby, M.D.*, simple movements through the mise-en-scène are more likely to be achieved via the zoom shot than by more conventional dollying.

temporal and spatial integrity contributes to an aesthetic of live theatrical performance, the zoom imitating the attentional focus of the audience member.

The following year, Kerns returned to Universal City to spend a further day
with Walter Strenge as he filmed *Owen Marshall, Counselor at Law*, a two-hour
feature for the World Premiere television series. This time, rather than presenting a general overview of shooting routines and techniques, Kerns framed his
observations within the context of Strenge's enthusiasm for the zoom lens.
Kerns notes, "With the recent improvement in the overall quality of varifocal
or 'zoom' lenses, it was inevitable that cinematographers would come to rely on
them as a general, all-purpose lens. Not only has the zoom lens replaced a number of primary lenses but, because of its unique ability to continuously change
the focal distance, is able to create the illusion that the camera is moving towards
or away from the scene. In a sense, the zoom lens can all but eliminate the dolly
in making moving camera shots." In this context, Kerns adds, "Strenge was on
the 21st day of a 23-day schedule. He said that so far he had photographed *every
scene* in the picture with the Angenieux 25mm-250mm lens. 'It has not been off
the camera except to be cleaned and checked each evening,' he added."[62] Strenge
emphasizes the versatility of the zoom, suggesting that in addition to replicating
shots made with a dolly, the zoom could capture shots "that would be difficult,
if not impossible, to capture with the camera moving on the dolly. For example,
this lens can travel down the length of a table, move up a staircase or jump across
some large prop. There is really no limit to the type of shot you can get with a
varifocal lens."[63]

Kerns's article on *Owen Marshall, Counselor at Law* has a significance beyond
its descriptions of production practices. It also engages, in a way that his article
on *Marcus Welby, M.D.*, does not, with considerations of the aesthetic impact of
the zoom lens and addresses a number of potential criticisms of the device. It
is a strident declaration of the benefits of the zoom lens, of a sort that had not
appeared in *American Cinematographer* since Richard Moore's article in 1965.[64]
Two self-evident themes are particularly pronounced: as good as the zoom
lens can be, it relies on technological progress (a good-quality lens) and skilled
operation (a highly professional crew). The importance of a well-trained, "professional" crew is complemented by Strenge's descriptions of his own use of the
zoom—compared with that of unspecified others. Strenge tells Kerns, "I prefer
to call [zoom lenses] *varifocal* lenses. Unfortunately the term 'zoom' has come to
mean for me a lot of aimless, wild shots into nowhere. When used properly, the
varifocal lens is a wonderful tool, but if used with wild abandon, it can become
rather boring. Varifocal is really a more accurate name because the lens combines a wide range of focal lengths housed in a single optical system."[65]

Strenge describes his own "secret" for the effective use of the zoom: he starts
the zoom when an actor moves or uses it in concert with a pan or tilt and, when

doing so, "feather[s]" the zoom so that it starts and finishes gradually. For this, he remarked, "a good, motorized zoom unit is essential." Kerns also describes in greater detail the operation of the "Joy Stick" electronic zoom control, which enabled its operator, Walter Bluemel, to zoom in or out at a consistent rate and to "'feather' his moves at the beginning and end so that it virtually duplicates the gradual starts and stops that a regular camera dolly makes." This level of electronic control, however, did not reduce the complexity of operation: while Bluemel "handle[d] the focal changes on the lens," fellow assistant camera operator Max Wolk "control[led] the focus knob."[66] As on the set of *Marcus Welby, M.D.*, studio operations still involved at least two pairs of hands on the camera.

The pilot episode of *Owen Marshall* shows comprehensive and complex use of the zoom shot, in excess of what appears in *Marcus Welby*. One interior shot, for example, begins with one character in the foreground and another in the background. The foremost character makes a drink and is followed across the set by a zoom shot. The camera rests, then follows the pair as they walk to a couch, where they sit down, a further zoom moving in to frame them in a two shot. The sequence is intercut with some singles, but the master shot follows purely with zooms. The episode also includes some relatively extreme and rapid transitions from two-shot compositions to head-and-shoulders singles. Frequently, such zoom shots are combined with other forms of camera movements—especially panning. This style can also be seen in the second-season episode "Love Child" (November 9, 1972), which, in addition to frequent zoom shots whenever characters move around the set, includes some considerably more "stylish" uses of the zoom that purposefully direct the visual and mental attention of the audience. In an early scene, the zoom pulls back from a medium shot of two young women in a swimming pool before resting on a new medium shot of Owen Marshall and his companion at the poolside, with the women in the background. In another scene, the zoom is used in combination with the panning camera to explore and break down the space in a hospital room; in the same scene, a trivial movement in staging (a character sitting down on the side of a bed) is depicted through an adjustment of the zoom lens. The zoom is also used to animate point-glance spatial relations, reflecting the attention of characters in the mise-en-scène; but in the more cramped interiors of *Owen Marshall*, such shots seem both more obvious and more intense. The zoom, finally, is also frequently used at the beginning and end of acts, pulling out of—or plunging back into—the narrative.

As examples of high-budget, high-profile 1970s television drama serials, *Marcus Welby, M.D.*, and *Owen Marshall, Counsellor at Law* offer an alternative view of the zoom than what is provided by a close focus on feature films produced at the same time. They represent the extreme development of techniques first developed during the 1950s and 1960s, in which zooms were introduced into standard filming setups in order to provide production efficiencies and increased flexibility for crews filming in cramped and often monotonous studio spaces. Other prominent shows of the same era showed a similar enthusiasm for the zoom shot: particularly important examples include *Ironside* (1967–1975), *Hawaii Five-O* (CBS, 1968–1980), and *Charlie's Angels* (1976–1981)—each of which is replete with zoom shots in both studio and location-filmed sequences.

The zoom, as the preceding chapters of this book make plain, was not invented in the 1970s. Nor was it exactly "rare" in pre-1970s film, having been used extensively in a range of high-profile Hollywood features from the mid-1960s onward. One thing *was* new in the 1970s, however. During this decade, the field of academic film studies began to find its voice. Alongside box-office success and Academy Awards, a new celebratory criterion emerged: films could be acclaimed by scholars, isolated as teaching examples, and valorized by detailed analysis. Certain 1970s auteurs benefited greatly from this new critical attention, and in the context of the zoom shot, few benefited more than Robert Altman. Altman's films make a particularly attractive case study of the zoom because they are so frequent and so unapologetically overt. Furthermore, they can readily be identified as a marker of his personal style.

The resulting discussions have tended to emphasize the thoughtful, deliberate nature of Altman's zooms. From Robin Wood's claim that Altman was the first director to "grasp" the zoom's "expressive potentialities" to David Cook's emphasis of the "systematic" and "structured" properties of Altman's zooms, there is the implication that others before Altman used the zoom carelessly or by accident or economic necessity.[67] Altman, it has been consistently and problematically argued, bestowed unique genius on the zoom and used it in powerful ways that few others could match. Altman's films remain the most salient examples of "zoom style" and continue to inspire valuable fresh work in film history and criticism. Hamish Ford has associated the zoom with what he describes as Altman's "porous frame," in which "those in front of the camera . . . enjoyed relatively unrestricted front-to-back and lateral bodily movement within the available space, while the team behind the camera forged images with equivalent freedom." For Ford, Altman's "ubiquitous" zooms create a frame "in a constant state of flux."[68] Jay Beck has noted that the combination of zoom lenses and wireless microphones used in *MASH* enabled Altman to create "complex audiovisual symphonies" that place the audience "in an active spectatorial position, being asked to sift through the audiovisual information in order to follow one of the potential narrative paths."[69] For Beck, the "zoom cinematography"—in combination with the complex, multilayered soundtrack—encourages a greater audience involvement in the film's unconventional narrative.

Altman, like a number of other TV Generation directors, first used the zoom on the small screen during the 1960s. In his earliest television work, zooms appear only occasionally. In a 1961 episode of *Bus Stop*, for example, the zoom emphasizes the shooting of a storekeeper during a holdup. A few years later, episodes of *Combat!* and *Kraft Suspense Theatre* show Altman becoming more adventurous, experimenting with the zoom as an insight into the subjective psychological state of key characters.[70] The most overt and coordinated of Altman's television zooms, however, are to be seen in "Once upon a Savage Night," an episode of *Kraft Suspense Theatre* in which a serial killer roams Illinois, pursued by the police.[71] The zoom is central to the visual style of this episode, and the long, dramatic zoom shots—not seen before in Altman's work—make it highly likely that this was one of his earliest opportunities to work with the newly available Angénieux 10:1 zoom lens. Zooms appear throughout the episode, highlighting the killer's crimes and heightening the sense of his malevolent psychology.

Altman's extensive use of the zoom in feature films did not emerge out of the blue but was heavily prefigured by his work in television. With increasingly flexible zoom lens technology and somewhat greater creative freedom, by the mid-1960s, he was able to benefit from the zoom's potential as a storytelling device rather than a mere money-saving technology. Altman made extensive creative use of the zoom throughout his feature-directing career, beginning with *Countdown* (1968). Dismissed by Robert Kolker because it was neither as stylish nor as unusual as Altman's later work, *Countdown* is a considerably more interesting film when compared with the television episodes mentioned previously. In the film, which narrates an ill-fated mission to send an astronaut to the moon, Altman continues to use the zoom as a means to highlight the inner thoughts of a character in a scene that has no dialogue. The zoom is the most notable feature of a powerful scene in which the protagonist, an astronaut named Stegler who is dangerously unprepared for his mission, is strapped into the lunar capsule. Locked inside the spaceship, hidden behind glass, Altman insistently zooms toward Stegler's face. The more the image fills the screen, the greater Stegler's terror appears, until finally the audience is confronted with his tearful, terrified face. In Altman's next film, *Cold Day in the Park* (1969), his psychologically motivated zoom is one of the film's key motifs. As Kolker notes, these zooms foster a sense of "isolation and inwardness."[72] Altman's use of the zoom in this film is highly strategic. For most of the film's duration, Altman repeatedly uses the zoom to demonstrate the isolation of Frances, a bored woman who takes hostage a fraudulently mute teenager. In the film's final scene, however, Altman reverses the usual pattern, using the zoom to demonstrate the horror of the nameless teenage boy as he realizes that he cannot escape her grasp.[73]

After *That Cold Day in the Park*, and for at least the first half of the 1970s, Altman's films—including *MASH* (1969), *Brewster McCloud* (1970), *McCabe & Mrs. Miller* (1971), *Images* (1972), and *The Long Goodbye* (1973)—adopted a style that made maximum use of the zoom. *MASH* continues Altman's fascination with zooming in and out of cluttered mise-en-scènes and through windows. An early scene in which Hawkeye arrives at camp and joins a group of nurses eating in the officers' mess tent is a case in point: the zoom transgresses the physical walls of the space, seeming to zoom through the gauze sidewalls of the tent. This motif can be traced in Altman's earlier work: in a voyeuristic scene in *That Cold Day* in which we watch through a series of windows as Frances attends a medical appointment, in the pondering zoom through the spacecraft hatch in *Countdown,* and in the zoom through the window of a diner in "Once upon a Savage Night."

Despite this continuity, *MASH* diverges from Altman's earlier style in important ways. There are far more zoom shots than in any previous film by Altman, and probably more than in any Hollywood feature that preceded it. In using the zoom so frequently, Altman also becomes more adventurous in how he uses it. Sometimes the zoom simply tightens a framing; sometimes it is coordinated with the soundtrack for extra emphasis (as in the sharp zoom-in as a jeep's tire is shot in the opening scene). Occasionally, the zoom combines with the panning camera to create the sense that the audience is embedded within the scene. This is most notable when, after being provoked by Hawkeye, Major Burns becomes physically violent and is sent away in a straitjacket. We see this scene from the apparent perspective of a single bystander, watching as a jeep carries Burns away. Rather than repeatedly moving from one perspective to another, Altman pans and zooms, maintaining a single physical position and perspective while continuing to pick up the reactions and dialogue of the various spectators.

McCabe & Mrs. Miller and *Images* feature the most extreme of Altman's zooms at this moment in his career. The cinematography of both films is preoccupied with depth and with making direct transitions into the depth of the mise-en-scène via the zoom. Here, Belton suggests, "Altman's zooms function like jazz improvisations superimposed on a fixed melody: whether motivated or not, they signal his presence as a narrator."[74] In *McCabe*, the zoom toward a banjo player strumming in a gambling parlor is a particularly strong example of the film's many zooms through cluttered and dimly lit interiors. The soundtrack is as confusing as the image: The low, overlapping chattering of the gamblers vies for attention with the banjo. The zoom advances slowly and uncertainly. It finally picks out the banjo player, but like the virtuoso single-take Steadicam shots often found in later films, part of the visual pleasure of the mobile frame lays in this uncertainty of the final destination. Zooms like these, Belton suggests, create "a very flat, dimensionless space which enhances the enclosed, claustrophobic nature of the film."[75] More broadly, the continual zooming in *McCabe* reflects a tonal consistency that unites the cinematography with other aspects of the film. The zoom is the distinctive visual counterpart to the film's distinctive soundtrack: as repetitive as the nondiegetic soundtrack (a continual restatement of the same harmony) and as overlapping as the film's multitrack diegetic speech.

Images offers further opportunities to examine the aesthetic consequences of these strategies. Altman and Zsigmond use the same suite of techniques as in *McCabe*. The zoom often retains the familiar didactic function in which the camera is a tool of literal description: the film's motifs are devices of seeing and imaging (in particular cameras and their lenses), which the zoom repeatedly picks out and flags for the audience's attention. However, the setting, plot, and tone of the film mean that other zooms have very different implications. It is *Images* that, in contrast to *McCabe*, demonstrates the reliance of the zoom-into-depth on a geometric, inorganic mise-en-scène: a cityscape or building interior. The *Images* camera often executes zooms of significant length, but these are as often onto a landscape as through a doorway and into a room. In the latter case, the profilmic seems transformed as the depth-signifying planes disappear from the frame edges, whereas in the former—partly because of the camera distance and partly because of the lack of proximity to the physical landscape—nothing melts away; the zoom's target is simply magnified. Inside a house, or within a city street, we appear to travel as a person might; when zooming across a valley or down a hillside, we adopt a more birdlike perspective and mobility.

Ultimately, this freedom of movement typifies some of the most stimulating and resonant zoom shots of the 1970s. The zoom's interactions with landscapes and the built environment, in particular, have preoccupied recent writers on the New Hollywood and nourished new perspectives on the technique. Amy Rust has explored how the zoom, alongside other technologies, shapes "vision and violence for the counterculture and capitalism" in the American cinema of the late 1960s and early 1970s. In *McCabe & Mrs. Miller*, Rust sees a powerful example of how the zoom can "figure fantasies of violent encounter" in Altman's films and beyond.[76] For Adam O'Brien, who approaches the subject from an ecocritical perspective and draws on *Easy Rider*, *Jaws*, and—once more—*The Conversation*, zooms serve to "emphasize, or at least suggest, the limitations of the camera in our world."[77]

Such variation in critical approaches and interpretations of the zoom reflects the technique's freedom of movement not only through on-screen space but also across genre and time period. For all that some cinematographers have fretted about anachronism, the zoom is effective in the period piece. As noted earlier, we find zooms used to lavish effect in *Barry Lyndon* (Stanley Kubrick, 1975). Yet far from clashing with and detracting from the eighteenth-century setting, it is as if the lavish, propulsive zoom shot was made precisely in order to heighten the absurd costume and behavior of the Regency aristocrat. Furthermore, having done so, it is no less capable of energizing the mud and chill of *McCabe &*

Mrs. Miller, and it is equally suited to depicting the contemporary cops (*Dirty Harry*), robbers (*The Thomas Crown Affair*), and private eyes (*The Conversation*) who populate the American mainstream cinema. Furthermore, from the 1960s and into the 1970s, the zoom boom is a global cinematic phenomenon, stamping its mark onto the cinemas of the European New Wave. Zooms contribute to the murderous horror of *Le Boucher* (Claude Chabrol, 1970), the neorealist spiritualism of *Il vangelo secondo Matteo* (Pier Paolo Pasolini, 1964), and the shocking provocations of *A Clockwork Orange* (Stanley Kubrick, 1971). From films like these, we learn that the zoom shot has no inherent suitability or any natural home. Rather, it is a technique as flexible as any other, capable of being put to use in narratives of any form and scenes of any nature.

The 1970s was a high point for the zoom. This was the moment at which it finally became fully embedded in film and television style, aided by the introduction of more sophisticated and useful supporting technologies. Though now a truly well-established technology, certain uses for the zoom remained novel: such ambitious, artistic, expressive uses as are found in the films of Robert Altman had not been seen before in American film, while the comprehensive use of the zoom in network television drama was also an innovation. In the years that followed, the zoom's prominence in film and television productions of this period became a marker of the era: within decades, directors and cinematographers would be using the zoom as one of the clearest and most efficient ways to lampoon seventies style. After the end of the 1970s, the changing approach to the zoom centered around three key developments. Hollywood cinema's style became faster, looser, and freer, partly influenced by changes in television, where portable video cameras replaced film equipment for many purposes. Meanwhile, as the free and easy "zoom cinematography" of the 1970s began to fall out of the fashion, the zoom was reborn as a key marker of the smart, self-conscious television situation comedy forms of the early 2000s. These changes were to finally transform the zoom beyond anything that cinematographers of the 1950s and 1960s could have envisaged or embraced.

7 · CONTEMPORARY ZOOMS

From first introduction to comprehensive embrace, it took about fifty years for the zoom lens to become a truly mature professional filmmaking technology. After the first zoom shots in late silent-era cinema, the zoom went through several cycles of technological development while stylistic approaches to the zoom as a narrative device shifted significantly. As interesting as they may have been, zoom shots in the late 1920s and early 1930s were rare and exceptional—spectacular effects provided by a cumbersome technology that did not seem to be supported by a sustained invention or marketing effort. In the late 1940s, when the Zoomar lens transformed television, Hollywood cinematographers were largely isolated from the changes it delivered. Gradually, following the introduction in the 1950s of Pan Cinor, Zoomar, and Angénieux zooms for 16mm and 35mm cameras, zoom shots came fully onto the horizon for professional directors and cinematographers. Even then, it took another twenty years—encompassing the introduction of Angénieux's powerful 10:1 zooms and the development of refined electronic zoom motors—before zooming became truly ubiquitous in Hollywood. This ubiquity came at a price: traditionalist cinematographers, always distrustful of flashy new devices that might draw attention to their craft, became increasingly critical of the new tendency to zoom overtly.

When the zoom lens was new, zoom shots had few associations or connotations; a sudden, punchy zoom shot could neither remind viewers of the film style of a past decade nor make a reference to another genre. More recently, the zoom has acquired more specific meanings and associations, stemming in part from its more limited and more cautious use. As the Steadicam became more attractive, it replaced some of the practical functions of the zoom. High-budget network television dramas like *ER* (NBC, 1994–2009) and *The West Wing* (NBC, 1999–2006) placed the immersive, fluid motion of the Steadicam at the center of their visual style, leaving zooms to lower-budget productions such as soap operas. Cable drama series such as *The Sopranos* (HBO, 1999–2007), *Six Feet Under* (HBO, 2001–2005), and *The Wire* (HBO, 2002–2008) similarly avoided the zoom, preferring tracking, panning, and the "cinematic" qualities of a more stable camera. Television drama's move away from the zoom created new stylistic opportunities: unstable, jolting zooms became a signifier of nervous energy or smartphone-age vérité. These techniques typified the visual style of *24* (Fox, 2001–2010) and were also seen in Hollywood features including *The Hurt Locker* (Kathryn Bigelow, 2008) and *Cloverfield* (Matt Reeves, 2008). Meanwhile, the zoom's decades-long association with news and documentary, magnified by the development of the camcorder, made it a useful signifier of self-conscious parodies of documentary, ranging from conventional "mockumentaries" such as *The Office* (2005–2013) and *Parks and Recreation* (2009–2015) to the quirkier *Arrested Development* (2003–present). In these shows, the zoom itself is part of the comedy.

As film style became more varied and flexible, the zoom became more acceptable and, often, less noticeable. John Belton, writing in 1980, summed up the zoom's interaction with broader changes in film style. For Belton, the zoom was "symptomatic of the evolution of the language of the cinema since the New Wave. Spatially distorting and inherently self-conscious, the zoom reflects the disintegration of cinematic codes developed before the Second World War. Now regularly used in combination with pans and tracks to extend their movements a few feet, the zoom has co-opted these codes from within."[1] After the 1970s, the zoom lens remained highly controversial. Many directors and cinematographers made a show of refusing to use it at all. Others did the opposite, making dramatic, overt zooms part of their visual style. But as Belton's account implies, there was also a middle way, which saw the zoom integrated more comfortably into the norms of feature cinematography and television drama. It became increasingly acceptable to zoom subtly, attempting to hide the zoom within a camera move, or to use "small zooms" to add a sense of energy, unpredictability, or vérité to footage. The introduction of an increasingly wide range of high-performance zooms marketed as "variable primes" capitalized on a tendency—which had always existed—for cinematographers to use a zoom in place of a battery of prime lenses. Though no different to standard zooms in terms of their basic design, by marketing zoom lenses as variable primes lens, manufacturers could appeal to camera operators who might otherwise have shunned the zoom lens.

For David Bordwell, the zoom is one example of a wide repertoire of camera and editing techniques that together define the restless, intensified nature of contemporary Hollywood cinema. Changes in the style of mainstream Hollywood cinema, identified by Bordwell as "intensified continuity," are typified by "rapid editing, bipolar extremes of lens lengths, reliance on close shots, and wide-ranging camera movements."[2] Zoom lenses, especially when designed explicitly as variable primes, contributed toward the development of this style. Variable primes offered camera operators and directors greater flexibility of focal lengths and enabled them to inject additional movement into scenes. Depicting the tense world of American bomb-disposal technicians in Iraq, Kathryn Bigelow used the zoom to evoke a greater sense of realism, creating a "jumpy" style that recalls vérité but is firmly grounded in the twenty-first century. Reviewing *The Hurt Locker*, Manohla Dargis eloquently described the "purposeful wobbliness" of the film's zoom, which "when deployed fast and with a tremble, as it is here . . . can also serve as a kind of visual punctuation, like an exclamation point." Besides this observation about the qualities of the zoom itself, Dargis also articulates the link between the literal zoom shot and the "zoomy effect" created by Bigelow's "propulsive use of close-ups and very long shots."[3] Some cinematographers, such as John Seale, have increasingly buried zoom shots within camera movement, multiplying the degree to which framing and camera position appears to change during scenes. Improvements in variable primes, and their increasing use, made it more tempting for camera operators to zoom modestly in order to add additional energy to their cinematography. Zeiss variable primes were used extensively in the shooting of *Gangs of New York* (Martin Scorsese, 2002), in combination with a highly mobile camera. The film's cinematographer, Michael Ballhaus, created "little zooms," explaining that he loved variable primes because "if you want to go a little wider or a little closer it's just a move of the finger."[4] Andrew Lesnie, on shooting *The Lovely Bones* (Peter Jackson, 2009), cited a similar advantage: Angénieux's 15–40mm Optimo lens enabled him to choose between the "nice and wide" 15mm end of the lens and the portrait potential of the 40mm setting. The infinite range of focal lengths in the middle was a convenient bonus. As Lesnie put it, "If I chose to ride the zoom during a shot, we had that option."[5] In professional filmmaking, the convenience and flexibility of the variable prime, usable at multiple focal lengths, was becoming more important than the ability to create a zoom shot.

Significant changes in zoom technology and style were not confined to professional cinematography. During the 1980s, amateur cinematographers began to swap 8mm cameras for portable video equipment. In television, the rise of the lightweight electronic newsgathering camera—ultimately used in applications far broader than newsgathering—led to an explosion in live and on-the-scene reporting. Electronic television cameras were becoming increasingly portable: they could now be operated on a shoulder and transmitted images by radio link. This had significant implications for the style of news coverage that appeared on television screens, and ENG cameras were soon used in the production of a wider range of—usually lower budget—television programming. Powered by batteries and connected to base stations via microwave link, these cameras required smaller, lighter lenses to maximize their portability. These factors combined to create some iconic moments of television coverage in which the facility of the zoom was central to camera operators' ability to acquire footage and viewers' ability to make sense of it. Zoom lenses helped enable a surge in the practice of shooting live TV coverage from news helicopters, of which the blanket coverage of the Los Angeles Police Department's pursuit of O. J. Simpson in 1994 is one of the most famous examples. Technological advances in video that had benefited television soon made an impact on consumer video technology, thanks to the further miniaturization and cost reduction of video cameras. By the end of the 1980s, portable video cameras were increasingly affordable, and by the 1990s, they were everywhere. Camcorders—nearly always with integrated zooms, easily operated via a thumb switch—became a mass-produced consumer product. They enabled the creation of another grimly iconic video sequence: George Holliday's video of the beating of Rodney King, in which the zoom was of critical importance. As this chapter explains, the zoom has retained a central but often overlooked role in the creation of images of great political and social importance.

"YOU DON'T CUT BREAD WITH A SAW"

Improvements in zoom lens technology during the 1970s were so fast and so dramatic that by 1976, the camera designer Ed DiGiulio declared that the technology had "come of age."[6] A great change had undoubtedly occurred: In the early 1960s, the zoom had been a relatively rare sight on a film set, and in the early 1970s, electronic zoom controls were in their infancy. Now, at the beginning of the 1980s, these technologies were indispensable, ubiquitous, and unremarkable. Indeed, by 1980, most of the desired qualities and functions of the zoom had been achieved—if not perfected—by equipment manufacturers. Camera operators could use zoom lenses with very high ratios that reached from ultrawide to ultratelephoto positions. The lenses were much faster and much sharper than earlier models. Auxiliary technologies offered a wider and more precise range of electronic controls, enabling zooms to be used precisely without having to place hands on the camera. This array of technologies—versatile, high-quality zoom lenses manipulated via electronically controlled motors—remains in use to this day. Manufacturers continue to refine the technologies and incrementally improve their products to keep up with ever-higher resolution digital image acquisition and increasingly complex motion control systems.

In the 1960s and 1970s, it had been developments in film technology that had made the most significant mark on the moving image. In the 1980s and 1990s, the focus shifted to television and video. As earlier chapters have demonstrated, zoom lenses for large television cameras—as used in studios and tethered to remote trucks—were at first developed in tandem with those designed for film. In the 1940s, there was little to differentiate a television zoom lens from a film camera zoom lens, aside from the shape of the mounting and the design of the housing. However, the design of film and television zoom lenses quickly diverged. Zooms for film cameras were designed to be as portable as possible while maintaining the high optical standards required for shooting on high-resolution film formats. Often this came at the expense of high zoom ranges. Television, meanwhile, needed higher zoom ratios to better cover live events from fixed and often distant camera positions. These cameras were often less portable, and electronic cameras were not routinely handheld. Thus by the end of the 1970s, typical TV camera zoom lenses were vast and heavy but versatile. When designing zooms for television, lens manufacturers competed to provide the longest possible range of focal length, and by the mid-1980s, they had managed to develop lenses capable of creating breathtaking zooms far in excess of what was generally available (or necessary for) film production. By 1983, Canon was marketing a 40:1 zoom lens, Angénieux a 42:1 lens, and Fujinon a 44:1 model.[7] The latter of these, a fifty-six-pound behemoth, offered television directors a 13.5–600mm range and featured a built-in 2:1 extender that increased the telephoto position to 1,200mm.[8] This was a focal length befitting of a telescope, and zooms of this design enabled exceptionally long zoom shots that could either transform close-ups of distant buildings into broad cityscapes or zoom from wide shots of sports stadiums to screen-filling close-ups of athletes' faces.

Though zoom lenses continued to improve, developments in a range of camera mobility technologies—including cranes, booms, and the Steadicam—rendered them less attractive for filmmakers who wanted to create a sense of physical movement.[9] Together, these developments obviated one of the strongest incentives to use the zoom. In the 1970s, the zoom's major attraction had been its ability to create apparent camera movement and flexibility of coverage without causing expensive delays for equipment repositioning. By the 1990s, Steadicams, hotheads, and lightweight cranes with enormous ranges of motion were increasingly serving the purposes for which zooms had earlier been advertised. Where zooms had once been marketed as potential replacements for the crane or dolly, now more flexible and cost-effective forms of camera movement were introduced. The Steadicam was improved and refined, while lighter and more flexible cranes meant that filmmakers could benefit from a stable camera mounting and a full range of motion. At the end of the crane arm, servo-controlled camera mounts known as hotheads enabled precise remote control of pan and tilt movements. Only the very largest cranes needed to be mounted on a heavy-duty truck; lighter equipment such as the Louma crane, Techno-crane, and Jimmy Jib could be loaded onto the back of a light- or medium-duty vehicle and positioned on a small base. Cranes such as these competed with the zoom lens by enabling rapid telescopic extensions and swift repositioning.

The 1970s had been the decade in which electronics spurred a great advance in the convenience and practicality of zoom lenses, but it was also the decade in which they were most dangerously overused. The zoom was voguish and yet hated. There was a fine line between using it with aplomb and amateurism, but nobody could agree where the line lay. With lavish, expressive zooms, Robert Altman and Stanley Kubrick had done some of their most celebrated work. But this was also the decade in which an irritated Billy Wilder wished aloud that he could "take away the zoom lens" from young directors—and from Kubrick. "Just don't let them have it," he said at an American Film Institute event in 1976.[10] By the 1980s, new camera-mobility technologies were becoming more attractive, and many cinematographers remained disillusioned with the zoom shot. Asked why he had barely used the zoom on the science-fiction romance *Somewhere in Time* (Jeannot Szwarc, 1980), cinematographer Isodore Mankofsky offered two explanations. The first was stylistic: the zoom, he explained, creates a certain "look" on film, limited to "moving straight in," allowing for none of the organic deviations of movement that would be created by a handheld camera. On top of this, practical considerations weighed heavy: the film's vast locations meant that time would have been wasted lighting wide sets to accommodate an infinite range of focal lengths. Far better, the cinematographer had concluded, to stick to "the old-fashioned school of filmmaking where you move your actors and you move your camera and you don't use the zoom to do the job."[11] Mankofsky's choice was to use prime lenses to create the look he and director Szwarc desired, but the Steadicam—new, growing in popularity, and undergoing constant improvement—was well poised to provide the physical mobility and flexibility that zoom lenses lacked.

Nostalgia for a simpler, plainer, more self-effacing style continued to discourage some cinematographers from showily operating their zoom lenses. This was not a view limited to high-budget features: television productions sometimes followed similar logic. Shooting *The Tracker*, a Western-style TV movie for HBO, director of photography George Tirl attempted to evoke the cinematography of John Ford. This, of course, meant avoiding visible zooms, which prompted Tirl to muse colorfully on the "correct" use of the technology: "Ford most likely wouldn't have used a zoom because it is a modern type movement. So when we zoomed in our film we tried to do it invisibly. These things are tools and every tool has to be used properly. You don't cut bread with a saw. You can get very 'newsreel' with a zoom. But that really isn't the purpose."[12] Even as "variable prime" zooms became more present on film sets, the debate over the use of the zoom lens continued— often as restatements of the same arguments about "use," "abuse," and the deleterious effects the technology could have on a cinematographer's craft. "People can get really lazy and just set up a zoom and move back and forth," complained cinematographer John Schwartzmann in 1996 while shooting *The Rock* for Michael Bay; in a similar vein, director James Mangold bemoaned the zoom's "very strange way of making you indecisive. If you want to change the frame a little, all you have to do is turn a ring, and to me there's something cheap about that."[13] Here we see the long-term legacy of views originally expressed in the 1950s and 1960s, for Schwartzmann and Mangold echo similar sentiments expressed by—among others—James Wong Howe and Karl Malkames decades previously.

Thus while zoom technology continued to evolve after 1980, the industrial conversation that surrounded its use remained rather static. Convention continued to hold that artistic cinematography should rely on either prime lenses or very good zooms used as variable primes. If zoom moves had to be seen on screen, they should ideally be concealed—as artfully as possible—within a camera move. Zooming overtly was an embarrassing trope of the 1970s and, for some, was ideally left in the history books. This was the motivation behind Woody Omens's avoidance of the zoom on the set of *Coming to America* (John Landis, 1988). As Omens explained, "The style of this picture was such that prime lenses were the way to do it. I've shot movies for years almost entirely with zoom lenses. I just feel that it may be time to go back to something more traditional in movies—the look we had before the zoom lens was invented."[14] Omens's wish for the industry to dispense with its zoom lenses was not to be granted: there are countless examples from the 1980s and beyond of films and television series that make ample and overt use of zoom shots. However, they did so in continually changing technological and stylistic contexts.

As films as diverse as *Wall Street* (Oliver Stone, 1987) and *The Royal Tenenbaums* (Wes Anderson, 2001) demonstrate, the big, punchy zoom shot never went away. *Wall Street* includes two particularly striking zoom shots at the start of a frenetic sequence in which shares in a steel company are purchased in order to bid up the company's price. The zoom thrusts across the trading floor toward a digital clock, marking the opening of the trading day; in the next shot, a similarly rapid zoom tightens the frame on Bud Fox (Charlie Sheen) as he works the room. For *The Witches of Eastwick* (1987), director George Miller and cinematographer Vilmos Zsigmond created an "outrageous look" with "heavy use of zoom lenses."[15] In many cases, occasional high-energy zooms provide a stark contrast with otherwise sedate cinematography. In *The Royal Tenenbaums*, an 11:1 zoom was reserved for a "series of pronounced snap-zooms," which contrasted with otherwise subtle camera movement.[16] Both in films and on television, computer-generated special effects made faster, deeper "zooms" possible. In *Spider-Man* (Sam Raimi, 2002), these digitally created zooms imitate the superhero's "supernaturally intense level of inspection."[17] As in earlier decades,

FIGURE 7.1. A sharp zoom surges toward a digital clock at the start of a high-intensity trading scene in *Wall Street* (Oliver Stone, 1987).

the zoom retained an ability to shock when its sudden plunging movements were juxtaposed with otherwise conventional cinematography and continuity editing.

Toward the end of the 1990s, film and television began to reach toward the kitsch and nostalgia value of the previous generation. The excessive zooms of the 1970s began to reappear as markers of a past style.[18] Filming the short-lived CBS crime drama series *Buddy Faro*, cinematographer Aaron Schneider attempted to concoct an "interestingly cheesy" style out of memories of "old television shows." As Schneider explained, deliberately mishandling the zoom was central to the pastiche: "At one point, we used a big fat zoom-in on a window for an establishing shot. It took us a few takes to purposefully execute the zoom improperly.... We centered heads in the frame and gave them 'too much' headroom. We all had a lot of fun trying to create a subtle comedy in the camerawork itself."[19] A straighter motivation for the reappearance of the overt zoom shot can be seen in *Munich* (Steven Spielberg, 2005). The film tells the story of a group of Mossad agents sent to Europe to assassinate the killers of Israeli athletes murdered at the

1972 Olympics. In keeping with its setting, Spielberg's film adopts elements of the decade's style. The director of photography, Janusz Kaminski, used a Cooke 25–250mm zoom lens to create a variety of zoom shots "characteristic of seventies movies." According to camera operator Mitch Dubin, a longtime collaborator with both Kaminski and Spielberg, the director agreed to include zooms in the film purely because of its 1970s setting.[20] Spielberg's decision is symbolic of the place of the zoom within early twenty-first-century filmmaking. The "perfection" of the zoom lens and its marketing as a variable prime has not led to its use as an overt substitute for the tracking or dollying camera. Rather than

FIGURE 7.2. Long high-angle zooms in *Munich* (Steven Spielberg, 2005) call to mind the cinema of the 1970s.

replace camera movement, the cinematic zoom shot has instead become a self-reflexive marker of eras and genres. It can stand for the films of the 1960s and 1970s but not for the classic Western or the silent feature.

Though zoom shots have remained present, a spirited refusal to use the zoom remained a perennial fixture of cinematography's industrial discourse. As in the previous decade, cinematographers and directors cited numerous reasons to avoid the zoom. *Star Trek: The Motion Picture* (1979) was filmed almost exclusively using prime lenses. In the view of the film's director of photography, Richard H. Kline, this—along with the avoidance of any "forcing" during film development—contributed to a "pristine look." The film, Kline remarked, "was a picture that called for prime lenses. It has a prime lens look and feel to it."[21] Another important science-fiction film of the same period, *Star Wars: The Empire Strikes Back* (Irvin Kershner, 1980), was also filmed without zoom lenses.[22] Across the decades, the zoom remained a cipher for "contemporary" cinematography, and this tended to preclude their use in period pieces. In *Down with Love* (Peyton Reed, 2003), Jeff Cronenweth "eschewed zoom lenses completely" in order to create a feeling of 1950s Technicolor.[23] Other cinematographers made a point of their avoidance of the zoom when "involvement" in the scene was a particularly important quality. After shooting *Sophie's Choice* (Alan J. Pakula, 1982), Nestor Almendros remarked on a scene in which the camera pulls back to reveal the protagonist (Meryl Streep) and her children in a cattle truck. "This pullback would have been simple with a zoom lens," he explained, "but it would not have had the same effect as a camera move. The audience would not have had the same sense of involvement with the characters in the scene that we obtained by having the camera actually inside the car."[24] In both feature and television production, the value of "real" camera movement was enhanced by the increasing acceptance of the Steadicam. While director of photography Donald Thorin boasted of using "no zooms on the entire show" in filming *Against All Odds* (Taylor Hackford, 1984), the Steadicam was used extensively.[25] Likewise, Gerald Finnerman avoided zoom lenses entirely on early episodes of *Moonlighting* (ABC, 1985–1989). His preference for the moving camera was boosted by the occasional use of a Steadicam rig for location work.[26] Swooping, gliding Steadicam shots were to become a staple of high-budget network television drama; the zoom, once seen in almost every shot of some 1970s television dramas, was to vanish.

As long, showy zooms fell out of favor, cinematographers increasingly used zoom lenses as convenient alternatives to a range of prime lenses. Cinematographers who admitted to fitting a zoom to a camera often hastened to assure their colleagues that this was purely for convenience. John A. Alonzo shot *Blue Thunder* (John Badham, 1983) "mostly with hard [prime] lenses. Even when we used a zoom lens, it was generally set at a fixed point."[27] Dean Cundey hardly ever took the zoom off the camera as he filmed *The Invisible Woman* (Alan J. Levi, 1983)—but, as the *American Cinematographer* reporter put it, this was "not so much for zooming as for a convenience in adjusting framing for a shot."[28] Zooms with a 5:1 ratio were increasingly preferred over the 10:1 Angénieux lenses that had been popular in the 1960s and 1970s. The 5:1 Cooke zoom lenses were a favorite choice, used widely across features and television series, including *Star Trek: The Next Generation* (1987–1994) and *Empire of the Sun* (Steven Spielberg, 1987).[29] A 6:1 Cooke zoom was used extensively by John Hora as he shot *Gremlins* (Joe Dante, 1984). Hora remarked, "Normally I try to leave the zoom lens in the truck or as far away as possible from the set and shoot everything in prime. However, on *Gremlins*, in all honesty, about 50% of the film was shot with a Cooke 10–60 zoom rented from Panavision, which I found to be excellent for our purposes."[30] Hora kept his set of primes close by, but his enthusiasm for the 6:1 zoom was an indication of the future popularity of shorter zooms. The shift away from Angénieux's 10:1 zoom lens is highlighted by a 1991 *American Cinematographer* article on the production of Alan Rudolph's *Equinox*, which describes Rudolph's "fascination with the 10:1 zoom," which by this point was regarded by the production's cinematographer, Elliot Davis, as "a very anachronistic tool."[31]

Cinematographers' increasing willingness to use zoom lenses in place of primes was partly a result of the increasing optical quality of zooms but also a response to the changing preferences and backgrounds of cinematographers themselves. When shooting *Flashdance* (Adrian Lyne, 1983), cinematographer Don Peterman had to adjust to a freer and less meticulously planned method of shooting, which relied on the flexibility of the zoom lens to grab a wide range of footage. According to Peterman, this was a result of Lyne's experience in shooting commercials: "He'll put the zoom on and shoot one at 40mm and then he'll say, 'Shoot this one at a hundred. Just shoot it. I don't care if you get half of the shot.' Then he'll use a piece of that. It's his style. He has always done that in commercials, you know, where you shoot 10,000 feet of film for a 60 second spot."[32] Other directors of photography found zooms attractive for different reasons. ABC's miniseries *The Winds of War* (Dan Curtis, 1983) was shot almost entirely using a 20–120mm Angénieux zoom lens, thanks to "substantial improvements in the sharpness and resolution of these zoom lenses" observed by the director of photography, Charles Correll. For Correll, the zoom was still not quite as sharp as he wanted it to be, but shooting consistently with a zoom lens offered an efficient way to obtain a consistent "look" across scenes.[33] In 1986, while filming *Ruthless People*, director Jan de Bont eschewed the Steadicam, regarding it as potentially "distracting and dangerous," and the zoom lens was used as a prime, alternating among a limited number of focal lengths.[34] Gradually, improvements in the quality of zoom lenses began to win over established cinematographers who had previously limited their use. Owen Roizman, who had previously restricted his use of the zoom to commercial shoots, shot almost all of *I Love You to Death* (Lawrence Kasdan, 1990) with a 17.5–75mm Panavision Primo lens.[35]

In parallel to these evolving preferences, lens manufacturers found new ways to market shorter, but faster, zoom lenses. In the late 1980s, Panavision introduced the Primo range of lenses, which included a zoom. Panavision president John Farrand explained that Primo zooms "resulted from the frustration of the cinematographer at not being able to intercut high-quality primes."[36] The set of lenses were closely color matched to facilitate intercutting, but some cinematographers found themselves using the zoom more extensively than Panavision may have anticipated. "Primo zoom," it turned out, was as workable a compromise as the name suggested. Jordan Cronenweth, in filming *Final Analysis* (Phil Joanou 1992), explained, "I respect the quality of [the Primo zoom] so much that I don't often have to change to a prime. You can use it to line up your shot because you can float back and forth and pick the lens that you want. But the difference between the primes and the zoom are so close now that we often shoot a good percentage of the run on the zoom."[37] In fact, Primo zooms were popular despite being widely regarded as *too* sharp. On the set of *Billy Bathgate* (Robert Benton, 1991), Nestor Almendros dealt with the Primo's unwanted sharpness by reverting to older zooms rather than placing diffusion filters in front of the lens.[38] Vilmos Zsigmond, facing the same problem while filming *Maverick* (Richard Donner, 1994), chose instead to use older zoom lenses in order to benefit from their softer quality.[39] This was a remarkable development after decades in which complex zoom optics led to softened and muddied images.

Arri, selling lenses manufactured by Carl Zeiss, was even more direct in its response to the growing preference for a short, high-quality zoom lens. For years, cinematographers who had used zoom lenses but had never "zoomed" explained that they viewed their lenses as "varifocals" or "variable primes." As early as 1978, Angénieux had introduced a 2.8:1 zoom lens, which it nicknamed a "variable prime . . . because of its image quality and normal focal length."[40] In the mid-1990s, Arri and Carl Zeiss formalized this nomenclature by introducing a set of three complementary zoom lenses marketed explicitly as "variable primes." The three lenses in the set each offered a relatively short range of focal lengths—16–30mm, 29–60mm, and 55–105mm—bucking the historic trend toward longer zoom ranges. The lenses won an Academy plaque in 1998, which hailed the firm for its development of "sharp, high-contrast, high-resolution images with minimized vignetting, superior to many prime lenses."[41] By reducing the zoom ratio of its variable primes, Zeiss was able to offer a much brighter lens with a lower T-stop than almost any competitor. This compromise proved particularly useful to Michael Ballhaus while filming *Sleepers* (Barry Levinson, 1996); the fast variable primes enabled his crew to capture scenes in low-light conditions while retaining the flexibility of the zoom lens.⁴² The lenses were marketed as a "complete lens system" with an "entire focal length range of 16mm to 105mm."⁴³ Of course, such a range could only be achieved by changing the lens on the camera twice, but this bold marketing strategy was a clear indication that lens speed was now regarded as a more important selling factor than zoom range.

After the 1970s, it became increasingly common for directors and cinematographers to attempt to hide their zooms from viewers by "burying" them within a camera movement. When filming *Annie*, cinematographer Richard Moore recast zoom shots as "optical dollies" in which "the focal length is drifted either tighter or looser to accommodate the shot, [facilitating] a fluidity of camera movement that is much more difficult to achieve if you're using a fixed focal length lens."⁴⁴ In filming *Titanic* (James Cameron, 1997), Russell Carpenter was "constantly massaging our focal lengths throughout scenes changing from, say, a 27mm on one shot to a 35mm and then to something else for the rest of the coverage." For this, they used 4:1 and 11:1 Primo zooms.⁴⁵ The cinematographer John Seale became a particularly vocal exponent of the "buried" zoom. Seale's camerawork in *The Talented Mr. Ripley* (Anthony Minghella, 1999) offers a particularly significant example of zooms that, while not concealed from the audience, are subtle enough to pass almost unnoticed. In certain scenes, the camera is in constant motion, zooming gradually in and out as multiple characters move within the frame. Seale boasted of using a Panavision 11:1 Primo lens to film almost the whole of the film, much to the imagined displeasure of his colleagues: "Some people may worry that I'm using the zoom as a zoom, and I suppose sometimes I do—but I also use the zoom as a multi-focal-length lens that I can adjust in shot whenever the camera or the actor moves. . . . With a zoom I can tighten up the frame gently or loosen up a bit to provide much more freedom for the actors to do what they want. I'll get in awful trouble [with other cinematographers] for saying this, but sometimes I'll move the camera just so I can tighten the zoom."⁴⁶ When Seale was able to operate the camera himself, he mounted the camera on a tripod and attached a zoom control to the pan handle, creating something "like a documentary camera." Yet because the zooms slowly traverse relatively short ranges of focal lengths and are often buried within panning movements, the zooms do not inject a vérité style into the cinematography. Instead, they contribute to the film's jazz aesthetic and queasy psychological uncertainty. For other filmmakers, burying zooms in camera movement was a component of a more efficient and flexible approach to production. Director James Foley described how he "had to learn to love zoom lenses" while shooting *Confidence* (2003) with director of photography Juan Ruiz Anchía. In search of efficiencies on a tight production schedule, Foley's distaste for the zoom, acquired at film school, gave way to greater pragmatism. The efficiency of shooting with a variety of zooms and variable primes saw principal shooting on *Confidence* concluded in only thirty-five days; the zoom shots themselves were "disguised" by their burial within camera movement.[47] These examples are representative of how, in the 1980s and 1990s, zoom lenses were improved and repackaged as variable primes. This adjusted form of marketing represented a capitulation, by equipment manufacturers, to a stubborn convention: the zoom should be avoided where possible and concealed where its use was essential. The zoom lens has become a more powerful, versatile, and ubiquitous tool, but the zoom shot has remained controversial and limited in its use.

"AS TIGHT AS WE CAN GO RIGHT NOW"

While cinematographers continued to disagree over the best uses of the zoom in high-budget film and television productions, producers of news footage and amateur video embraced the zoom and used it to devastating social and political effect. It is a given that zoom lenses remain vital for televised sports and other live public events. On top of this, the magnifying power of the zoom has been a key enabler of the contemporary on-the-scene television news camera operator. Zoom lenses have been as important as helicopters in enabling live aerial television shots, while the zoom, now standard equipment on the camcorder, has also boosted the abilities of the citizen journalist.

In the early 1990s, two video sequences grabbed the attention of television viewers in the United States and far beyond—and zoom lenses were essential to the production of both. In the early hours of March 3, 1991, officers of the Los Angeles Police Department gave chase to a car driving at speed along Interstate 210 through the San Fernando Valley. When the car finally stopped, three men emerged. From across the street, a man named George Holliday picked up a Sony Handycam portable video camera. Holliday filmed as a group of officers violently beat one of the occupants of the car, an African American man named Rodney King.[48] After capturing just over eight minutes of footage, Holliday shared the tape with KTLA, a local television station. The station broadcast the footage, and the beating of King became international news. Holliday's Handycam footage had produced vivid testimony of police brutality: as Stephan Talty wrote in *Film Comment* a few weeks later, "When the video was broadcast on national television, it was as if a longstanding rumor had been confirmed by a new technology, as if a new microscope now widely available to the public had given us pictures of a ravaging, diseased cell."[49]

A little more than three years later, on June 17, 1994, the former football star and film actor O. J. Simpson led police on a slow chase along Interstate 405. As Simpson's Ford Bronco headed north toward Brentwood, a swarm of television news helicopters assembled a few thousand feet above. Their footage was beamed by microwave radio link to local television base stations, and from there to millions of homes across the United States. Every major network, and the cable news channel CNN, broadcast live footage of the pursuit. The reality of the chase collided with that Friday night's scheduled television—sports on some channels, light drama on others. But as Walter Goodman reflected in the *New York Times* two days later, the chase made a "strange show," not least for the lack of access it offered viewers to the protagonist. "The on-screen chatter never stopped," wrote Goodman, "but you could hear almost nothing from the scene itself; the images in our sights held their silence and their secrets."[50] This sense of detachment from the event may have been increased by the flat, long-distance telephoto shots obtained from helicopters aloft. However, that the chase could be captured at all was an indication of the continuing centrality of the zoom lens in live television.

In the 1940s and early 1950s, the likely impact of television on journalism had been unclear. Whether television could contribute to journalism was hotly debated. Any uncertainty melted away as the 1950s progressed. Television was not to be limited to cigarette commercials and cowboy serials: national networks and their local affiliates covered everything from presidential races to local politics. TV news showed itself able to capture moments of national triumph and disaster, and in doing so, it became enmeshed in the civic and political life of the United States. For much of this time, news filming was the preserve of a professional elite. What could be recorded and transmitted was determined by the allocation and availability of camera equipment and the willingness of networks and their affiliates to transmit material. Starting in the mid-1970s, these limitations eased as the technologies of television newsgathering changed. Stations that had once relied on 16mm film cameras switched to new portable electronic cameras, which recorded onto videotape. Videotapes had a larger capacity than film reels, and synchronized sound was easier to acquire. Furthermore, images from portable electronic cameras could be beamed directly back to stations via microwave relay. Live images no longer required a studio-sized camera linked by cables to a TV truck. A camera could be on an operator's shoulder, in a car, or in a helicopter above the scene. Images could be viewed live from these locations without the need for film processing. While many early portable electronic cameras allowed users to change lenses, on early models, this was more difficult than on film cameras thanks to the increased precision and complexity of the image-capturing surface. These factors meant that electronic cameras required a more complex and sensitive "lineup" process than their film cousins.[51] A zoom lens, once matched and calibrated to a camera, was far more likely to remain attached to the camera.

Video cameras designed for use by amateurs quickly followed, replacing the 8mm cine cameras that had been used to make home movies. Portable video recording had been available to serious amateurs since the late 1960s: equipment such as the Portapak saw wide use by artists and activist documentary makers, who experimented with the potential of the new medium.[52] However, the weight and expense of the equipment limited their appeal to home users. Proud parents were relatively unlikely to be filming their children's birthday parties with such cumbersome equipment. It took the arrival of the camcorder to free amateur filmmakers—now videographers—from the limitations of film. Theirs was no longer a short-duration, one-shot recording medium; handheld camcorders could record for up to two hours—if the battery could keep up. If something more interesting happened once the tape was full, earlier footage could be overwritten. Pictures could be reviewed instantly, or—if something of particular note was captured—the tape could be handed over to a television station for further dissemination. When combined, these technological advances were a potent combination. The cultural effects of the video revolution have been written about in some detail, but what has been forgotten, because it was not a new technology when portable video cameras arrived, is the enduring importance of the zoom lens in enabling the work of a generation of citizen journalists and digital witnesses.

Some of the earliest palm-sized camcorders on the market in the 1980s did not feature zoom lenses: both Sony's CCD-M8 Handycam and JVC's Video-Movie GR-C9—brought to market in 1985 and 1987, respectively—offered a fixed focal length lens. By contrast, Sony's larger CCD-V8 offered a motor-controlled 6:1 optical zoom lens covering focal lengths from 11.5mm to 70mm, promising potential buyers that the zoom lens would "help you be more inventive."[53] Kodak and JVC also developed camcorders that, while slightly larger, provided their users with medium-range zoom lenses.[54] Sony, disappointed by poor sales of the compact but zoomless Handycam, completely redesigned their smallest portable video camera. When the revised, "passport sized" Handycam CCD-TR55 appeared on the market in 1989, it offered similar zooming abilities to the larger models in the product range.[55] Since the early 1990s, a zoom lens has been a standard feature of nearly all camcorders. In amateur hands, the zoom has proved particularly important to witnesses and bystanders because it has enabled them to record footage while remaining in a place of safety.

Thus as he filmed the beating of Rodney King, Holliday remained at a considerable distance—about one hundred feet—from the incident, relying on the zoom to capture a closer view of what was happening in front of him. His footage is marked by repeated zooms in and out, which continually reestablish the context of the event.[56] Holliday shot for around eight minutes, of which only a relatively small portion was widely broadcast. John Thornton Caldwell has drawn attention to the murky, low-resolution qualities of the footage, describing it as "essentially electronic noise."[57] The zoom helped overcome the disadvantages of the low-fidelity camcorder. The clip most often broadcast on television begins on Holliday's close-up of the officers surrounding King and ends just after Holliday zooms out. The zoom helped create a sense of narrative and spatial integrity and completeness that was essential to the credibility of Holliday's tape. Indeed, the prosecutor in the case against the four LAPD officers tried for the assault described the tape as "the most objective piece of evidence you could have."[58] Without the camcorder's integrated zoom lens, Holliday's record of the incident could not have been as compelling, credible, or comprehensive. Indeed, without a zoom lens, it may never have been recorded in the first place.

The same is true of footage of the O. J. Simpson chase. In this instance, no case can be made for the zoom lens as a protector of the camera operators' safety; they were protected from harm by their location a few thousand feet above the action. The Simpson chase, iconic in its own right, helped the "helicopter-televised chase to become a genre in itself."[59] By this point, however, aerial news coverage delivered by helicopter was already a staple of American news broadcasting. One of the earliest dedicated news helicopters was developed by KTLA's chief engineer John Silva in the late 1950s. Though the camera and transmitter used for the experiment needed to be radically stripped down to make it light enough, the zoom lens was an essential component in transmitting meaningful footage from the air and was included in the original setup.[60] Shooting television images from a helicopter demanded special skills and a new approach. One of the earliest helicopter news cameramen "discovered pretty quick that [he] couldn't make fast pans and zooms when [the helicopter was] in motion," because the vibration of the aircraft made keeping the camera steady difficult and reduced the viability of long focal lengths. Nevertheless, the airborne news reports delivered from the "Telecopter" were a ratings hit, and the station soon invested in larger and more powerful aircraft with improved cameras. Each new helicopter boasted a more powerful zoom lens.[61]

Early footage shot from KTLA's Telecopter is scarce. What does survive vividly demonstrates the importance of the zoom in making the helicopter news footage viable. KTLA's coverage of the collapse of the Baldwin Hills Dam in December 1963 offers a particularly dramatic example. The pictures, included in an extant newsreel, shows how KTLA's airborne camera operator was able to zoom dramatically down toward the initially modest dam breach, achieving a sufficiently close view to show churning water pouring through the gap.[62] A similar effect is seen in footage of the Watts Riots: a clip from images shot by the Telecopter first shows an indistinct pall of smoke emerging from one of a number of buildings before zooming down to capture flames roaring out of first- and second-floor windows.[63] Today these pictures are accessible only in remediated form, as preserved newsreel, or as historical online video. In each example, only a dramatic few seconds of television footage have been included in the presentation, but these are clips drawn from longer periods of coverage originally watched live by hundreds of thousands of people. These excerpts point toward the very early establishment of a now familiar grammar of airborne television news coverage. Only the zoom could enable the continual juxtaposition of wide-angle context with closeup drama. It was this capacity to continually refresh and reframe the viewer's perspective that made helicopter news footage so compelling.

During the O. J. Simpson chase, helicopter-borne zoom lenses were used simply to keep the chase framed as it unfolded. Yet this function was as important to the coverage of the chase as the helicopters themselves. The iconic image of the O. J. Simpson chase is that of Simpson's white Ford Bronco traveling along a highway. Yet this flashbulb memory does little to represent the length and diversity of television coverage of the chase. Pursuing police cars kept a substantial distance from Simpson's vehicle, presenting a live storytelling challenge for pilots and camera operators aloft. Maintaining a tight framing on Simpson's Bronco told no story: it showed merely a car traveling alone along an apparently

FIGURE 7.3. As news helicopters swarmed above the pursuit of O. J. Simpson, zoom lenses moved in and out, searching for a shot of the fugitive while telling the story of the chase.

quiet freeway. Zooming out to a wider angle transformed the visual narrative, revealing the dozen chasing police cars, spectators on bridges and on-ramps, rubbernecking traffic in the opposing lanes, and the long shadows cast by buildings in the early evening sunshine. However, it also revealed the sedate pace of the pursuit. Camera operators in the helicopters, under frequent instruction from news directors and from anchors commentating on the ground, therefore settled into a pattern of zooming in and out. When the cameras pulled back their zoom lenses, extreme wide shots provoked commentary on the actions of the police, on the traffic situation in the surrounding streets, and on the interaction of the news helicopters with the flight paths of airplanes coming in and out of Los Angeles International Airport. Tighter shots heightened the sense of a speedy pursuit while satisfying viewers that the camera was zoomed in as far as was possible. News anchors commentating on the case repeatedly noted, somewhat apologetically, that the closest possible shot—with the car centered in the frame—was "as tight as we can go right now" and regretted that the zoom was not sufficiently powerful to show the face of the passengers. Here a film editor might have cut to a close-up, but the best that the zoom lenses in the helicopters could manage was still a long shot by Hollywood standards.

"EMBRACE THE SCHTICK"

Just as the zoom has remained an essential film production technology, it has also continued to make a significant impact on the style and production logistics of drama and comedy television. However, away from news and sports coverage, in the domain of the network drama or sitcom, the zoom has seen more circumscribed use. The zoom shot is not often seen in so-called quality television, which has preferred a cinematic style. Instead, the zoom shot has come into its own in the mockumentary genre, where over-the-top zoom shots pastiche the documentary genre and signal to viewers a strong sense of irony and self-parody.

The overt zoom is rarely to be seen in high-budget cable shows like *The Sopranos, Six Feet Under, The Wire,* and *Breaking Bad,* which—along with some network dramas like *The West Wing* and *ER*—have been identified by scholars as belonging to a category of "quality television." This may be because one of the stylistic markers of quality television is its "cinematic" nature. This is a controversial and contested term, often clumsily applied to denote a form of television that seems to rise above the ordinary and is thus deserving of special critical acclaim.[64] Despite the flaws in this way of talking about television, it is inarguable that most of the series that form quality television's loose critical canon follow the stylistic norms and formal conventions of feature film more closely than those of the network television drama, three-camera sitcom, or soap opera. As Caldwell points out, film was the dominant mode of production for American television shows, whether quality or "nondescript," but from the 1980s, "cinematic values brought to television spectacle, high-production values, and feature-style cinematography."[65] More recently, Janet McCabe has used the example of *Boardwalk Empire* to demonstrate how Martin Scorsese applied his own vision to the "high-end image-making techniques" of quality cable drama. Scorsese's approach to *Boardwalk Empire*, McCabe argues, evokes the look and feel of American cinema in the early twentieth century.[66] As she points out, Scorsese was only one of many high-profile American film directors to have directed cable television series since 2000.[67] This followed a trend, from the mid-1980s, for expensive commercials directed by lauded feature film directors.[68] While specific shows might evoke particular genres in their attempt to be "cinematic," as a whole, such television loosely attempts to evoke the look and feel of classical Hollywood film form and style. In recent years, this has come to mean, inter alia, shooting on high-quality film stock, in widescreen, with subtle lighting. Focus pulls, crane shots, and complicated camera moves might all figure into this sense of the cinematic, but there is no fixed definition from which to generate a checklist.[69]

Cinematic television is perhaps easier to define by what it tends to exclude, and a "cinematic" approach to form and style leaves little room for the zoom shot. High-budget "quality" television drama in the 1990s and 2000s tends to reject the zoom in favor of physical movement of the camera—including crane shots and, often, the Steadicam. At the most serious end of the quality spectrum, a stable camera is preferred. In a typical hour-long episode of *The Sopranos* or *Six Feet Under*, for example, the camera moves far less than it would in a typical forty-two-minute "hour" of network television drama. The faster pace of *ER* and *The West Wing* demanded more camera movement, but directors and cinematographers of these shows opted to deliver this via immersive "walk-and-talk" Steadicam shots, and this trend spread far beyond these trailblazing examples. This approach to form and style continues at the dawn of a new age of "quality" television commissioned by video-on-demand services like Netflix. *House of Cards* and *Better Call Saul* both follow the example set by their HBO forerunners. While neither straightforwardly film nor television, they look and feel more like film. Over the past two decades, there has been no major network, cable, or video-on-demand series that has eschewed physical camera movement in favor of the zoom—no stylistic equivalent of *Marcus Welby, M.D.* Indeed, the role played by the zoom in *Marcus Welby, M.D.*—substituting for tracking and dollying in order to cover the action as quickly and efficiently as possible—has been supplanted by the tendency to cover scenes from numerous angles and leave directorial decisions for the editing suite. The zoom in contemporary television drama does not navigate space and does not contribute toward production efficiency, and so it has little to offer a run-of-the-mill television drama. Meanwhile, because the zoom retains the odor of 1970s schlock, it cannot contribute toward the much-desired "cinematic" style of high-budget television.

This does not mean that all recent high-end television drama has been shot exclusively with prime lenses or at fixed focal lengths. These series follow a strategy familiar from feature cinematography, using a combination of prime and zoom lenses, and zooming only very gradually, so as to "creep" or (as Bordwell puts it) "prowl" toward characters.[70] In high-end cable drama series, the zoom is used minimally and is often reserved for special purposes. The pilot episode of *Six Feet Under*, for all its quirky tone and stylistic innovation, avoids the zoom almost entirely. But it makes an exception for a short, stylized, handheld scene in which Nate Fisher recalls seeing a coffin returned to grieving relatives on a beach in Italy. The series premiere of *The Sopranos*, which sets the tone for the cinematography throughout the show's run, features only one identifiable zoom shot: a very brief, and very slow, push-in toward a statuette in Jennifer Melfi's office. In the final episode of the show's first season, creeping zooms add extra emphasis to a series of moments at which various characters are about to be shot to death. In the final episode of the fifth season, zooms combined with unsteady handheld camerawork heighten the sense of dramatic tension as Tony Soprano provokes his sister Janice into an argument. Another HBO series, *The Wire*, shot on 35mm so as to create "more of a feature look," relied heavily on a Panavision 11:1 zoom for location shooting. A profile of the show's cinematographer, Ute Briesewitz, described how the zoom enabled quick coverage of "several angles and sizes." However, Briesewitz—who shot most of the first two seasons of *The Wire*—was clear that her aim was to conceal zoom shots within camera movements.[71]

When the zoom appears in network television drama during this period, it is most often as part of a strategic divergence from the stylistic norms of the medium. The concluding episode of the sixth season of *The West Wing* offers one of the most striking examples of a show suspending its usual cinematographic rules and presenting an episode shot in an entirely different style. "2162 Votes" focuses on the efforts of two competing candidates to capture the presidential nomination at the Democratic National Convention. The familiar style of the series—elegantly lit scenes covered by graceful camera moves—is upended in favor of an edgy, nervous, vérité aesthetic. The camerawork in most scenes is marked by whip pans, lens flares, and rapid focus pulls—along with frequent zooms. The zoom darts in and out, capturing and reframing characters as they move through the screen. In the episode's documentary-style scenes, each stylistic component is exaggerated. There is more lens flare, more whip pans, and more camera movement than would be found in a true documentary. The zoom is also used in a heightened fashion: constant small adjustments of focal length remind the viewer of their privileged access to backroom deals and strategy. *The*

West Wing's great attraction, as a series, is its behind-the-scenes access to seldom-revealed political discussions. But this attraction loses its novelty after six seasons, and so "2162 Votes," through its camerawork and faster-than-usual editing, uses documentary tropes to refresh the episode's voyeuristic sensibility. Like the cine camera footage in *Capricorn One*, the episode's approach is not only heightened documentary but an overworked pastiche of documentary style designed for a maximal contrast with the few scenes—back at the White House—in which the show's usual style is maintained. "2162 Votes" is not the only episode in which an overblown vérité style is employed—a scene earlier in the same season in which Toby Ziegler (Richard Schiff) and Josh Lyman (Bradley Whitford) fight in a White House office is another example—but it is the most sustained and powerful example of how the overt zoom shot is occasionally permitted within the cinematic stylistic conventions of a contemporary network drama series.

By far, the most significant use of the zoom in early twenty-first-century television has been as a marker of the mockumentary genre, of which *Arrested Development*, *The Office*, *30 Rock*, *Curb Your Enthusiasm*, and *Parks and Recreation* are particularly prominent examples. What links sitcoms such as these, according to Ethan Thompson, is that they "look different and are made differently from comedies in the past"; they are, to use a term Thompson adopts from Brett Mills, examples of a "comedy verité" form.[72] They are also prime examples of "self-reflexive" television, and the zoom is a vital marker of this self-reflexive style.[73] In the case of mockumentary, the cinematography and editing of a show's

FIGURE 7.4. In a feverish season-ending episode set at a political convention, *The West Wing* breaks with its usual style and adds vérité-style zoom shots and whip pans.

FIGURE 7.5. Propulsive zooms, whip pans, and fidgeting focus pulls characterize the self-conscious mockumentary style of sitcoms such as *Parks and Recreation*.

entire run diverges from what is standard for the sitcom. As typical examples, *Arrested Development* (Fox, 2003–2006; Netflix, 2013–), *Parks and Recreation* (NBC, 2009–2015), and *Modern Family* (ABC, 2009–) make lavish use of the handheld camera. Alongside these shows' unstable frames, whip pans, and focus pulls, viewers are presented with an unstoppable stream of zooms that continue unabated from cold open to closing credits. If the zoom seems the most overt marker of mockumentary to the viewer, it may be similarly important to the crew. Describing his approach to the first season of *Arrested Development*, director of photography James Hawkinson made clear the centrality of the zoom to the show's visual style: "The show was to be shot in cinema-vérité style, with obvious and deliberate camera operation, and the directors and I developed our own set of rules that would both justify and mitigate the style of the camera-work. First, there was the extremely important employment of the zoom lens. . . . My mantra to my very competent operators, Greg Harrington and Ian Dodd, became 'embrace the schtick.' In that same spirit, each day after viewing dailies, I would give out the 'Golden Stick Award' to whichever operator excelled in telling a visual joke with the zoom."[74]

Zooms are thus among the most prominent markers of the mockumentary genre, and in their repetition, they serve an essential function in continually restating the show's generic classification. This may be why the zooms in early episodes of *Parks and Recreation* are so much more pronounced and exaggerated than those seen in later episodes: the zoom helps remind an audience not yet fully familiar with the show and its rules of operation that they are watching an exaggerated, self-reflexive mockumentary. But the zoom plays a deeper and more involved role than merely marking a genre. Unlike the focus pull or the mere condition of unsteady framing, the zoom helps set up, reveal, and emphasize punchlines. The unrehearsed style is often painstakingly rehearsed: in both *Parks and Recreation* and *Modern Family*, camera operators zoom in close coordination with scripted dialogue, moving in or out between clauses of speech or before punchlines. Here, the zoom does some of the work of the laughter track, orienting viewers to the intended humor.

As much as the zoom has been used in mockumentary to emphasize and create humor, it has become in certain contexts the object of the joke and an enduring shorthand for nonprofessional or lower-standard cinematography. Comedy features like *Delirious* (Tom Mankiewicz, 1991) and *The Cable Guy* (Ben Stiller, 1996) mocked zoom shots found in television soaps and courtroom coverage, while the primetime television sitcom *Friends* (NBC, 1994–2004)

FIGURE 7.6. The "Golden Stick Award": there's always a zoom in *Arrested Development*.

included dramatic scene-ending zoom shots in its occasional parodies of the daytime soap opera *Days of Our Lives* (NBC, 1965–).[75] Film mocks television, primetime mocks daytime, and everybody mocks the amateur. Overdone zoom shots have been a key stylistic component of the "low-resolution reality" aesthetic of mockumentary and the "found footage" film.[76] While filming *Interview with the Assassin* (Neil Burger, 2002), Richard Rutkowkski exploited "the tropes of video camerawork, such as focus problems, bad zooms, uncontrolled highlights—things that you would control if you were shooting a theatrical feature on film."[77] The zoom has a double function in *The Blair Witch Project* (Daniel Myrick and Eduardo Sánchez, 1999), distinguishing between two formats—film and video—while simultaneously contributing toward the film's central conceit of amateurism. The opening shot calls attention to the particularly imperfect aesthetics of the video camera: the unseen camera operator, zooming out and focusing on Heather Donahue (playing herself), complains, "You look a little blurry there, let me zoom out." In the montage of shots that follow, the frequent zooms draw constant attention to the amateur nature of the production. The camera operators often zoom too far: shooting footage of the production's first slate, Donahue overextends the camcorder's zoom. The slate is misframed, and when it moves, Donahue cannot follow it, leading to an incomprehensible series of out-of-focus shots. These zooms effectively contrast with the film's 16mm footage, which is far more sedate: the opening scenes of the crew's documentary are presented as a series of stable, steadily framed shots of gravestones and the surrounding countryside. Just as in the few snatched frames of amateur film seen in *Capricorn One*, in *The Blair Witch Project*, the zoom is a convenient shorthand for amateurism.

CONCLUSION

Today, zoom shots are barely noticed, so familiar are they and so well integrated into film and television production practice and visual grammar. But such familiarity risks concealing the ongoing political and social significance of the technology. Adding a zoom lens to a television camera is far more than simply adding a convenient accessory. The zoom transforms television's fixed perspective, enabling the camera to enhance and enlarge subjects within its view. When used in this way in sports coverage, soap operas, or sitcoms, its advantages seem trivial. Yet the zoom continues to impact contemporary politics across the globe. As Marwan Kraidy recounts, after the assassination of the Lebanese prime minister Rafiq Hariri led to anti-Syria protests in Beirut, the Syrian president Bashir al-Assad gave a speech in which he "criticized the performance of Lebanon's television channels, accusing them of inflating the size of the demonstrations by using narrow camera angles. 'Zoom out,' he said (using the English expression), challenging unnamed Lebanese channels sympathetic to the opposition rallies, and it would become clear that the demonstrations were small."[78] After Assad's speech, Kraidy notes, "the English expression 'Zoom Out' entered the political lexicon." Both sides used the metaphor to attack one another, and a Beirut newspaper "published a column titled 'In Praise of "Zoom In"' noting 'the camera's hypocrisy as it plays.'"[79]

A decade later, during the Republican primaries prior to the 2016 U.S. presidential election, zoom lenses again played a central role in a political campaign. In September 2015, Donald Trump began to attack the media's coverage of the crowds attending his rallies. At a rally at the Oklahoma State Fair, he made a "zooming-in" motion with his hand and complained that the cameras focused only on him, never showing the true number of attendees at his rallies. As Trump knew, the zoomed-in pool camera isolated him on the stage. It disconnected him from the crowds and made him look like any other politician. With the camera still tightly framing him, Trump declared that even though he had attracted a crowd of many thousands, the media would report "a nice crowd of six or seven hundred people." As the crowd got angrier, Trump addressed the cameras directly. As the *Washington Post* reported, "Trump pointed to the small island of national and local reporters packed onto a riser in the sea of Oklahomans. 'Hey, cameras: Can you do us a favor?' Trump said. 'Take the cameras off me and pan the crowd. Pan it. Be honest. Go ahead, pan it. . . . They don't want to pan it! Pan those cameras!'"[80] In response, at least one of the television cameras at the venue zoomed out and ranged around the crowd. The effect created was remarkable. As the camera zoomed out, the image of Trump changed dramatically. He was no longer a politician on a dais but a leader among followers. Demanding that the cameras zoom out (though Trump rarely, if ever, used the word) and pan around the crowd became a regular part of Trump's stump speech throughout the primary campaign. In venue after venue, Trump would stop his speech and address the news cameras. While denouncing the media for misrepresenting his campaign, he would enlist his audience's support in demanding that the cameras pan across the crowds. Sometimes, the cameras would remain fixed on their shot of Trump, but often they would zoom out and pan to show a crowd angry at the media. Though candidates and officials had manipulated television for decades, there was little precedent in American politics for a candidate who would attempt to personally direct the zoom lens of a television camera.

Like many film and television production technologies, the problem solved by the zoom lens is easily grasped, and the basic solution has not changed dramatically for many years. Cinematographers and directors sometimes wish to alter the scale of the images they wish to capture without the cost or labor of moving the camera or changing the lens. Equally, they may wish to change the shot scale gradually and fluidly while film runs through the camera. The earliest zoom lens patent, filed almost a century ago by Rolla T. Flora, outlines these dual problems and describes a single solution: the zoom lens. Flora's design was primitive, hand-made, and limited in its capabilities. Yet we see its vestiges in modern zoom lens designs. Gradually, zoom lenses have become more complex. Different design approaches have been attempted, encouraged by the introduction of powerful computing technology, precision engineering, and novel synthetic materials. Flora's early lens—which was probably challenging to operate and likely produced dark, poorly focused images—has given way to reliable, high-quality, semiautomated zoom lenses manufactured at a range of sizes and qualities to suit all users, from the professional cinematographer to the camcorder-wielding amateur. The historical narrative that has described this progression has often been formed of breakthrough solutions, firsts, and comings-of-age—at which, each optical innovator in turn declares, the zoom is finally "perfect." In truth, the development of the zoom lens has been punctuated by failures, false starts, and confrontations.

By tracing the zoom's slow, fraught path to ubiquity, we can learn a great deal about the broader development of mainstream American film and television, from the earliest roots of these media to their contemporary manifestations. For cinematographers, the zoom has acted variously as a challenge, an irritant, and a provocation. It has been a challenging technology because it has offered a deceptively simplistic solution to a "problem" not always regarded as such by cinematographers. Early patents and advertisements for zoom lenses invited motion picture producers to consider the efficiencies inherent in moving the zoom lens instead of moving the camera. Cinematographers, however, have often taken a different view. They have seen, in the zoom lens, a challenge to their preferred way of working, in which genuine camera movement is preferable to the "false" movement of the zoom lens. As the final chapter of this book has shown, a variety of apparently undesirable associations have attached themselves to the zoom: it is often dismissed as a "modern-type" movement redolent of newsreel or television, which encourages laziness and indecision among those who use it. These views are not somehow natural ways to talk about a zoom lens; rather, they are the result of professional cinematographers' ambivalence about and negotiation with the affordances of zoom lens technology.

The zoom's unique visual effect has left an indelible mark on the twentieth- and twenty-first-century moving image. Sometimes this mark is so clear that we cannot miss it, as in the films of Robert Altman and John Frankenheimer or in the television dramas of the 1970s. Elsewhere, the zoom hides in plain sight, a generic convention of live television made almost invisible by its familiarity. This may seem an outsized influence for what now seems an unremarkable optical device. Yet without the zoom, much of live television would be impractical, and many iconic film sequences would be impossible. The zoom has challenged the creativity of directors and camera operators of all levels and provoked innovation in optical design and mechanical engineering. As film, television, and digital moving-image media continue to develop, the zoom will continue to reveal the distant subject, shock the audience, and challenge the cinematographer.

ACKNOWLEDGMENTS

This book began, almost a decade ago, as a doctoral research project at the University of Exeter. I would never have got that far without the love and support of my parents. I am grateful for the wise advice of my supervisors, Steve Neale and James Lyons, and to the Arts and Humanities Research Council for funding the project. I am equally grateful to my colleagues and friends—especially Helen Hanson, Phil Wickham, Lisa Stead, Emma Bird, and Kiri Thompson—who made living in and studying at Exeter such a pleasure.

This work has been greatly strengthened by material discovered in a number of libraries and archives. History is nothing without archives, and it is the archivists and librarians who make the work possible. I am grateful to Heather Smedberg and her colleagues in the Mandeville Special Collections Library at the University of California, San Diego; Dorinda Hartmann at the Wisconsin Center for Film and Theater Research in Madison; and Mark Quigley at the Archive Research and Study Center at UCLA. I have been further aided by the staffs of the Library of Congress in Washington, DC; the National Archives and Records Administration at College Park, Maryland; and the Margaret Herrick Library in Los Angeles, California.

Over the course of the research and writing of this book, many people have generously contributed their thoughts and feedback. Jason Jacobs, Steven Peacock, Adrian Danks, Lisa Dombrowski, and Patrick Keating have all helped shape this work in different ways. Part of chapter 3 originally appeared, in a different form, in the journal *Technology and Culture*, where it benefited from the keen eye of Barbara Hahn and several anonymous readers. I am profoundly grateful to Leslie Mitchner and Murray Pomerance at Rutgers University Press for enthusiastically receiving my proposal and for their patience on the long road to the final draft.

While finishing the book, I was working in the Department of Media Arts at Royal Holloway University of London, and I am particularly thankful for the support and patience of John Ellis. Meanwhile, my friends in the Southern Broadcast History Group have provided many entertaining diversions over the past several years.

Most of all, I thank my wife, Demelza Hookway, for her endless patience and inspiration and our daughter, Milly, for being the most welcome distraction an author could hope to have. I dedicate this book to them.

NOTES

CHAPTER 1. INTRODUCTION

1. "Drama at the Touch of a Lever," *International Photographer* 6, no. 12 (January 1935): 11.

2. This model, described by Douglas Gomery as the "neoclassical economic theory of technical change," has been applied to numerous studies of technology within and beyond film history. See Douglas Gomery, "The Coming of Sound: Technological Change in the American Film Industry," in *Film Sound: Theory and Practice*, ed. Elizabeth Weis and John Belton (New York: Columbia University Press, 1985), 5–24.

3. For a useful guide to the relevant trade journals and the new opportunities afforded by digital platforms, see the dossier "Technology and the Trade Press," *Velvet Light Trap*, no. 76 (Fall 2015): 49–67.

4. Barry Salt, *Film Style and Technology*, 2nd ed. (London: Starword, 1992); John Belton, "The Bionic Eye: Zoom Esthetics," *Cinéaste* 11, no. 1 (Winter 1980–1981): 20–27.

5. Chris Cagle, "Classical Hollywood, 1928–1946," in *Cinematography*, ed. Patrick Keating (New Brunswick, N.J.: Rutgers University Press, 2014), 34–59.

6. Patrick Keating, "Introduction," in *Cinematography*, ed. Patrick Keating (New Brunswick, N.J.: Rutgers University Press, 2014), 4.

7. "Sawyer Award Kicks Up Controversy," *Daily Variety*, March 26, 1990, 6, 22.

8. See Keating, "Introduction," 6; David Bordwell, Kristin Thompson, and Janet Staiger, *The Classical Hollywood Cinema* (London: Routledge and Kegan Paul, 1985).

9. "Experiment in Terror," *American Cinematographer* 43, no. 5 (May 1962): 321.

10. Gerald Hirschfield, "Low Key for 'Fail Safe,'" *American Cinematographer* 44, no. 8 (1963): 483.

11. Herb A. Lightman, "'The Outrage'—Off-Beat Photography Is One of Its Virtues," *American Cinematographer*, April 1964, 198.

12. Joseph V. Mascelli, "Use and Abuse of the Zoom Lens," *American Cinematographer* 38, no. 10 (October 1957): 652–653, 677.

13. David A. Cook, *Lost Illusions*, vol. 9 (Berkeley: University of California Press, 2002), 361.

14. Cook, 362.

15. Peter Wollen, "Cinema and Technology: A Historical Overview," in *The Cinematic Apparatus*, ed. Teresa de Lauretis and Stephen Heath (London: Macmillan, 1980), 20.

16. Bernard F. Dick, *Anatomy of Film*, 2nd ed. (New York: St. Martin's, 1990), 51.

17. Robert Edmonds, *The Sights and Sounds of Cinema and Television: How the Aesthetic Experience Influences Our Feelings* (New York: Teachers College, Columbia University Press, 1982), 17–18.

18. Stuart M. Kaminsky, "The Use and Abuse of the Zoom Lens," *Filmmakers Newsletter* 5, no. 12 (October 1972); "General Camera Corporation," *American Cinematographer* 45, no. 7 (July 1964): 389.

19. Paul Joannides, "The Aesthetics of the Zoom Lens," *Sight & Sound* (Winter 1970): 40–41.

20. Dick draws a similar parallel between the zoom and "italics [misused] by inexperienced writers." See Dick, *Anatomy of Film*, 50.

21. Kaminsky, "Use and Abuse," 21.
22. Belton, "Bionic Eye."
23. David Bordwell, *On the History of Film Style* (Cambridge, Mass.: Harvard University Press, 1997), 246–247.
24. Bordwell, 247.
25. Geoffrey Nowell-Smith, *Making Waves: New Cinemas of the 1960s* (New York: Bloomsbury, 2013), 102–103.
26. In the context of the 1950s, "home cinematography" takes the place of "home video," but zoom lenses were definitely available for 8mm cameras by the late 1950s. See "The New Pan Cinor 20mm to 60mm Variable Focal Length Lens for 16mm Cameras," *Bolex Reporter* 2, no. 3 (1952): 16.
27. William C. Wees, "Prophecy, Memory and the Zoom: Michael Snow's Wavelength Reviewed," *Ciné-Tracts* 4, nos. 2–3 (Fall 1981): 79.
28. Wees, 79–80.
29. Donato Totaro states that the zoom in the film has a "teleological purpose": "Where is it heading"? He further says that "Snow's own description that the film was a 'summation of . . . religious inklings' supports a reading of the zoom's trajectory . . . as a transcendental journey where the spectator is 'carried' from one space/time to another." See "Wavelength Revisited," *Offscreen* 6, no. 11 (2002), http://offscreen.com/view/wavelength.
30. *Wavelength* is returned to repeatedly by film theorists whose task is to discuss the zoom lens. This may simply be because the film consists of one long zoom shot. What is surprising is that there also exist discussions of *Wavelength* that make no mention of the film's zoom. Noël Burch, for example, refers only to "the advance of the camera," complicating yet again the common declaration that the zoom is instantly distinguishable, and therefore different, from the track. See Noël Burch, *Life to Those Shadows*, trans. Ben Brewster (Berkeley: University of California Press, 1990), 258. See also Wees, "Prophecy, Memory," 18.
31. Donald Skoller, "Aspects of Cinematic Consciousness," *Film Comment* 8, no. 3 (1972): 51.
32. Vivian Sobchack, "The Active Eye: A Phenomenology of Cinematic Vision," *Quarterly Review of Film and Video* 12, no. 3 (June 1990): 25.
33. Sobchack, 25–26.
34. Jennifer M. Barker, "Neither Here nor There: Synaesthesia and the Cosmic Zoom," *New Review of Film and Television Studies* 7, no. 3 (September 2009): 311, 312.
35. Garrett Stewart, *Framed Time: Toward a Postfilmic Cinema* (Chicago: University of Chicago Press, 2007), 283.
36. Barker, "Neither Here nor There," 312.
37. Barker, 312.
38. This technique has numerous names, including "dolly zoom," "Hitchcock zoom," "*Vertigo* effect," "trombone shot," "contra-zoom," and "*Jaws* shot." See, respectively, Jinhee Choi, "Leaving It up to the Imagination: POV Shots and Imagining from the Inside," *Journal of Aesthetics and Art Criticism* 63, no. 1 (February 2005): 22; Thelma Wills Foote, "Happy Birthday, Nola Darling! An Essay Commemorating the Twentieth Anniversary of Spike Lee's 'She's Gotta Have It,'" *Women's Studies Quarterly* 35, nos. 1–2 (2007): 224; Simon Spiegel, "Things Made Strange: On the Concept of 'Estrangement' in Science Fiction Theory," *Science Fiction Studies* 35, no. 3 (2008): 381; Richard Berger, "The 'Trombone Shot': From San Francisco to Middle Earth via Amity," *Big Picture*, March 2009, 28; "Obituary: Roy Schneider," *Times*, February 12, 2008.

39. Sobchack, "Active Eye," 27.

40. Colleen Lucille Birchett, "The Effects of Television on the Descriptive Writing of College Students" (PhD diss., University of Michigan, 1986).

41. Sun-Kyung Hong, "Television Viewing and Cognitive Styles" (PhD diss., University of Alabama, 2006).

CHAPTER 2. DRAMA AT THE TOUCH OF A LEVER

1. "Quirk Is Hit by Silent Susie; Savvy? No? It's Army Lingo," *Los Angeles Herald*, August 10, 1918.

2. *Oxford English Dictionary Online*, s.v. "zoom," accessed June 2017, http://www.oed.com/view/Entry/233040.

3. "President Starts Abroad: Last Glimpse of the President's Ship 60 Miles at Sea," *New York Times*, December 5, 1918, 1.

4. "'Air Bows' to Wilson Punished; Say LA Man Endangered President," *Los Angeles Herald*, December 5, 1918, 1; "Capers in Airplane for Wilson Costly," *Sacramento Union*, December 10, 1918, 5.

5. "Plane to Deliver Dry Goods," *Los Angeles Herald*, August 1, 1919, 13.

6. "Flying Upside Down Thrills," *Sausalito News*, August 30, 1919, 3.

7. "Why Those Who Long to Fly Need Not Fear Airsickness," *Los Angeles Herald*, August 19, 1919, 18.

8. "Bill Would Put Rein on Airmen," *Sacramento Union*, April 7, 1921, 5; "German Plane to Be Used on Armistice Day," *Los Angeles Herald*, October 28, 1921, A13.

9. "Harry E. Herndon," advertisement, *Los Angeles Herald*, December 3, 1920, A12.

10. "General Gasoline and Lubricants," advertisement, *Madera Tribune*, December 29, 1925, 2.

11. Mervyn Heard, *Phantasmagoria: The Secret Life of the Magic Lantern* (Hastings: Projection Box, 2006), 99.

12. Heard, 97.

13. Vincent Ilardi, *Renaissance Vision: From Spectacles to Telescopes* (Philadelphia: American Philosophical Society, 2007), 4.

14. Ilardi, 46–47.

15. Peter Abrahams, "Ignazio Porro; Ignaz Peter Paul Porro," europa.com, June 9, 2005, http://home.europa.com/~telscope/porro.doc.

16. Priska Morrissey, "Naissance et Premiers Usages du Zoom," *Positif*, February 2008, 89.

17. Rudolf Kingslake, *A History of the Photographic Lens* (London: Academic Press, 1989), 133–134; T. R. Dallmeyer, *Photographic Lens*, 756,779, issued April 5, 1904.

18. "[Cinematographer William F.] Alder, by means which have defied all expert analysis or explanation, improvised some mysterious device which enabled his camera to follow action, to truck, dolly and zoom with a sophisticated facility that seems often quite out of the reach of many a present-day studio so lavishly equipped with tracks, trucks, cranes and lenses of variable focal length." See James Card, "George Eastman House of Photography," *Film Quarterly* 16, no. 2 (1962): 40.

19. Barry Salt claims that *The Grand Duchess and the Waiter* (Malcolm St. Clair, 1926) includes a zoom shot. See *Film Style and Technology*, 2nd ed. (London: Starword, 1992), 185. However, neither of the versions I have seen—a 16mm print held by the British Film Institute and an 8mm print dating from the 1960s—includes such a shot.

20. Kingslake, *Photographic Lens*, 155; C. C. Allen, *Optical Objective*, 696,788, issued April 1, 1902.

21. A. König, *Variable Power Telescope*, 1,094,724, issued April 28, 1914.

22. Richard Koszarski, *An Evening's Entertainment: The Age of the Silent Feature Picture, 1915–1928* (Berkeley: University of California Press, 1994), 145.

23. Rolla T. Flora, *Photographic Apparatus*, 1,790,232, issued January 27, 1931.

24. Flora, *Photographic Apparatus.*

25. Joseph Walker and Juanita Walker, *The Light on Her Face* (Hollywood, Calif.: ASC, 1984), 266–267.

26. Joseph Walker, *Camera*, 1,898,471, filed September 21, 1929, and issued February 21, 1933.

27. This chapter has been greatly strengthened by reference to Mark Medin's identification of a range of early zoom shots in a post for David Cairns's *Shadowplay* blog. See Mark Medin, "Zoom," *Shadowplay* (blog), September 14, 2012, http://dcairns.wordpress.com/2012/09/14/zoom/.

28. See, for example, Marsha Oregon, "Making 'It' in Hollywood: Clara Bow, Fandom, and Consumer Culture," *Cinema Journal* 42, no. 4 (Summer 2003): 83.

29. Lucy Fischer, *American Cinema of the 1920s: Themes and Variations* (New Brunswick, N.J.: Rutgers University Press, 2009), 241.

30. Fischer, 243.

31. Patrick Keating, "The Silent Screen, 1894–1927," in *Cinematography*, ed. Patrick Keating (New Brunswick, N.J.: Rutgers University Press, 2014), 11–16.

32. "The B&H Cooke Varo Lens with Variable Focus and . . . Variable Magnification," *International Photographer*, January 1932, 1.

33. Kingslake, *Photographic Lens*, 305.

34. Arthur Warmisham, *Improvements in Variable Focus Lenses*, 398,307, issued September 14, 1933; Arthur Warmisham and Irving Cisski, *Lens of Variable Equivalent Focal Length*, 1,947,669, issued February 20, 1934.

35. Our understanding of their presentation is based on a paper subsequently published in the journal of the SMPE. See Arthur Warmisham and R. F. Mitchell, "The Bell & Howell Cooke Varo Lens," *Journal of the Society of Motion Picture Engineers* 19, no. 4 (October 1932): 329–339.

36. Warmisham and Mitchell, 338.

37. Warmisham and Mitchell, 337.

38. Warmisham and Mitchell, 337.

39. "New B&H Lens Eliminates Crane Shots in Professional Movies," *American Cinematographer* 12, no. 10 (February 1932): 31.

40. "The Bell & Howell Cooke Varo Lens," *International Photographer* 7, no. 4 (May 1935): 17; "New Cooke F 1.3 Speed Panchro Lens," *International Photographer* 7, no. 9 (October 1935): 11.

41. "Drama at the Touch of a Lever," *International Photographer* 6, no. 12 (January 1935): 11.

42. "Now Casting—the B&H Cooke Varo Lens," *International Photographer* 5, no. 4 (May 1933): 11.

43. "Army Air Corps Studies New 'Zoom' Lens," *Motion Picture Projectionist* 5, no. 7 (May 1932): 26.

44. "Army Air Corps Studies New 'Zoom' Photographic Lens," *American Cinematographer* 13, no. 1 (May 1932): 44.

45. Outtakes from this newsreel can be seen through the online digital video repository of the Moving Image Research Collections of the University of South Carolina. See "Aerial Photography of Windy City—Outtakes," Fox Movietone News Story 14–312 and 14–313, filmed on April 27, 1932.

46. Ray Fernstrom, "The Newsreel World," *International Photographer* 5, no. 5 (June 1933): 18.

47. Notes accompanying *Gaumont British News*, no. 468, June 23, 1938.

48. John Belton, "The Bionic Eye: Zoom Esthetics," *Cinéaste* 11, no. 1 (Winter 1980–1981): 24.

49. George Turner, "Cinemasters: Milton Krasner, ASC," *American Cinematographer* 67, no. 9 (September 1986): 40.

50. For *Island of Lost Souls*, see Paramount Pictures Production Records, folder 00879, Margaret Herrick Library. For *Four Feathers*, see Paramount Papers Scripts, F-683.

51. See Paramount Production Papers, folder 01058, Margaret Herrick Library.

52. David Bordwell, *On the History of Film Style* (Cambridge, Mass.: Harvard University Press, 1997), 313.

53. For *Thunder Below*, see Paramount Production Papers, folder 01826, Margaret Herrick Library. For *King of the Jungle*, see folder 00927 in the same collection.

54. "SMPE Requests National Standards for Motion Picture Industry," *Journal of the Society of Motion Picture Engineers* 19, no. 4 (October 1932): 393.

55. D. Samuelson, "Equipment Inventions That Have Changed the Way Films Are Made," *American Cinematographer* 75, no. 8 (August 1994): 76.

56. Salt, *Film Style*, 207.

57. "Industrial Grocers Go in for Talkies," *American Cinematographer* 13, no. 4 (August 1932): 43.

58. M. E. Gillette, "The Use of Films in the US Army," *Journal of the Society of Motion Picture Engineers* 26, no. 2 (February 1936): 182.

59. Laurence J. Roberts, "Cameras and Systems: A History of Contributions from the Bell & Howell Co. (Part I)," *SMPTE Journal* 91, no. 10 (October 1982): 944.

60. A. N. Goldsmith, "Problems in Motion Picture Engineering," *Journal of the Society of Motion Picture Engineers* 23, no. 6 (December 1934): 352.

61. Kingslake, *Photographic Lens*, 156.

62. "The Durholz Lens," *International Photographer* 4, no. 2 (March 1932): 7.

63. Salt, *Film Style*, 207.

64. Otto B. Durholz, *Variable Focus Lens Unit*, 1,950,166, issued March 6, 1934.

65. "A New Zoom Lens," *American Cinematographer* 12, no. 11 (March 1932): 16.

66. "Durholz Describes His Novel Lens," *International Photographer* 4, no. 3 (April 1932): 10.

67. Lewis L. Mellor and Arthur Zaugg, *Variable Equivalent Focal Length Lens*, 2,159,394, issued May 23, 1939, col. 1.

68. Lodewyck J. R. Holst, William Mayer, and Harry R. Menefee, *Lens System*, 2,130,347, issued September 20, 1938, col. 1.

69. John G. Capstaff and Oran E. Miller, *Photographic Objective*, 2,165,341, issued July 11, 1939, col. 1.

CHAPTER 3. TAKE ME OUT TO THE BALL GAME

1. Melvin Maddocks, "Television," *Christian Science Monitor*, May 1, 1958, 14.

2. Dennis Deninger, *Sports on Television: The How and Why behind What You See* (New York: Routledge, 2012), 8–21.

3. Rudolf Kingslake, *A History of the Photographic Lens* (London: Academic Press, 1989), 170.

4. "Register of Frank Back Papers," Mandeville Special Collections Library, University of California, San Diego, https://library.ucsd.edu/speccoll/findingaids/mss0568.html; Transcript, *Zoomar, Inc. vs. Paillard Products, Inc.*, in Irving R. Kaufman Papers, Library of Congress, Washington, D.C., boxes 8 and 9.

5. Spencer Klaw and Brendan Gill, "The Talk of the Town," *New Yorker*, November 22, 1947.

6. "Resume, Dr. Frank G. Back," August 26, 1980, Frank Back Papers, Mandeville Special Collections Library, University of California San Diego, box 2, folder 6; see also "Personalia," *Journal of the Optical Society of America* 53, no. 1 (January 1953): 206.

7. "Letter, L. D. Wallick to Frank G. Back," September 26, 1944, Frank Back Papers, box 3, folder 26.

8. *Zoomar v. Paillard*, 38.

9. Frank G. Back, *Varifocal Lens for Cameras*, 2,454,686, filed July 30, 1946, issued November 23, 1948.

10. *Zoomar v. Paillard*, 312.

11. *Zoomar v. Paillard*, 307, 309.

12. Frank G. Back, "A Positive Vari-focal View-Finder for Motion Picture Cameras," *Journal of the Society of Motion Picture Engineers* 45, no. 6 (1945): 468.

13. Back, *Varifocal Lens*; Zoomar (Registered Trademark), 432,534, issued September 2, 1947.

14. Kingslake, *Photographic Lens*, 170.

15. *Zoomar v. Paillard*, 318; "Brochure," in NBC records, box 596, folder 32.

16. "Par Reel Tried Zoomar Lens on World Series," *Daily Variety*, October 7, 1947, 9.

17. A. H. Weiler, "Betty Smith Looks at the South—Garbo Considers," *New York Times*, October 12, 1947, X5.

18. *Zoomar v. Paillard*, 29.

19. "'Zoomar' in Action," *Boxoffice*, October 11, 1947, 47.

20. *Paramount News* 7, no. 13 (1947), accession 2,746, record group 200, Motion Picture Collection, National Archives and Records Administration (NARA), College Park, Maryland.

21. "'Zoomar' Lens a Boon for Newsreels," *Variety*, October 8, 1947, 18.

22. Vol. 7, no. 15 of 1947, accession 2,746, record group 200, Motion Picture Collection, NARA.

23. Vol. 7, no. 19 of 1947, accession 2,746, record group 200, Motion Picture Collection, NARA.

24. "Promotional Materials," n.d., NBC records, box 596, folder 32.

25. *Zoomar v. Paillard*, 304.

26. *Zoomar v. Paillard*, 302.

27. Evidence of Zoomar lenses in use in Hearst newsreels can be seen, for example, in the December 15, 1947, edition of *News of the Day*, VA12490M, UCLA Film and Television Archive.

28. "Pro Football Championship Battle! Yankee Stadium, New York City," *News of the Day*, Hearst newsreel, December 15, 1947, V12490M, UCLA Film and Television Archive.

29. "Cleveland Wins World Series! Fifth Game! Final Game! Cleveland Ohio and Boston, Massachusetts," *News of the Day*, Hearst newsreel, October 11, 1948, VA6120M, UCLA Film and Television Archive.

30. "New Tele Lens Gives Longshot or Closeup without Switching," *Billboard*, April 26, 1947, 15.

31. "New Lens for Televising Simplifies Operation," *Boxoffice*, May 10, 1947, 53.

32. Communications between Zoomar and NBC, and among personnel within NBC, are documented by an extensive series of interoffice memos, letters, cables, and contracts held within the NBC records.

33. Noran E. Kersta, "Memo to John F. Royal," May 15, 1947, NBC records, box 596, folder 32, Wisconsin Center for Film and Theater Research (WCFTR), Madison, Wisconsin.

34. R. E. Shelby, "Letter to O. B. Hanson," August 7, 1947, NBC records, box 596, folder 32, WCFTR.

35. "Letter of Agreement," October 3, 1947, NBC records, box 596, folder 32, WCFTR.

36. Noel Jordan, "Memo to Warren Wade," November 24, 1947, NBC records, box 596, folder 32, WCFTR.

37. Jordan, "Memo to Warren Wade."

38. F. C. Wilbur, "Letter to R. E. Shelby," December 19, 1947, NBC records, box 596, folder 32, WCFTR.

39. "Jerry Fairbanks Group Returns from Hawaii," *Boxoffice*, October 25, 1947, 49; "Technical," *Broadcasting-Telecasting*, November 10, 1947, 60.

40. "Songwriter to Make 16mm for Nontheatrical Use," *Boxoffice*, November 22, 1947, 64.

41. "Poppele Calls Audience Data TV's Big Need," *Billboard*, December 20, 1947, 16.

42. "Zoomar in Rose Bowl," *Broadcasting-Telecasting*, December 15, 1947; "Zoomar for KTLA," *Broadcasting-Telecasting*, March 22, 1948.

43. Television Zoomar Corp, "Television Zoomar Manual," ca. 1951, Frank Back Papers, box 4, folder 2, Mandeville Special Collections, University of California San Diego.

44. Refer to the discussion in chapter 1 and see, especially, Joseph V. Mascelli, "Use and Abuse of the Zoom Lens," *American Cinematographer* 38, no. 10 (October 1957): 652–653, 677.

45. Erik Barnouw, *Tube of Plenty* (Oxford: Oxford University Press, 1975), 102.

46. James R. Walker and Robert V. Bellamy, "Baseball on Television: The Formative Years, 1939–1951," *Nine* 11, no. 2 (Spring 2003): 1–4.

47. Cy Wagner, "Tele's Baseball Coverage All Right but Lacks Interest," *Billboard*, April 24, 1948, 15.

48. "Hub Ballcasts like Last Year," *Variety*, April 19, 1950, 43.

49. "Threat to WPTZ Sports Perch Seen in Philly Football, Series Setups," *Variety*, September 20, 1950, 27.

50. "TV Baseball Rough Diamond," *Billboard*, May 20, 1950, 6.

51. Haviland F. Reves, "WWJ Zooms Coverage with 35 on Sked," *Billboard*, May 20, 1950, 6.

52. Herm, "Tele Still on the Ball in B.B. Coverage; Cameras on the Spot for Openers," *Variety*, April 23, 1952, 23.

53. Herm, "TV's Slick Performance on World Series, with a Minimum of Frills," *Variety*, October 10, 1951, 24.

54. "Series Coverage down to Fine TV Point; No Changes," *Variety*, October 1, 1952, 1.

55. "TV Turns in a Solid, Workmanlike Job on Series, Sans Gimmicks," *Variety*, October 7, 1953, 47; Mark, "World Series," *Variety*, October 6, 1954, 36.

56. Sam Chase and Jerry Franken, "Louis-Walcott Fight," *Variety*, December 13, 1947, 16.

57. Sam Chase, "Hockey Games," *Billboard*, December 27, 1947, 16.

58. "Derby Telecast," *Broadcasting-Telecasting*, May 23, 1949, 4; "WXYZ-TV Sells 5-Hour Boat Race to Chevvy," *Billboard*, June 11, 1949, 15.

59. "WPTZ at US Open," *Broadcasting-Telecasting*, June 19, 1950, 6; "TVing of Polo Matches Offered as 3G Package," *Variety*, May 9, 1951, 31.

60. Haviland F. Reves, "Tugboat Race," *Billboard*, June 2, 1951, 6.

61. After the introduction of the Zoomar lens, Joseph Walker created a heavily modified version of the motion picture zoom lens he had developed in the 1920s (see previous chapter). Walker redeveloped the lens on behalf of the Don Lee Broadcasting System. Renamed the "Electra-Zoom," the lens featured a motor that enabled the operator to zoom in or out smoothly. The Electra-Zoom was marketed to television stations within and beyond the United States, but its actual impact is hard to gauge. It may be the case that on some occasions, trade journal references to the "Zoomar" lens refer generically to the Electra-Zoom.

62. "Simple TV Remote," *Broadcasting-Telecasting*, November 15, 1948, 106.

63. June Bundy, "Industry Hits All Time High on Tough Macarthur Assignment," *Variety*, April 28, 1951, 3; Bert Briller, "Iconoscopes Invade Ike Inaugural, Capturing Color, Capers, Camera-Derie," *Variety*, January 21, 1953, 33.

64. "Remote Telecasting," *Broadcasting-Telecasting*, August 25, 1952, 80.

65. Rees, "Jaycee Parade," *Variety*, June 17, 1953, 34.

66. Don, "Attempted Suicide," *Variety*, September 30, 1953, 34.

67. "TV Zooms in a Tornado," *Variety*, April 16, 1958, 35.

68. Victor Ford, "How Zoomar Aids TV Photography," *American Cinematographer* 30, no. 6 (June 1949): 202, 214.

69. Tim Hollis, *Hi There, Boys and Girls! America's Local Children's TV Shows* (Jackson: University Press of Mississippi, 2001), 100; James Pinkerton, "It's 'Super-Circus' for Canada Dry," *Broadcasting-Telecasting*, March 13, 1950, 49.

70. R. W. Stewart, "The Convention via Video," *New York Times*, June 27, 1948, X9.

71. Stewart, X9; Jack Gould, "Television and Politics," *New York Times*, July 18, 1948, X7.

72. Soule Gardner, "How TV Will Take You to Conventions," *Popular Science*, June 1952.

73. Mary Ann Watson, *The Expanding Vista: American Television in the Kennedy Years* (Durham, N.C.: Duke University Press, 1994), 209–210.

74. Jack Gould, "TV at the Crossroads: A Critic's Survey," *New York Times*, March 9, 1952.

75. "TV as a Political Force," *New York Times*, June 8, 1952.

76. Gardner, "Take You to Conventions."

77. "Far Cry from Radio-Only Era," *Variety*, July 9, 1952, 23; see also Charles A. H. Thomson, *Television and Presidential Politics* (Washington, D.C.: Brookings Institution, 1956), 18.

78. "NBC Set to Cover '52 Political Drive,'" *New York Times*, January 1, 1952, 30.

79. Thomson, *Television and Presidential Politics*, 37.

80. Florence S. Lowe, "More Assurance, Polish, Flavor Mark TV Webs' Coverage of Dems," *Variety*, July 22, 1952, 1.

81. "Television Showed the Floor to History's Biggest Audience," *Life*, July 21, 1952, 19.

82. "TV Spies Mrs. Howard Doffing Shoes on Dais," *New York Times*, July 11, 1952, 9.

83. Abel, "TV for President!," *Variety*, July 16, 1952, 2.

84. Jack Gould, "Radio and Television," *New York Times*, July 8, 1952, 34.

85. The source is a C-SPAN rebroadcast of a portion NBC's live coverage of the convention, originally broadcast on July 9, 1952, and rebroadcast by C-SPAN on March 8, 1989. At the time of writing, the 1988 rebroadcast could be viewed at "1952 Floor Fight on Seating of GA Delegates," C-SPAN, July 9, 1952, https://www.c-span.org/video/?3987-1/1952-floor-fight-seating -ga-delegates.

86. Jack Gould, "The Year's Summary," *New York Times*, December 28, 1952, X11.

87. Causing confusion in some historical accounts, Paul Willemen, for example, states that "Paramount deployed a zoomar lens in the late '20s." Willemen, "The Zoom in Popular Cinema: A Question of Performance," *Rouge*, no. 1 (2003), http://www.rouge.com.au/1/zoom.html.

88. Irving R. Levine, "Soviet Continues TV Expansion, 25th Station Goes on the Air," *Variety*, September 25, 1957, 35.

89. Abel, "S-B Plugs 75 Standards in 'TV Song Production Book'; Big 3 to Categorize 500," *Variety*, October 29, 1952, 46; Rose, "Alcoa Hour," *Variety*, November 30, 1955, 40; "Television Showed the Floor," 18.

CHAPTER 4. UNLIMITED HORIZONS

1. Peter Brunette, *Roberto Rossellini* (Los Angeles: University of California Press, 1996), 222; Warren Buckland, *Directed by Steven Spielberg* (London: Continuum, 2006), 10.

2. Gérard Bandelier, "La SOM, Société d'Optique et de Mécanique," archive.org, n.d., http://web.archive.org/web/20001029235133/www.leprogres.fr/Fex-indo/som/som1.htm.

3. Rudolf Kingslake, *A History of the Photographic Lens* (London: Academic Press, 1989), 171.

4. "'Pan-Cinor'—Novel Variable Focus Lens with Seven Elements," *American Cinematographer* 31, no. 6 (June 1950): 205.

5. "The New Pan Cinor 20mm to 60mm Variable Focal Length Lens for 16mm Cameras," *Bolex Reporter* 2, no. 3 (1952): 16.

6. "Zoom for Really Professional Shots with the New Pan Cinor Lens," *Bolex Reporter* 2, no. 4 (Fall 1952): 24–25.

7. Sid O'Berry, ". . . and Just Zoooooooom," *Bolex Reporter* 3, no. 2 (Spring 1953): 24.

8. Arthur Rowan, "The Pan Cinor—Variable Zoom Lens for 16mm Cameras," *American Cinematographer* 34, no. 10 (October 1953): 490; "Zoom for Really Professional Shots," *Bolex Reporter* 2, no. 4 (Fall 1952): 24–25.

9. Rowan, "Pan Cinor," 508; Harry Pennington, "The Pan Cinor Lens," *Bolex Reporter* 3, no. 2 (1953): 26.

10. Willis Cook, "The Pan Cinor-60 for TV," *Bolex Reporter* 5, no. 2 (Spring 1955): 19.

11. "Now! Direct View through Your New Pan Cinor Zoom Lenses," *Bolex Reporter* 5, no. 3 (Summer 1955): 19.

12. Robert H. Hess, "The New Pan Cinor-70 at the Summit!," *Bolex Reporter* 6, no. 1 (Christmas 1955): 20–21.

13. "Zoomar," advertisement, *American Cinematographer* 34, no. 10 (October 1953): 495; "Zoomar," advertisement, *American Cinematographer* 34, no. 11 (November 1953): 557; "Zoomar," advertisement, *American Cinematographer* 34, no. 12 (December 1953): 604; "Zoomar," advertisement, *American Cinematographer* 35, no. 1 (January 1954): 10.

14. Alvin D. Roe, "The Zoomar Varifocal Lens for 16mm Cameras," *American Cinematographer* 35, no. 1 (January 1954): 27; "Film Readied to Show Use of Zoomar on Small Camera," *Broadcasting-Telecasting*, December 28, 1953.

15. Roe, "Zoomar Varifocal Lens," 27.

16. Parts of this chapter and those that follow draw on evidence from the trial transcript in the case of *Zoomar, Inc. vs. Paillard Products, Inc.* The *Zoomar v. Paillard* transcript consists of 616 continuously numbered pages divided among four folders in two storage boxes at the Library of Congress in Washington, D.C., box 8, folders 5 and 6 (covering pp. 1–148a, 149–292a of the transcript) and box 9, folders 1 and 2 (pp. 293–454, 455–616). The judgement was published in the *Federal Supplement* and is referenced as 152 F. Supp. 328.

17. Joseph E. Gortych, "Lens Design Patents: The View from Court-Space," *Optics & Photonics News*, June 1996, 31.

18. The finding in this case abbreviates these patents as '686 and '817. The same form used in what follows.

19. Kaufman was well known for having sentenced Ethel and Julius Rosenberg to death earlier in the decade. It is not clear which of the Shereff brothers—Louis or Harry—represented Back during the trial, as the transcript merely names "Mr. Shereff." The Shereff brothers ran a general legal practice and do not seem to have had substantial experience in fighting high-stakes intellectual property cases. The defense attorneys appointed by Paillard, by contrast, acted in numerous such cases during the 1950s, especially those concerning patent infringement and validity.

20. *Zoomar v. Paillard*, 27–28.

21. *Zoomar v. Paillard*, 65.

22. *Zoomar v. Paillard*, 104.

23. "Zoom Lens Rights Are Held Invalid," *New York Times*, June 6, 1957, 52.

24. Erik Barnouw, *Tube of Plenty* (Oxford: Oxford University Press, 1975), 213.

25. William Boddy, *Fifties Television* (Chicago: University of Illinois Press, 1990), 75.

26. Joseph V. Mascelli, "Use and Abuse of the Zoom Lens," *American Cinematographer* 38, no. 10 (October 1957): 652–653, 677.

27. Joseph V. Mascelli, "How 'All-Star Golf' Is Shot for TV," *American Cinematographer* 39, no. 1 (January 1958): 26–27, 57.

28. Hal Erickson, "Night Court," *Encyclopedia of Television Law Shows* (Jefferson, N.C.: McFarland, 2009), 196.

29. Erickson, 196.

30. Joseph V. Mascelli, "Filming Courtroom Dramas for Television," *American Cinematographer* 40, no. 1 (January 1959): 33.

31. Mascelli, 33.

32. Mascelli, 56.

33. "Episode 7," *Night Court USA*, Alpha Home Entertainment, 2005.

34. John Belton, "The Bionic Eye: Zoom Esthetics," *Cinéaste* 11, no. 1 (Winter 1980–1981): 20–27.

35. "Time of Delivery," *Philco Television Playhouse*, NBC, October 31, 1954, VA18862T, UCLA Film and Television Archive.

36. "President," *Alcoa Hour*, NBC, May 13, 1956, VA2372T, UCLA Film and Television Archive.

37. Michael Rosen, "John Frankenheimer," Archive of American Television, March 21, 2000, http://www.emmytvlegends.org/interviews/people/john-frankenheimer.

38. "Eloise," *Playhouse 90*, CBS, November 22, 1956, VA15522T, UCLA Film and Television Archive.

39. "Days of Wine and Roses," *Playhouse 90*, CBS, October 2, 1958, VA2085T, UCLA Film and Television Archive.

40. "The Comic," *Peter Gunn*, NBC, October 12, 1959, VA6129T, UCLA Film and Television Archive.

41. "Wings of an Angel," *Peter Gunn*, NBC, April 18, 1960, VA3631T, UCLA Film and Television Archive.

42. "The Brain Picker," *Mr. Lucky*, CBS, February 6, 1960, VA4368T, UCLA Film and Television Archive.

43. "Diagnosis Danger," *Alfred Hitchcock Hour*, March 1, 1963, CBS Television.

44. "The Dark Labyrinth," *Alcoa Premiere*, ABC, March 21, 1963, T35880, UCLA Film and Television Archive.

45. "Solo for B-Flat Clarinet," *Breaking Point*, ABC, September 16, 1963, VA19296T, UCLA Film and Television Archive.

46. "A Cardinal Act of Mercy, Part 1," *Ben Casey*, ABC, August 26, 1963, VA2468T, UCLA Film and Television Archive.

47. "Ben Casey. Cardinal Act of Mercy. Part 1," UCLA Library Catalog Holdings Information, https://cinema.library.ucla.edu/vwebv/holdingsInfo?bibId=6870.

CHAPTER 5. CREEPERS AND NECK-SNAPPERS

1. "What's New," *American Cinematographer* 43, no. 9 (September 1962): 524–528.

2. "Gordon Enterprises," advertisement, *American Cinematographer* 44, no. 1 (January 1963): 3.

3. Joseph Brun, "Odds Against Tomorrow," *American Cinematographer* 40, no. 8 (August 1959): 479.

4. See, for example, *I Spy* (NBC, 1965–1968) and *They Shoot Horses, Don't They?* (Sydney Pollack, 1969).

5. Darrin Scot, "Shooting '-30-' on a Single Set," *American Cinematographer* 40, no. 12 (December 1959): 760.

6. Scot, 760.

7. Scot, 760.

8. Scot, 760.

9. George A. Mitchell, "Multiple Cameras Cut Shooting Time of 'Hell to Eternity,'" *American Cinematographer* 41, no. 7 (July 1960): 436.

10. Patrice-Hervé Pont, *Angénieux* (Paris: Éditions du Pécari, 2003), 15.

11. Rudolf Kingslake, "The Development of the Zoom Lens," *Journal of the Society of Motion Picture and Television Engineers* 69, no. 8 (August 1960): 540.

12. Pont, *Angénieux*, 19.

13. Pont, 180.

14. Herb A. Lightman, "The Angénieux Story," *American Cinematographer* 56, no. 3 (March 1975): 328.

15. Pont, *Angénieux*, 193, 201.

16. "What's New," *American Cinematographer* 37, no. 4 (April 1956): 202.

17. John Forbes, "Motor-Driven Zoom Lens," *American Cinematographer* 41, no. 12 (December 1960): 746.

18. "Motor Drive for 35mm Zoom Lenses," *American Cinematographer* 43, no. 10 (October 1962): 632.

19. "Camera Equipment Company," advertisement, *American Cinematographer* 44, no. 10 (October 1963): 561.

20. "What's New," *American Cinematographer* 44, no. 7 (July 1936): 388.

21. "Camera Service Center," advertisement, *American Cinematographer* 44, no. 10 (October 1963): 617.

22. "General Camera Corporation," advertisement, *American Cinematographer* 45, no. 7 (July 1964): 389.

23. Richard Moore, "New Uses for Zoom Lenses," *American Cinematographer* 46, no. 7 (July 1965): 438.

24. Hal Mohr, "Zoom Uses," *American Cinematographer* 46, no. 8 (August 1965): 491.

25. Jay Donohue, "Focal Length and Creative Perspective," *American Cinematographer* 47, no. 7 (July 1966): 500.

26. Herb A. Lightman, "The Photography of 'Hud,'" *American Cinematographer* 44, no. 7 (July 1963): 414–416.

27. Herb A. Lightman, "'The Outrage'—Off-Beat Photography Is One of Its Virtues," *American Cinematographer* 45, no. 4 (April 1964): 198.

28. Herb A. Lightman, "Capturing on Film the Mythical Magic of 'Camelot,'" *American Cinematographer* 49, no. 1 (January 1968): 30.

29. Lightman, 33.

30. Lightman, 33, 48.

31. "The Boston Location Filming of 'The Thomas Crown Affair,'" *American Cinematographer* 49, no. 8 (August 1968): 742.

32. Herb A. Lightman, "Filming 'Planet of the Apes,'" *American Cinematographer* 49, no. 5 (April 1968): 277.

33. Herb A. Lightman, "The Director-Cameraman Relationship," *American Cinematographer* 49, no. 5 (May 1968): 364–365.

34. Warren Buckland, *Directed by Steven Spielberg* (London: Continuum, 2006), 10.

35. Michael Rosen, "John Frankenheimer," Archive of American Television, March 21, 2000, http://www.emmytvlegends.org/interviews/people/john-frankenheimer.

36. Herb A. Lightman, "Birdman of Alcatraz," *American Cinematographer* 43, no. 6 (June 1962): 354–355, 384.

37. Stuart M. Kaminsky, "The Use and Abuse of the Zoom Lens," *Filmmakers Newsletter*, 1972, 23.

38. David Bordwell, Kristin Thompson, and Janet Staiger, *The Classical Hollywood Cinema* (London: Routledge and Kegan Paul, 1985), 44.

39. David Bordwell, *Poetics of Cinema* (New York: Routledge, 2008), 24.

40. Todd Rainsberger, *James Wong Howe, Cinematographer* (San Diego, Calif.: A. S. Barnes, 1981), 233.

41. Scott Eyman, ed., *Five American Cinematographers: Interviews with Karl Struss, Joseph Ruttenberg, James Wong Howe, Linwood Dunn, and William H. Clothier*, no. 17 (Metuchen, N.J.: Scarecrow, 1987), 83.

42. Dennis Bingham, "Shot from the Sky: The Gypsy Moths and the End of Something," in *A Little Solitaire: John Frankenheimer and American Film*, ed. Murray Pomerance and Barton R. Palmer (New Brunswick, N.J.: Rutgers University Press, 2011), 225–226.

43. In addition to these dramatic zooms, in *The Gypsy Moths*, Frankenheimer also uses the zoom to adjust framing during scenes set in the parachute team's aircraft.

44. Rainsberger, *James Wong Howe*, 255.

45. The sole exception to this is during a confrontation between Alva and Legate. Other moments of particular drama are reinforced by camera movement: when Alva's mother remarks "she and JJ got married," Alva's shock is shown through a rapid track-in, not a zoom.

46. Salt misidentifies these shots as forming the film's opening sequence. See Barry Salt, *Film Style and Technology*, 2nd ed. (London: Starword, 1992), 258.

47. During this period, Pollack was also somewhat involved in the production of *The Swimmer*. However, most available sources agree that the majority of the film was shot by Frank Perry prior to Pollack's involvement: Meyer credits Pollack with "one sequence," and a report in *Variety* said that this was a "sequence involving Janice Rule." See Janet L. Meyer, *Sydney Pollack: A Critical Filmography* (Jefferson, N.C.: McFarland, 1998), 11; "New York Sound Track," *Variety*, January 18, 1967, 19.

48. Meyer, *Sydney Pollack*, 57.

CHAPTER 6. THE ZOOM BOOM

1. Geoffrey Nowell-Smith, *Making Waves: New Cinemas of the 1960s* (New York: Bloomsbury, 2013), 103.

2. Charles Tepperman describes in great detail the diversity of amateur cinematography and its links to professional practice in *Amateur Cinema: The Rise of North American Moviemaking, 1923–1960* (Oakland: University of California Press, 2015).

3. "Bolex Showcase," *Bolex Reporter* 5, no. 4 (Spring 1954): 14.

4. Martin Zipin, "Temple University Goes TV . . . Portrays Tyler School of Fine Art," *Bolex Reporter* 3, no. 4 (Fall 1953): 18–19.

5. "How to Use the Pan Cinor Zoom-Type Lens," *Bolex Reporter* 3, no. 4 (Fall 1953): 24–26.

6. Les Barry, "Follow the Action with Pan Cinor," *Bolex Reporter* 7, no. 4 (Fall 1957): 12–13.

7. Merrill F. Sproul, "To Zoom . . . or Not To Zoom," *Bolex Reporter* 10, no. 3 (Summer 1960): 18–19.

8. "New: Bolex Zoom Reflex P-1," *Bolex Reporter* 11, no. 2 (1961–1962): 12.

9. "New Ideas in Photography from Kodak," *Popular Science*, November 1960, 208; "Zooms You Right into the Splash of a Trout Battle!," *Popular Science*, July 1962, 161.

10. "New Palm-Size Movie Camera," *Popular Science*, July 1968, 106.

11. Henry Provisor, *8mm/16mm Movie-Making* (New York: American Photographic, 1970), 16.

12. Jerry Yulsman, *The Complete Book of 8mm Movie Making* (New York: Coward, McCann & Geoghegan, 1972), 36.

13. Bradley Schauer, "The Auteur Renaissance, 1968–1980," in *Cinematography*, ed. Patrick Keating (New Brunswick, N.J.: Rutgers University Press, 2014), 87.

14. G. H. Cook and F. R. Laurent, "Recent Trends and Developments of Zoom Lenses," *Journal of the Society of Motion Picture and Television Engineers* 80, no. 8 (August 1971): 631.

15. Yoshiya Matsui, "Use of Calcium Fluoride for Zoom Lenses of High Quality for Cinematography and Television," *Journal of the Society of Motion Picture and Television Engineers* 80, no. 1 (January 1971): 22.

16. "Industry Activities," *American Cinematographer* 54, no. 5 (May 1973): 516.

17. Milton Forman, "The Trial of the Catonsville Nine," *American Cinematographer* 53, no. 7 (July 1972): 774–776, 818–822.

18. Marshall Brown, "Professional and Profitable Filming in Super-8," *American Cinematographer* 53, no. 2 (February 1972): 164–167.

19. Herb A. Lightman, "The Canon Story," *American Cinematographer* 54, no. 8 (August 1973): 994.

20. This silence in the trade press may be why Barry Salt suggests that Canon "did not try to make zooms covering a focal length change of 10 to 1." See Barry Salt, *Film Style and Technology*, 2nd ed. (London: Starword, 1992), 279. A detailed *American Cinematographer* profile of Canon published in 1973 mentions exactly such a lens.

21. Herb A. Lightman, "Behind the Scenes of 'Hello Dolly,'" *American Cinematographer* 51, no. 2 (February 1970): 116–119, 130–131, 166, 170–171, 176–178.

22. David B. Nowell, "Shooting the Aerial Sequences for 'Capricorn One,'" *American Cinematographer* 58, no. 12 (December 1977): 1290; "Second Unit Filming for 'A Bridge Too Far,'" *American Cinematographer* 58, no. 4 (April 1977): 442.

23. "New Fuji Film Ultra Multi-layer EBC Coating Technique an Answer to Camera Flare Problem," *American Cinematographer* 54, no. 3 (March 1973): 304–305.

24. "The Moving Camera," *American Cinematographer* 55, no. 6 (June 1974): 689.

25. Dick Neville, "Television Newsfilm Problems," *Journal of the Society of Motion Picture and Television Engineers* 80, no. 3 (March 1971): 159.

26. Ellen Wolf, "Camera Inventor Clicks Another Oscar," *Variety*, March 4, 2002, 26.

27. Forman, "Trial of the Catonsville Nine."

28. Herb A. Lightman, "The 44th Annual Academy Awards Presentation," *American Cinematographer* 53, no. 5 (May 1972): 490–493.

29. David A. Cook, *Lost Illusions* (Berkeley: University of California Press, 2002), 79. For a very thorough analysis of Kubrick's use of the zoom in *Barry Lyndon*, see Jeffrey Scott Bernstein, "The Zooms in *Barry Lyndon*," jeffreyscottbernstein.com, n.d., http://www.jeffreyscottbernstein.com/kubrick/images/BARRY%20LYNDON.pdf.

30. "Photographing Stanley Kubrick's 'Barry Lyndon,'" *American Cinematographer* 57, no. 3 (March 1976): 321.

31. Scott Henderson, "The Cinema Products Story," *American Cinematographer* 56, no. 5 (May 1975): 574–576, 580–584, 598–607.

32. "The First Feature Use of Steadicam-35 on 'Bound for Glory,'" *American Cinematographer* 57, no. 7 (July 1976): 778.

33. John Jurgens, "Steadicam as a Design Problem," *SMPTE Journal* 87, no. 9 (September 1978): 590.

34. Charles Loring, "The Unique Video West Instant Replay System," *American Cinematographer* 51, no. 2 (February 1970): 140.

35. Herb A. Lightman, "The Wrath of God on Location," *American Cinematographer* 53, no. 3 (March 1972): 258–331.

36. Lightman, "Behind the Scenes."

37. Herb A. Lightman, "On Location with 'Fiddler on the Roof,'" *American Cinematographer* 51, no. 12 (December 1970): 1204–1207.

38. Herb A. Lightman, "Wild Rovers: Case History of a Film," *American Cinematographer* 52, no. 7 (July 1971): 657.

39. "The Last Picture Show: A Study in Black and White," *American Cinematographer* 53, no. 1 (January 1972): 103.

40. Karl Malkames, "To Zoom or Not to Zoom," *American Cinematographer* 55, no. 6 (June 1974): 713.

41. Herb A. Lightman, "James Wong Howe, ASC Talks about His Photography of 'Funny Lady,'" *American Cinematographer* 56, no. 1 (January 1975): 32–33, 116.

42. "Last Seminar with a Hollywood Legend," *American Cinematographer* 57, no. 9 (September 1976): 1010.

43. Howard Schwartz, "An American Film Institute Seminar with Gordon Willis, ASC," *American Cinematographer* 59, no. 10 (October 1978): 979.

44. "The Filming of 'Tora! Tora! Tora!,'" *American Cinematographer* 52, no. 2 (February 1971): 124–127, 174–176, 178–181.

45. Bill Keil, "On Location with 'Lost Horizon,'" *American Cinematographer* 54, no. 4 (April 1973): 412.

46. John A. Alonzo, "Behind the Scenes of 'Chinatown,'" *American Cinematographer* 56, no. 5 (May 1975): 572.

47. "Photographing the French Connection," *American Cinematographer* 53, no. 2 (February 1972): 216.

48. Herb A. Lightman, "The New Panaflex Camera Makes Its Production Debut," *American Cinematographer* 54, no. 5 (May 1973): 616.

49. James Crabe, "The Photography of 'Rocky,'" *American Cinematographer* 58, no. 2 (February 1977): 205, 221.

50. David Hammond, "'Action Unit' Lives Up to Its Name While Shooting 'The Towering Inferno,'" *American Cinematographer* 56, no. 2 (February 1975): 168.

51. Philip H. Lathrop, "The Photography," *American Cinematographer* 55, no. 11 (November 1974): 1333.

52. John Belton, "The Bionic Eye: Zoom Esthetics," *Cinéaste* 11, no. 1 (Winter 1980–1981): 25–27.

53. David Bordwell, *On the History of Film Style* (Cambridge, Mass.: Harvard University Press, 1997), 246–251.

54. Cook, *Lost Illusions*, 361–366.

55. Cook, 165.

56. "Journey into Darkness," *Arrest and Trial*, ABC, December 8, 1963, T35022, UCLA Film and Television Archive.

57. "The Jar," *Alfred Hitchcock Hour*, CBS, February 14, 1964, VA3070T, UCLA Film and Television Archive.

58. "A Dangerous Proposal," *Run for Your Life*, NBC, January 3, 1968, T22010, UCLA Film and Television Archive.

59. Robert V. Kerns, "A Day on the Set of 'Marcus Welby, MD,'" *American Cinematographer* 51, no. 3 (March 1970): 265.

60. Kerns, 267.

61. Kerns, 269.

62. Robert V. Kerns, "Using the Zoom Lens Creatively," *American Cinematographer* 52, no. 3 (March 1971): 226. However, in the same article, Kerns notes that Strenge, exceptionally, had used a 25mm lens to capture a wide shot (228).

63. Kerns, 227.

64. Richard Moore, "New Uses for Zoom Lenses," *American Cinematographer* 46, no. 7 (July 1965): 438–441.

65. Kerns, "Using the Zoom Lens," 227.

66. Kerns, 228, 270.

67. Robin Wood, "Smart-Ass & Cutie-Pie," *Movie 21* (Autumn 1975): 8; Cook, *Lost Illusions*, 362.

68. Hamish Ford, "The Porous Frame: Visual Style in Altman's 1970s Films," in *A Companion to Robert Altman*, ed. Adrian Danks (Chichester: Wiley-Blackwell, 2015), 119, 132.

69. Jay Beck, *Designing Sound* (New Brunswick, N.J.: Rutgers University Press, 2016), 58–59.

70. "The Volunteer," *Combat*, ABC, January 22, 1963; "The Long Lost Life of Edward Smalley," *Kraft Suspense Theatre*, NBC, December 12, 1963.

71. "Once upon a Savage Night," *Kraft Suspense Theatre*, NBC, April 24, 1964.

72. Robert Kolker, *A Cinema of Loneliness*, 4th ed. (Oxford: Oxford University Press, 2011), 411.

73. For a fuller discussion of these examples and a broader view of Altman's progression from television to film, see Nick Hall, "Just a Station on His Way? Altman's Transition from Television to Film," in *A Companion to Robert Altman*, ed. Adrian Danks (Chichester: Wiley-Blackwell, 2015), 68–91.

74. Belton, "Bionic Eye," 25.

75. Belton, 25.

76. Amy Rust, *Passionate Detachments: Technologies of Vision and Violence in American Cinema, 1967–1974* (Albany: State University of New York Press, 2017), 118.

77. Adam O'Brien, *Transactions with the World* (New York: Berghahn Books, 2016), 190.

CHAPTER 7. CONTEMPORARY ZOOMS

1. John Belton, "The Bionic Eye: Zoom Esthetics," *Cinéaste* 11, no. 1 (Winter 1980–1981): 27.

2. David Bordwell, *The Way Hollywood Tells It: Story and Style in Modern Movies* (Berkeley: University of California Press, 2006), 121.

3. Manohla Dargis, "The Work of War, at a Fever Pitch," *New York Times*, January 7, 2010, http://www.nytimes.com/2010/01/10/movies/awardsseason/10darg.html.

4. Rachael K. Bosley, "Native Sons," *American Cinematographer* 84, no. 1 (January 2003): 45.

5. Gray Simon, "Watchful Spirit," *American Cinematographer* 91, no. 1 (January 2010): 51.

6. Ed DiGiulio, E. C. Manderfield, and George A. Mitchell, "An Historical Survey of the Professional Motion-Picture Camera," *SMPTE Journal* 85, no. 7 (July 1976): 484.

7. Richard Patterson, "Video Lenses," *American Cinematographer* 64, no. 9 (September 1983): 24–92.

8. "What's New," *American Cinematographer* 64, no. 6 (June 1983): 24.

9. Bordwell, *Hollywood Tells It*, 154–155.

10. Billy Wilder and Robert Horton, *Billy Wilder: Interviews* (Jackson: University Press of Mississippi, 2001), 115.

11. "Filming in the Time Warp of Two Different Eras," *American Cinematographer* 61, no. 7 (July 1980): 720.

12. Nora Lee, "'Magic of the Silver Box' for the Tracker," *American Cinematographer* 69, no. 3 (March 1988): 59.

13. Eric Rudolph, "The Rock Offers No Escape," *American Cinematographer* 77, no. 6 (July 1996): 73; Chris Pizzello, "High Noon Hits the New Jersey Turnpike," *American Cinematographer* 78, no. 9 (September 1997): 60.

14. Nora Lee, "Coming to America—a Lavish Comedy," *American Cinematographer* 69, no. 8 (August 1988): 48.

15. Bob Fisher, "Witches of Eastwick: An Outrageous Look," *American Cinematographer* 68, no. 6 (June 1987): 64–70.

16. Jon Silberg, "Intellectual Angst," *American Cinematographer* 83, no. 1 (January 2002): 54.

17. Ron Magid, "Making 'Spidey Sense' Tingle," *American Cinematographer* 83, no. 6 (June 2002): 52.

18. As Adam O'Brien points out in his excellent ecocritical discussion of the zoom in the New Hollywood, "If one were to direct a spoof of, or homage to, this period, it is hard to imagine not using [the zoom] lens." Adam O'Brien, *Transactions with the World* (New York: Berghahn Books, 2016), 179.

19. Bob Fisher, "Swanky Modes," *American Cinematographer* 79, no. 10 (October 1998): 66.

20. B. Benjamin, "The Price of Revenge," *American Cinematographer* 87, no. 2 (February 2006): 38–39.

21. Richard Kline, "Behind the Camera on 'Star Trek: The Motion Picture,'" *American Cinematographer* 61, no. 2 (February 1980): 181.

22. David Samuelson, "The Photography of 'Stars Wars: The Empire Strikes Back,'" *American Cinematographer* 61, no. 6 (June 1980): 615.

23. Hugh Hart, "Production Slate: Scenic Surrealism and Retro Romance; That Touch of Pink," *American Cinematographer* 84, no. 5 (May 2003): 29.

24. "Sophie's Choice," *American Cinematographer* 64, no. 4 (April 1983): 56–57.

25. Donald Chase, "Against All Odds," *American Cinematographer* 65, no. 3 (March 1984): 52.

26. Bob Fisher, "Tender Loving Care for Moonlighting," *American Cinematographer* 67, no. 7 (July 1986): 40–48.

27. Bob Fisher, "Cinematography in the 1600 Zone," *American Cinematographer* 64, no. 5 (May 1983): 92.

28. Richard Patterson, "Making 'The Invisible Woman,'" *American Cinematographer* 64, no. 4 (April 1983): 106.

29. Nora Lee, "'Star Trek'—the Voyages Continue," *American Cinematographer* 68, no. 11 (November 1987): 80; Dale Kutzera, "'Empire of the Sun'—an Exotic Journey," *American Cinematographer* 69, no. 1 (January 1988): 48.

30. Paul M. Sammon, "John Hora and Gremlins," *American Cinematographer* 65, no. 11 (November 1984): 77–78.

31. Ron Magid, "Equinox: 'Twin Bill' with a Twist," *American Cinematographer* 74, no. 4 (April 1993): 84.

32. Robert Veze, "Photography for Flashdance," *American Cinematographer* 64, no. 5 (May 1983): 72.

33. Bob Fisher, "Behind the Scenes on 'The Winds of War,'" *American Cinematographer* 64, no. 1 (January 1983): 103.

34. Samir Hachem, "Schemes and Dreams of Ruthless People," *American Cinematographer* 67, no. 7 (July 1986): 31.

35. David Heuring, "I Love You to Death: Humor in Black," *American Cinematographer* 71, no. 4 (April 1990): 54.

36. Benjamin Bergery, "Inside Panavision," *American Cinematographer* 78, no. 2 (February 1997): 31.

37. Michael Singer, "Final Analysis: Freudian Suspense, Shot with Style," *American Cinematographer* 73, no. 3 (March 1992): 47.

38. Rick Baker, "Almendros Illuminates Billy Bathgate," *American Cinematographer* 72, no. 11 (November 1991): 28.

39. Bob Fisher, "Zsigmond Shows Strong Hand on Maverick," *American Cinematographer* 75, no. 11 (November 1994): 62.

40. "New Products and Developments," *SMPTE Journal* 87, no. 11 (November 1978): 796.

41. See the Academy of Motion Picture Arts and Sciences Awards Database, awardsdatabase .oscars.org.

42. George Turner, "Revenge Served Cold," *American Cinematographer* 77, no. 10 (October 1996): 40–42.

43. Arnold & Richter Cine Technik, *Carl Zeiss / Arriflex Variable Primes* (Munich: Arnold & Richter Cine Technik, 1996).

44. "Behind the Cameras for the Filming of 'Annie,'" *American Cinematographer* 63, no. 6 (June 1982): 565–566.

45. David E. Williams, "A Perfectionist's Guide to Super 35," *American Cinematographer* 78, no. 12 (December 1997): 34–35.

46. Jay Holben, "Alter Ego," *American Cinematographer* 81, no. 1 (January 2001): 60.

47. Chris Pizzello, "Con Artistry: Confidence," *American Cinematographer* 84, no. 5 (May 2003): 97.

48. "Illuminated by Headlights," *New York Times*, March 18, 1991, B7.

49. Stephan Talty, "Family Record," *Film Comment* 27, no. 3 (May 1991): 52.

50. Walter Goodman, "Television, Meet Life. Life, Meet TV: Too Real for Television," *New York Times*, June 19, 1994, E1.

51. Anton Wilson, "Cinema Workshop," *American Cinematographer* 61, no. 1 (January 1980): 16.

52. Deirdre Boyle, "From Portapak to Camcorder: A Brief History of Guerilla Television," *Journal of Film and Video* 44, nos. 1–2 (Summer 1992): 67–79.

53. "Once Again, You've Got to Hand It to Sony," *Popular Science*, January 1986, 15.

54. James B. Meigs, "Home Video," *Popular Mechanics*, February 1986.

55. "Sony Goes to Battle for Its Favorite Child," Sony, n.d., https://www.sony.net/SonyInfo/ CorporateInfo/History/SonyHistory/2-02.html.

56. At the time of writing, Holliday's full video could be viewed at "Rodney King Beating Video Full Length Footage Screener," YouTube video, posted by "multishowtvweb," March 12, 2015, https://www.youtube.com/watch?v=sb1WywIpUtY.

57. John Thornton Caldwell, *Televisuality: Style, Crisis, and Authority in American Television* (New Brunswick, N.J.: Rutgers University Press, 1995), 305.

58. Elysse Leonard, "'Racial Rashomon': Reading Rodney King in *Dark Blue* (2002) and *Malcolm X* (1992)," Seventh Art, n.d., http://www.theseventhart.org/essays/The-Seventh-Art-Rodney-King-Malcolm-X-Dark-Blue.pdf.

59. Paul Mason Fotsch, *Watching the Traffic Go By: Transportation and Isolation in Urban America*, 1st ed. (Austin: University of Texas Press, 2007), 163.

60. "The Whirlybird Story," *Broadcasting*, April 25, 1960, 58.

61. Stephen Joiner, "Zoom Shot," *Air & Space*, April 30, 2009, http://www.airspacemag .com/history-of-flight/zoom-shot-57396049/. Several years before his death, John Silva gave a detailed oral history of his career, including the development of news helicopters for KTLA, to the Academy of Television Arts and Sciences Archive of American Television project. At the time of writing, his interview could be accessed at "John Silva," Archive of American Television, n.d., http://www.emmytvlegends.org/interviews/people/john-silva.

62. "Flood Disaster: Dam Break Damage Reaches $15 Million," YouTube video, posted by "Weather Underground," May 17, 2011, https://www.youtube.com/watch?v=sjfa-c8KUDw.

63. "Historic KTLA Footage of the 1965 Watts Riots in Los Angeles," *Los Angeles Times*, 2016, http://www.latimes.com/la-me-historic-ktla-footage-of-the-1965-watts-riots-in-los-angeles -video-20150716-premiumvideo.html.

64. For an enlightening discussion of the critical implications of "cinematic television," see Brett Mills, "What Does It Mean to Call Television 'Cinematic'?," in *Television Aesthetics and Style*, ed. Jason Jacobs and Steven Peacock (New York: Bloomsbury Academic, 2013), 57–66; Deborah Jaramillo, "Rescuing Television from 'the Cinematic': The Perils of Dismissing Television Style," in *Television Aesthetics and Style*, ed. Jason Jacobs and Steven Peacock (New York: Bloomsbury Academic, 2013), 67–75.

65. Caldwell, *Televisuality*, 12.

66. Janet McCabe, "HBO Aesthetics, Quality Television and Boardwalk Empire," in *Television Aesthetics and Style*, ed. Jason Jacobs and Steven Peacock (New York: Bloomsbury Academic, 2013), 192.

67. McCabe, 189.

68. Caldwell, *Televisuality*, 10.

69. One of the best explanations of the formal and stylistic properties of "cinematic television" may be found in a video essay by Matt Zoller Seitz and Chris Wade, "What Does 'Cinematic TV' Really Mean?," *Vulture*, October 2015, http://www.vulture.com/2015/10/ cinematic-tv-what-does-it-really-mean.html.

70. Bordwell, *Hollywood Tells It*, 135.

71. Eric Rudolph, "Points East: The Dark Side of 'Charm City,'" *American Cinematographer* 84, no. 6 (June 2003): 119–120.

72. Ethan Thompson, "Comedy Verité? The Observational Documentary Meets the Televisual Sitcom," *Velvet Light Trap*, no. 60 (Fall 2007): 63; Brett Mills, "Comedy Verite: Contemporary Sitcom Form," *Screen* 45, no. 1 (Spring 2004): 63–78.

73. Ruth Mackay, "Reflexive Modes and Narrative Production: Metatextual Discourse in Contemporary American Narrative," *Canadian Review of American Studies* 44, no. 1 (April 2014): 65–84.

74. James Hawkinson, "Filmmaker's Forum: Breaking Sitcom Rules on 'Arrested Development,'" *American Cinematographer* 85, no. 2 (February 2004): 107–108.

75. Pat Hilton, "Fun Filled Fantasy for Delirious," *American Cinematographer* 72, no. 2 (February 1991): 38–44; Michael X. Ferraro, "Global Village Idiot," *American Cinematographer* 77, no. 7 (July 1996): 77–84.

76. For a discussion of "low-resolution realism" in contemporary Hollywood cinematography, see Christopher Lucas, "The Modern Entertainment Marketplace, 2000–Present," in *Cinematography*, ed. Patrick Keating (New Brunswick, N.J.: Rutgers University Press, 2014), 141–146.

77. Jean Oppenheimer, "A Lone Gunman," *American Cinematographer* 32, no. 12 (December 2002): 75.

78. Marwan M. Kraidy, *Reality Television and Arab Politics: Contention in Public Life* (Cambridge: Cambridge University Press, 2010), 174–175.

79. Kraidy, 174.

80. Jenna Johnson, "Donald Trump Says the Media Underestimates His Crowds—and Him," *Washington Post*, September 27, 2015, suburban ed., sec. A.

SELECTED BIBLIOGRAPHY

Barker, Jennifer M. "Neither Here nor There: Synaesthesia and the Cosmic Zoom." *New Review of Film and Television Studies* 7, no. 3 (September 2009): 311–324.

Belton, John. "The Bionic Eye: Zoom Esthetics." *Cinéaste* 11, no. 1 (Winter 1980–1981): 20–27.

Bordwell, David. *On the History of Film Style.* Cambridge, Mass.: Harvard University Press, 1997.

———. *The Way Hollywood Tells It: Story and Style in Modern Movies.* Berkeley: University of California Press, 2006.

Caldwell, John Thornton. *Televisuality: Style, Crisis, and Authority in American Television.* New Brunswick, N.J.: Rutgers University Press, 1995.

Cook, David A. *Lost Illusions.* Vol. 9. Berkeley: University of California Press, 2002.

Hall, Nick. "Closer to the Action: Post-war American Television and the Zoom Shot." In *Television Aesthetics and Style,* edited by Jason Jacobs and Steven Peacock, 277–287. New York: Bloomsbury Academic, 2013.

———. "Just a Station on His Way? Altman's Transition from Television to Film." In *A Companion to Robert Altman,* edited by Adrian Danks, 68–91. Chichester: Wiley-Blackwell, 2015.

———. "Zoomar: Frank G. Back and the Postwar Television Zoom Lens." *Technology and Culture* 57, no. 2 (25 May 2016): 353–379. doi:10.1353/tech.2016.0061.

Joannides, Paul. "The Aesthetics of the Zoom Lens." *Sight & Sound* 40, no. 1 (Winter 1970–1971): 40–42.

Kaminsky, Stuart M. "The Use and Abuse of the Zoom Lens." *Filmmakers Newsletter,* 1972.

Keating, Patrick, ed. *Cinematography.* New Brunswick, N.J.: Rutgers University Press, 2014.

Kerns, Robert V. "Using the Zoom Lens Creatively." *American Cinematographer* 52, no. 3 (March 1971): 226–228, 270–272.

Kingslake, Rudolf. "The Development of the Zoom Lens." *Journal of the Society of Motion Picture and Television Engineers* 69, no. 8 (August 1960): 534–544.

———. *A History of the Photographic Lens.* London: Academic Press, 1989.

Lightman, Herb A. "The Angénieux Story." *American Cinematographer* 56, no. 3 (March 1975): 326–329, 342–347.

Malkames, Karl. "To Zoom or Not to Zoom." *American Cinematographer* 55, no. 6 (June 1974): 712–713.

Mascelli, Joseph V. "Use and Abuse of the Zoom Lens." *American Cinematographer* 38, no. 10 (October 1957): 652–653, 677.

Moore, Richard. "New Uses for Zoom Lenses." *American Cinematographer* 46, no. 7 (July 1965): 438–441.

Morrissey, Priska. "Naissance et Premiers Usages du Zoom." *Positif,* no. 564 (February 2008): 88–93.

Nowell-Smith, Geoffrey. *Making Waves: New Cinemas of the 1960s.* New York: Bloomsbury, 2013.

O'Brien, Adam. *Transactions with the World.* New York: Berghahn Books, 2016.

Pont, Patrice-Hervé. *Angénieux*. Paris: Éditions du Pécari, 2003.

Rust, Amy. *Passionate Detachments: Technologies of Vision and Violence in American Cinema, 1967–1974*. Albany: State University of New York Press, 2017.

Salt, Barry. *Film Style and Technology*. 2nd ed. London: Starword, 1992.

Sobchack, Vivian. "The Active Eye: A Phenomenology of Cinematic Vision." *Quarterly Review of Film and Video* 12, no. 3 (June 1990): 21–36.

"Technology and the Trade Press." *Velvet Light Trap* 76 (Fall 2015): 49–67.

Willemen, Paul. "The Zoom in Popular Cinema: A Question of Performance." *Rouge*, no. 1 (2003). http://www.rouge.com.au/1/zoom.html.

INDEX

Page numbers in *italics* refer to figures.

ABOUT THE AUTHOR

NICK HALL works in the Department of Media Arts at Royal Holloway, University of London. His research focuses on technology and style in postwar British and American film and television. This is his first book.